P9-AOO-102

Writing for Interactive Media

Jon Samsel and Darryl Wimberley

ALLWORTH PRESS
NEW YORK

© 1998 Jon Samsel and Darryl Wimberley

All rights reserved. Copyright under Berne Copyright Convention, Universal
Copyright Convention, and Pan-American Copyright Convention. No part of
this book may be reproduced, stored in a retrieval system, or transmitted in
any form, or by any means, electronic, mechanical, photocopying, recording,
or otherwise, without prior permission of the publisher.

04 03 02 01 00 99 98   5 4 3 2 1

Published by Allworth Press
An imprint of Allworth Communications
10 East 23rd Street, New York NY 10010

Cover design by Douglas Design Associates, New York, NY

Page composition/typography by Sharp Des!gns, Inc., Lansing, MI

ISBN: 1-58115-005-9

Library of Congress Catalog Card Number: 98-72754

Printed in Canada

You are the bows from which
your children as living arrows
are sent forth.

KAHLIL GIBRAN

This book is dedicated to our arrows.

Table of Contents

Part II. Interactivity and Narrative

Acknowledgments

We would like to extend our gratitude to our families (especially Cheyenne Samsel; Joelle Samsel; Jeanine Samsel; John and Joan Samsel; Jeanne Valenti; Doreen Shafer; Doris Wagner; and Doris Samsel) and to all the writers, teachers, visionaries, companies, organizations, and friends who have contributed so much to this endeavor. A special thank-you goes out to Neal Stephenson; Larry Kay; Douglas Gayeton; Carolyn Miller; Terry Borst; Todd Krieger; Michael Kaplan; John Sanborn; Greg Roach and HyperBole Studios; Jeffrey Sullivan; Larry Tuch; Archie Kleingartner and Kate Winegark (University of California, Los Angeles); Michael Joyce; Tim Neil; Joyce Honeychurch, Ph.D., and Terry Wimberley, Ph.D. (Florida Gulf Coast University); Vladimir Lange (Lange Productions); Chris Josephes; Deborah Todd; Charles Austin; Scott Rosenfelt; Harry Youtt; Paul Palumbo; John Tarnoff (Personality Factory); David Greene (Creative Spark); Molly Schneider (UCI Extension); Dana De Puy Morgan (Apple Computer); Cristina Bogossian; Mark Bernstein (Eastgate Systems, Inc.); Kenneth Lee (Objective Reality, Inc.); Brigette Callahan, Tom Gundlock and An Nguyen (Amiable Technologies, Inc.); Paul Provensano (Fox Interactive); John F. Barber, Ph.D. (Northwestern State University); Chris Kingry (Fox Interactive); Jacques Boulanger (JBI Localization); Richard Thompson; Clancy Fort; Kimia and Gary Willison—and all the caffeine junkies at the Monday Night Multimedia Coffee Club; Jim Sauve; Carl Bressler; Ken Locker (MGM); and finally, Tad Crawford, Nyier Abdou, and the entire staff at Allworth Press.

Introduction

The late great Orsen Welles once said, "Everything you need to know about filmmaking can be learned in two to three days." I don't know whether to believe that statement or not. I suppose that for a man who wrote and directed several of the most critically acclaimed films of all time, this was no overstatement. But I can almost guarantee that if those words were uttered by any other contemporary filmmaker, he or she would have been run out of town faster than you could shout, "Faster Pussycat! Kill! Kill!"

It is unlikely that a writer can learn everything he or she needs to know about *interactivity* in a day or two—let alone, within the pages of a single book. The daily bombardment of new tools, techniques, and technology is daunting—to the point, some even say, of polluting the creative landscape. One wonders if the technological gold rush will ever slow down long enough for our creative souls to catch up. I hope so. There is so much to learn and so much to see and explore.

The ever-expanding world of "new media" eagerly awaits its first *Citizen Kane* and *Casablanca* in much the same way as the information age searches for meaning in a fistful of fiber optic wire. As long as we live in a society where the technology tail waves the creative dog, we will continue to be inundated with new information at a dehumanizing pace. I am reminded of a commencement address given by John Nathan, a professor at the University of California at Santa Barbara, to the graduating class of the School of the Arts and Humanities. Nathan said, "New technology's voracious appetite for data has spawned a new profession. This profession is called content creation. It is up to us, the humanists and the artists, to restore some balance and perspective to . . . the Information Age."

That speech made a significant impact on my approach to living in a digital world. Nathan's words have given me the courage to ask the storyteller, Where? and the technologist, Why? My journey has taken me on an exhaustive quest to answer a deeply profound, two-part question: What is this thing called interactivity and what exactly is the writer's role in it?

Until now, there have been precious few resources for interactive writers and designers. With that in mind, the "best creative practices" of those artists on the front lines of the digital revolution will be examined in this book to provide some guidance and insight into the emerging field of interactive writing.

The first part of this book introduces the key skills and concepts every interactive writer needs to know in order to be cyberliterate such as how to plan and structure your interactive ideas, create dynamic flowcharts, and how to organize the written document.

In part two, we'll explore what all good stories have in common. We'll take a hard look at what makes interactive texts different from novels, films, and television, and see what those differences mean for the interactive writer. We'll talk about immersion and the seamless experience. We'll discuss how three-act structure fits into interactive narrative and consider how to develop characters for interactive dramas. Finally, we'll gather around the campfire for conversations with some of today's most celebrated "story-artists."

Part three takes us away from narrative as we delve into hypertext fiction and the World Wide Web. We'll deconstruct MGM's online rock 'n' roll murder mystery, *Paul Is Dead,* and reconstruct the role-playing saga known as *Myst.*

Part four explores the art of informational multimedia. Topics of interest include corporate uses of interactive multimedia, interactive education, and CD-ROM tutorials. We'll show writers how to implement instructional methodology into their concept documents. We'll also talk about how writers can build more productive and engaging Web sites.

Finally, part five tackles frequently asked questions concerning writers of all skill levels. Topics include the importance of networking, advice on dealmaking, tips on creativity, dealing with rejection, how best to follow up submissions, and common mistakes to avoid when writing interactive documents.

We live in an exciting age where the story and the teller are merging in a garden of forking paths. The audience is no longer a passive but an active participant in all that interactivity has to offer. New methods of communication and expression must be forged. And more and more it is the writer—the electric scribe of the Information Age—who leads the charge.

I.

Form
and
Function

1 Skills You'll Need

My father's definition of an expert is somebody who has done something once. And I've also heard it described about "experts" that an "ex" is a has-been and a "spurt" is a drip under pressure. I believe that those who fancy that they know it all have peaked. We are in a young industry and I suppose it makes more sense that we behave like youths: having fun, experimenting, doing naughty things, disobeying our elders, learning how to grow up, and seeing a universe of many possibilities.

LARRY KAY

Interactive writer and producer Greg Roach says that "the underpinnings of successful interactive design" require a "geometric understanding of the spatial possibilities of what the medium represents." Sounds like a mouthful, doesn't it? But writer and designer Michael Kaplan paints a similar picture of the interactive writer when he describes interactive writing as an "amalgam of math and storytelling." Besides math and storytelling skills, I would add that interactive writers also need to have a working knowledge of how digitally constructed texts are designed. That is, they should understand how the logic of programming affects their stories, and should understand how designers use procedural rules to realize at the machine level what the writer puts on the page.

Most writers experience some frustration when moving from books or stage plays or scripts to the interactive screen. This is chiefly because interactive writing demands competency in areas not usually second-nature to writers in the older technologies. For purposes of illustration, let's imagine writing as a strictly "right-brain" activity; an activity related to a writer's grasp of oratory, prose, and history. For contrast, we'll call skills related to math "left-brain" activities. The interactive writer has to rely heavily on the left *and* right hemispheres of the brain. And to participate in a text's design, the interactive writer has to track left- and right-brain activity simultaneously. Interactive writers have a whole set of concerns alien to writers of older media. A text's logic, the procedural rules that determine its design, the technology that communicates the user's interaction with the text—all of this stuff has to be taken into account on the printed page of the interactive script. The interactive scripter must therefore be able to nurture and develop creative ideas while constructing abstract systems of order and logic for the digitally based technology through which the text will be presented.

You could sum this up by saying that the interactive writer must be competent in storytelling, mathematics, and design. This probably explains why so few writers follow through with their interactive urges. And among those who do, it's obvious that failure is more common than success. This is understandable. It's not the writer's fault; it's just that jealous right brain claiming turf! But skills related to mathematics, abstract thinking, logical progression, the ability to see patterns in chaos, and so on are essential for creators of interactive content. "Left-brain thinking," as Kaplan and Roach acknowledge, is an indispensable tool in the interactive writer's bag.

Roger Schank once said that we may choose what to remember, but we are not free to forget at will. Interactive writers don't have the luxury of forgetting, or ignoring, those dimensions of multimedia production that are unfamiliar or arduous. Difficult though it may be, creative artists in this arena have to change the way they think. Interactive writers must learn the rules that govern the new form, and then apply that newfound knowledge to their interactive projects. Do that and your future as an interactive writer/designer is virtually unlimited!

What's the process like, then, this acquisition of left-brain skills? Well, it starts by understanding that interactive writing begins with the transformation of the printed page into an active matrix displayed on the computer screen. Printed pages have long been "interactive" in the sense that they allow the reader to choose any page at random, sample a few lines of text, jump into the index to search for a particular subject of interest, or close the book when the eye grows weary.

That kind of activity, familiar to all of us, *can* be interactive. But most of the time it's not. Most people read books linearly, from page one to the final word, paragraph by paragraph, chapter by chapter, verse to verse. In a book, the author has determined every aspect of content and presentation from the plot down to the most minute detail of scenery, and most readers are all too happy to be the passive recipients of the writer's labor.

Interactive texts are different. Michael Joyce says that what makes interactive texts different from books is that the interactive text can "change every time you read it." The problem with that characterization, as almost any reader will tell you, is that books change with each reading, too. People commonly read the same book over and over and never have the same experience twice. No two people reading a book come away with the same experience.

It's not correct to suggest, either, that readers of books are simply passive recipients of the author's intent. Many readers are extremely active, interacting with books in a myriad of ways, whether anticipating the author's stance in a polemic or guessing the bad guy in a whodunit. Thriller, political treatise, poem—the ways in which printed texts and readers can interact are vast.

However, digitally based texts invite a user's interaction in ways distinguished both in scale and in kind from older technologies. Many interactive texts, for example, particularly interactive fiction or games, practically beg the user to change the sequence in which information or incident is presented. The options that these texts offer their users are much more varied, and intrusive, than the kind of participation invited by a printed text.

Virtual technologies and printed technologies make different demands on their writers. Suppose, for a moment, that you'd like to write an interactive mystery. You're going to do a virtual Sam Spade, or Hercule Poirot. The writer of a printed text would go to a great deal of trouble to create a single, integrated sequence of cause and effect that *cannot* be changed. Readers of these texts will generally follow the novelist's single path from the body in the bathtub to the heroic declaration that "the butler did it!"

You can't change the sequence of events established in a printed mystery and expect to have anything make sense. Read an Agatha Christie and see what I mean; change one detail, move one incident from its established niche to another, and very likely you will be unable to discern the logic of Ms. Christie's work at all. But the same story, placed in the hands of an interactive writer, will be handled much differently.

One of the interactive writer's first goals is to make multiple sequences of incidents logically compatible and interesting. To do that, the interactive writer has to put the *user* in the driver's seat, providing an arena in which users are required to participate in ways that alter both the text's content and its presentation. Users cannot be passive in a multimedia text, even if they wanted to. They *must* make choices. They *must* intrude on the text.

It is this imperative, this demand that the user make choices affecting the text's content and presentation, which distinguishes an interactive script from scripts intended for nondigital technologies. And it's the user's *desire to participate* that gives interactive writers a space to create, which is different from the place provided by novels or plays or films.

"I think there have been a lot of writers who over the past two generations have been trying to figure out how to break the confines of a book," claims writer/designer/director Douglas Gayeton. "A book starts on page one and goes to the end. I think if those people were starting now, they would be doing interactive. Because, interactivity is all based upon the principle of nonlinear thought. And that is the way we think. I could talk to you and never finish a sentence—or finish an idea—because our minds are like that. And I think that's why people have gravitated toward interactivity. Not because it's a fad, but because it really captures the dimensionality of thought. That thought is not a linear process, it's a multiplane, multidimensional process. And a story that allows you to assimilate and capture the essence of how our thinking processes work is a tremendously fascinating and exciting thing."

The central consideration to keep in mind at all times when writing interactive properties is the *user experience*. Writers must consider the actions (and inaction) of the audience with the same depth and urgency afforded to the interactive concept being presented. Otherwise, the writer is simply embellishing a linear project with entertaining click-ons, cul-de-sacs, and side games.

The question one must ask next is, How can this best be accomplished? Interactive writers—whether they are building Web sites, CD-ROM games, or informational kiosks—must provide a framework for all possible user interactions to take place. Ultimately, the depth of user interactivity is influenced by the following factors:

Immersion
- Is belief suspended enough to draw the user into the world of the application?
- How captivating or believable is the application?

Exploration
- How much freedom does the user have within the application?
- What does the user discover along his or her journey?

Response
- How can the user communicate or interact with characters, objects, and activities within the application?

Satisfaction
- What does the user learn from the application?
- What can the user take away from the experience?
- How pleasurable or satisfying was the experience?
- How likely is the user to repeat the experience?

Legendary game designer Chris Crawford asserts that interactivity "breaks interaction down into three steps—listening, thinking, and speaking—each of which must be performed well in order to sustain a good interaction. The first two steps, listening and thinking, are poorly understood and difficult to execute with a computer. The third step, expression, is most similar to existing expository forms of entertainment and has therefore, unsurprisingly, been the most fully developed of the three steps—and it has also been overemphasized."

Understand Your Audience

What, then, does the audience want? What functionality and features do they really need? Who are the target users of your interactive application? What outcomes are expected by the user? The answers to each of these questions will shape both the content and the design methodology of your interactive system.

As a writer/designer of interactive systems, it is imperative that you devise a method of defining the "conditions of use" for your application in advance of any production work.

To better identify your target audience, you may want to ask yourself the following questions:
- What is the age and education level of my target user?
- How experienced is the person with interactive technology?
- What is the gender/cultural background of my target audience?
- Will my audience access this application from home or the office?
- How often will my audience interact with the application?
- Will my target user interact alone or with a group?
- What type of computer equipment does my target user own?
- In what type of environment will my audience use the application?

- Does the user have any preconceptions about the application? If so, what are they and how might they impact the quality of the interactive experience?

Define Your Objective

Many writers jump right into their interactive media projects without first identifying the purpose, objective, or goal of their work. Is the main purpose to entertain, inform, educate, or move the soul? Every interactive project differs in what it tries to achieve. For example, a music store kiosk may intend to transmit concise data on every musical act known to have released an album in the past fifty years. A role-playing CD-ROM adventure may aim to enchant its audience. An interactive training program may aspire, on the other hand, to educate the user for a practical application.

When you establish a clear objective, goal, and intent, you create a solid foundation for your project. If the writer fails to do this, how can the user be expected to relate to an interactive project? Establishing clear objectives will help you focus your message, explain your ideas to others, and develop a deeper passion for the subject matter. You will also find it easier to stick to your production timetable and stay within budget.

Remember, just because you *can* make something interactive, it doesn't mean you *should*. It's a good idea for writers to conduct a question-and-answer session about their project before any writing begins. Ask yourself questions such as:

- Why this project?
- What are the primary goals of the project?
- What do my target users want/expect from the application?
- What do I want my audience to feel while interacting with this project?
- Does my content merit an interactive format?
- Why am I the best person to spearhead this project?
- What is my passion for the subject matter?
- How can we, as creative artists, alter the confines of the medium itself?
- What unique interactive features might be added to enhance the content?
- What time frame do I have to work with?
- What are my time and budget constraints?
- What projects compete with mine?
- Will this project use primarily existing content?

- How scalable is the content? (Can it be easily changed/updated?)
- What are the most compelling features of this application?

What Is an Interface?

An interface combines your computer mouse with the icons found on your computer screen. It gives the user a means to connect with your interactive text. The computer interface is often referred to as the "look and feel" of an interactive system. The media displayed on a computer screen are dynamic and interactive. Their relationship to the user is constantly being altered by the actions of the user. If designed properly, the interface helps a user navigate a computer system. If designed poorly, the interface interferes with a user's objectives.

Interface design—the art of building the look and feel into an interactive system—is a process that encompasses everything a user can, might, and will interact with. This "whole user interaction"—sight, sound, and touch—must be meticulously planned by the interactive design team in order to achieve the optimum end-user experience. In fact, Apple Computer, pioneer of the graphical user interface (GUI) that is the underlying basis of the Mac operating system (now mimicked by Windows systems), created the Apple *Human Interface Guidelines,* a meticulous document that helped standardize interface design methodologies.

Why standardize at all, you ask? How do we gage the effectiveness of a user-interface design? From where do these design methodologies originate?

Northwestern University professor John F. Barber, Ph.D., explains: "One school of thought says we should follow paradigms that are already in place. I think there is a great deal of that happening today. The print-based cultural ideology and all its socioeconomic-political baggage has carried over into what we are doing in digitally mediated forms of communication such as the Internet. In some ways I would argue that that is good because we really don't have any other models to follow. We have World Wide Web 'pages' and they are set up like the pages of a book. But it's a 'scrolling' book rather than a 'turning-the-page' book. We are certainly confined by the limited dimensions of a monitor's display face. People don't have multiple monitors at their disposal so we can't do things like deconstruct an image and put part of it on one monitor and part of it on another."

In his book *The Metaphysics of Virtual Reality,* Michael Heim provides an insightful description of the user interface:

What then, is an interface? An interface occurs where two or more information sources come face-to-face. A human user connects with the system, and
the computer becomes interactive. . . . Interface means more than video hardware, more than a screen we look at. Interface refers also to software or to
the way we actively alter the computer's operations and consequently alter
the world controlled by the computer. Interface denotes a contact point where
software links the human user to computer processors. This is the mysterious, non-material point where electronic signals become information. It is
our interaction with software that creates an interface. Interface means the
human being is wired up.

Greg Roach looks at the user interface from a gaming point of view: "When
it comes to the user interface, our goal is to create something that is invisible—
where the content is its own interface. The tools the player needs to communicate with the environment and the other characters are completely out of sight
until you want them, and then they're there immediately. A big part of the
VirtualCinema [his company's patented gaming engine] experience is that
you're inside of this character—you embody this character and, for the most
part, you look out through their eyes and control their actions.

"We also play with character emotions. At certain key points in time, a
set of emotion icons will appear onscreen. These allow you to interrupt the
action as it is occurring in front of you and inject an emotional response into
the scene. That's one of the ways in which these psychological variables are
impacted. Sometimes psychological variables decrement based upon a choice
of phrase to another character. Sometimes they are based on the emotional
states that you choose via these emotion icons. Sometimes they're triggered
by physical objects in the environment—if you pick up and read the divorce
papers in your apartment, that action further implements your 'loss variable.'
The user is not aware that any of this is going on. If players are aware of it,
then we have failed."

Ideally, then, the most powerful interface designs are those that seamlessly
meld navigational tools (icons and other symbols) with graphic images. The
right mix creates a unique identity—an atmosphere and theme for your application that is like no other.

Many writers do not go on to design the interface of their interactive applications. This job is usually left to the lead graphic designer or production
designer. However, this does not mean that the writer does not need to spend

some time understanding what makes an interface work. On the contrary, smart interactive writers take the time to learn the basic tenants of design. How can a writer be so bold as to think he or she can create an interactive experience without being able to explain—even in general terms—how the user will actually interact with the system? Imagine trying to write a feature film without ever having watched a movie!

What should a writer know about interface design? Let's look at the major issues covered in Apple's *Human Interface Guidelines*, along with a few commonsense approaches to design and interaction, to see if we can find some answers.

Unity of Style

Follow the rules of good graphical design—try not to crowd your screen with too much content; use fonts that are pleasing to the eye; use lots of white space (yes, less is better); stick with a specific color scheme; design for the screen with a sense of balance, when possible; and use images instead of text (one image speaks louder than a chunk of words).

Unity of Vision

The writer's style and vision makes or breaks the unity of an interactive application. The moment that unity is broken, the user is lost. How does the writer approach his or her material? Corporately, so that the user says, "I am being sold—I am experiencing marketing content repurposed for the Web." Or poetically, with the use of a melodious phrase and a lyrical eye that sees images instead of solid character, symbols instead of people?

Unity of Metaphors

You can take advantage of your user's knowledge about the environment in which they live by using metaphors to communicate the key concepts and features of your application. For example, if you are creating an interactive training application for school teachers, you may want to use the classroom as your location metaphor, using familiar images found in a classroom (books, a blackboard, desks, a clock, file folders) as onscreen icons to represent the what and where the user needs to go in the application and interact with the material needed. When used well, metaphors quickly draw users into the application and help them navigate the application more intuitively. Be consistent—use variations of the same metaphors throughout the application.

Unity of Environment

A user should always feel empowered and in control of the application via the interface and should never feel that the computer has "automatically" taken actions that could arbitrarily change the user's preferences, destroy data, or force the user to waste time. Well-designed interfaces are also forgiving of user's mistakes and are stable enough to recover "gracefully" if the user makes mistakes, supplies inappropriate data, or attempts to take an action that might result in the irreversible loss of data.

Nodes and Links: The Brick and Mortar of Interactivity

If it is to be believed that structure is the backbone of an interactive application, then "nodes" are the bricks and "hypertextual links" are the mortar that links all the various media elements together. Let's take a look at these two strange words—"nodes" and "hypertext"—and examine what they mean to the interactive writer.

The word "hypertext" was first coined in the sixties by Theodor Nelson, a researcher and scientist best known for propagating *Xanadu*—a system of worldwide, interconnected texts. Many scholars insist that Nelson's "hypertext" is a predecessor to theories first posed by Vannevar Bush in his article, "As We May Think," which was published years earlier in the *Atlantic Monthly*. In the article, Bush claims that "the human mind . . . operates by association . . . in accordance with some intricate web of trails carried by the cells of the brain." He goes on to describe "memex," a system that stores, records, and communicates user information. "When numerous items have been joined together to form a trail, they can be reviewed in turn, rapidly or slowly, by deflecting a lever like that used for turning the pages of a book. It is exactly as though the physical items had been gathered together to form a new book. It is more than this, for any item can be joined into numerous trails."

Hypertext, then, is a structure of linked text or other media (hypermedia) through which a user can navigate and interact. Hypertext is made up of linked nodes (localized fields of data, interconnected) and these nodes are made up of any type of data you want to place there.

In *The Metaphysics of Virtual Reality*, Michael Heim writes, "The term hypertext refers to the existence of an unnoticed or additional dimension . . . when written words and phrases have an extra dimension, they are like crystals with infinite facets. You can turn over an expression and view it from any number of angles, each angle being another twist of the same text. Words and

phrases appear juxtaposed or superimposed. The sense of a sequential literature of distinct, physically separate texts gives way to a continuous textuality.
Instead of a linear, page-by-page, line-by-line, book-by-book approach, the user
connects information in an intuitive, associative manner. Hypertext fosters a
literacy that is prompted by jumps of intuition and association."

In his tome *Of Two Minds: Hypertext Pedagogy and Poetics,* noted hypertext
novelist Michael Joyce further clarifies the role of writer and reader within a
hypertextual system. Joyce asserts, "Borrowing from the conventions of print
culture, those who view, combine, or manipulate hypertexts are commonly
referred to as readers, while those who create, gather, and arrange hypertexts
are called writers. Yet hypertext challenges and, many say, obviates these dis-
tinctions. Hypertext readers not only choose the order of what they read but,
in doing so, also alter its form by their choices."

Joyce's assertion needs to be tempered. As Janet Murray notes in her book
Hamlet on the Holodeck, readers of hypertext do not originate anything. That
is, readers of hypertext can only choose options that a writer/designer origi-
nates and that exists, virtually, as a coded set of procedural rules that do not
change with a reader's participation.

A node is a "place," "space," "module," or "page" that contains "themati-
cally grouped" information (text, images, sound, animations, and so on). Nodes
are commonly referred to as Web pages, content modules, scenes, locations,
and even chapters.

For example, a writer looking to create a biography node about the life of
John F. Kennedy can fill that node with any type of information he or she can
dream of: a time line listing all the major events in Kennedy's life; a text biography; or a Flash animation encapsulating the assassination of JFK (see fig.
1.1).

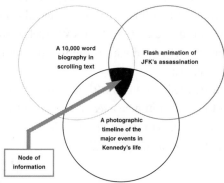

Fig. 1.1. Node for *Kennedy: A Biography*

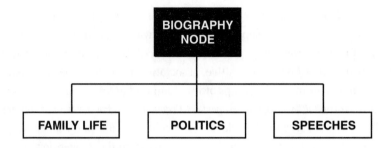

Fig. 1.2. JFK's oval office cluster

Nodes interconnect with other nodes via hyperlinks. So the node titled "Kennedy: A Biography" might link to three other related nodes: "Family Life," "Politics," and "Speeches" (see fig. 1.2).

Several years back, a UCLA writing instructor by the name of Jim Sauve gave a presentation on interactivity at a conference held in Bloomfield Hills, Michigan. Suave said that nodes can nest other nodes. In other words, a writer can build one node inside of another node. A visual analogy might be something like the structure of an atom. If an atom is a node, then an electron would be a node nesting within the atom node. For example, a writer might decide to take a thumbnail image from the famed Zapruder film and make *it* the hypermedia link between the JFK biography node and a nested, twenty-second Flash animation of the Kennedy assassination. That same biography node might contain a graphic icon of a musical node, hyperlinked to a nested speech node.

Sauve went on to say, "When you connect one node to another, you build relationships." That statement is very true. You don't need to know *how* relationship-building works at this time—this is a learned activity that may take many years to master. But you do need to ask yourself some important questions about the interconnectivity of your content—the who, what, where, why and how questions such as:

- What exactly do the hyperlinks within a node connect to?
- What type of media should be used to represent these links?
- Why should this node connect to that node?
- How can this best be accomplished?

When You Link Nodes, You Activate User Pathways

As we have learned, it is the writer's job to determine what content should appear within each node and how nodes interlink with one another. As we further define these hypertextual relationships, we begin to create a complete range of possible user experiences. Writers, in a sense, are the system architects who determine each aspect of an interactive application—from what the users can do and where they can go to what can happen on the screen.

It is important that the interactive writer make every attempt to organize his or her content in a way that:

- Best divides up the core information
- Achieves the key objective of the application
- Delivers a powerful user experience
- Keeps track of all the content
- Defines the relationship between each node of content
- Prompts the user to interact with the application

How to Assemble a Node

One way to build on your ideas is to follow your intuition and freely associate seemingly random concepts. A patchwork of uncensored ideas begins to develop. The key here is to allow for the free flow of uncensored ideas. Many creative artists tend to get hung up on the fine details, editing their ideas as they go. This stifles the creative process. Don't be so hard on yourself. Unleash all your ideas—the good and the bad.

It is important that you start off by building a creative foundation—a brainstorming session where you first list the major goals and objectives of your application. Next, focus on the content that will make up your project. In just a few short minutes, you can easily create a visual cluster of ideas for any concept you are thinking of developing. With all the crucial elements laid out as visual clusters on a page, you can elaborate on the best ideas and delete the ideas that don't work.

Using a cluster map (see fig. 1.3), jot down a key word that lies at the core of an idea or objective in the center rectangle. Then fill in the connecting ovals with the first impressions your mind associates with that word. When you have a cluster of ideas that revolve around a central premise, goal, objective, location, theme, or topic, you have a *node* of information. The combined sum of each element of a cluster (the central rectangle plus its connecting ovals) equals one complete node.

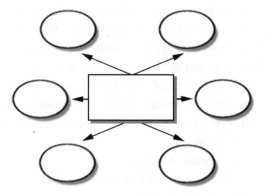

Fig. 1.3. Cluster map of one complete node

A writer can create a cluster of ideas that might eventually contain hidden or nested elements *within* that node. For example, the writer of *Kennedy: A Biography* might want the user to navigate an exploratory environment such as an oval office node in an attempt to uncover several hidden links or hot spots. The act of discovery might enhance the user experience. The discovery process might also be a foundational component of the application's content architecture (see fig. 1.4).

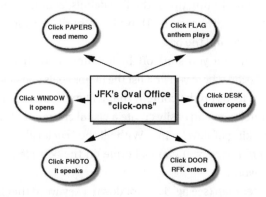

Fig. 1.4. JFK's oval office cluster

Another example of nested nodes is *Big Warm Bear Arms*, an interactive program created by writer/designer Greg Roach. The opening screen presents users with a collage node filled with images to explore. Clicking on an image such as the clock node triggers a nested linear story sequence. After that sequence plays out, the user is returned to the collage node to make yet another choice. The user's choices are multilinear, but the "play path" of each individual node is linear. Each nested node tells a piece of the overarching story. Consequently, the user "builds" a unique narrative for *Big Warm Bear Arms* with each click of the mouse (see fig. 1.5).

Fig. 1.5. Screen shot from *Big Warm Bear Arms*, by Greg Roach, winner of the 1993 QuickTime Film Festival award for Best Narrative. Reprinted by permission.

Fabricate a Flowchart

A flowchart (also referred to as a map, matrix, or site map) is simply a graphical representation of the application's design structure. Flowcharts are used to identify the sequence of nodes—how many and what they connect to—which in turn defines all possible user pathways through an application.

Nodes are usually represented as circles. Arrows are used to connect one circle to another, and the direction of these arrows identifies the flow of the program. All possible user's choices can be analyzed by examining the flowchart (see fig. 1.6).

Many Web sites allow users to access a site map directly from the home page. A site map is akin to the floorplan maps commonly found in shopping malls. Users can scan the map for their favorite store, identify their location on the map, and chart a course to that location in a matter of seconds. Web visitors like site maps because they can quickly scan the entire contents of a site

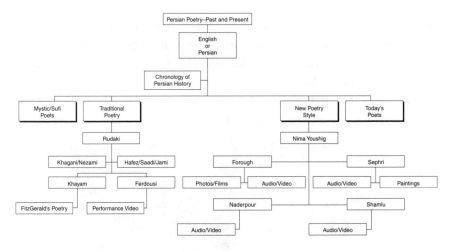

Fig. 1.6. Flowchart from Kimia Willison's interactive CD-ROM proposal, *Persian Poetry—Past and Present*.

and hyperlink to the information they need—quickly and efficiently—rather than wasting a lot of time and energy searching and scrolling an entire Web site. If you jump ahead to chapter 15, you can inspect an actual site map from the MGM Web series *Paul Is Dead* (see fig. 15.7).

In chapter 2, we will examine how to create a design structure that best demonstrates the type of user interaction you envision for your interactive system. As you build your design structure diagrams and combine them with other charts and graphs, you will be creating a master flowchart for your entire interactive project.

Other Ways to Organize Interactive Content

One of the most difficult tasks in writing and designing interactive applications is deciding how to divide up the various pieces of information, devising intelligent ways to keep track of it, and specifying what relationship you want the user to have with it.

Here are a few ideas for how to best organize the content for an interactive presentation:

Assemble a Table of Contents or Outline
Some writers like to organize the major elements of their interactive applications by creating a table of contents or outline that easily explains the range

of all topics to be discussed/explored in the work. Table of contents and outlines are easy to assemble, can be modified easily, and provide crucial information at a glance. Some writers organize their written material by "acts" or "chapters." There is no right way of doing this. Use whatever metaphors work for you.

Sequencing

Many narrative writers go so far as to tell their tales (from beginning to end) in a series of twelve sequential sentences. Then, they flush out the details by writing a description of each sequence—listing the major conflicts/challenges and/or objectives of the work.

Create a Character Matrix

If you are writing an interactive experience that tells a story, inevitably, you will be creating characters. One trick writers use to build characters quickly is to construct a character matrix, a chart that defines all necessary character information such as background story (backstory), physical characteristics, occupation, temperament, and inner story).

This initial overview of the things that challenge interactive writers and that are unique to interactive texts is a lot for writers to digest—especially for writers who come from traditional disciplines such as journalism, screenwriting, or copyediting. Writing for interactive media is a different monster. Writers need to think trilaterally—as writers, designers, and visitors—if they hope to master this new form.

The next chapter will demonstrate the importance of framing your interactive content in a design structure that best accomplishes the perceived range of action that should be built into your system—and, ultimately, experienced by the user. Creating the widest possible "depth of choice" is always preferable but not always easy to achieve. The trick is to design a system's structure and *not* its presentation. The solution is to create a system of interlocking geometric maps that outline what a single user can do and where he or she can go in any given application.

So activate your left brain and shake loose those cobwebs. It's time to conceptualize—time to build some design structures!

2

Structure Out of Chaos

Writing is easy. All you do is sit staring at a blank sheet of paper until the drops of blood form on your forehead.

GENE FOWLER

Whether or not you are aware of it, our world is structured into a series of shapes and patterns and sounds that trigger pleasure in us. This systematic organization is part of our intuitive nature—it allows us to structure sensory information into consciousness, thought, and language. It's the way we humans are designed.

In the interactive world, design structure is more than notes scribbled on a napkin or a complex flowchart depicting sequential scenes of an application in rich detail. Interactive design structure fulfills two important duties: it defines the navigational boundaries of the user experience and it is the framework that holds all the creative elements of an interactive work together.

You are now ready to make some pretty important decisions that will have a serious impact on the ability of the user to navigate your interactive application. As an interactive writer, it is your job to identify the user's *perceived* range of action—keeping in mind that "what the user can do" directly corresponds with the "rules and pathways you create."

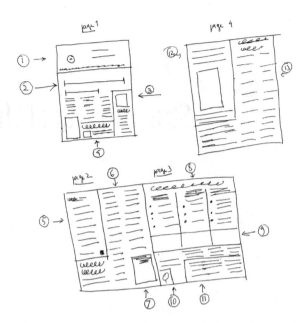

Fig. 2.1. Jacques Boulanger's notes on creating an electronic newsletter, scribbled on a napkin. Copyright 1998, JBI Localization. Reprinted by permission.

For example, an interactive environment such as *Myst* [the groundbreaking first-person point of view adventure game created by Robyn and Rand Miller], which has a wide range and depth of choice, may be perceived as more interactive than a conditional branching system with limited choices. This is true, in part, because of the navigation methodology built into the system—a methodology that emphasizes the program's "critical objective" over a "critical path" mentality. A critical objective is a centralized aim, goal, or action whereby the end user's overall path of discovery stresses a "means to an end," rather than fulfilling an immediate task. Key elements within such an application are revealed over time as the user navigates through the application. A critical path is a single correct path a user must follow to successfully complete an application. This is a procedural approach to completing a task.

The distinction between a critical objective and a critical path is significant. Many players confess that what they like best about playing *Myst* is "exploring the environment." Finishing the game is much less important.

In her essay "The Garden of Merging Paths," Rebecca Solnit writes, "Much recent attention to interactive media proposes that it makes the passive viewer become actively engaged. What is interesting about these products is that they map out a number of choices, but the choices are all pre-selected . . . that is, the user cannot do anything or go anywhere that the creator has not planned; as usual with computer programs, one must stay on the path and off the grass (by which analogy hackers do get off the path, a subversive success that keeps them in the park). We could chart the game as a series of forks in the road, in which each choice sets up another array of choices, but the sum total of choices has already been made. Thus the audience becomes the user, a figure who resembles a rat in a conceptual version of a laboratory maze. The audience-user is not literally passive; he is engaged in making choices, but the choices do not necessarily represent freedom, nor does his activity represent thinking."

Douglas Gayeton, who has worked on high-profile projects such as *Plug In* (AOL), *Waking Hours* (Boxtop/IXL), *Johnny Mnemonic* (Sony ImageSoft), *and Vanishing Point* (MSN/Sunshine Digital), claims, "The geography of an interactive space is an illusion . . . it's a directed experience. You only need to art direct (or write) what the viewer will see. If a location is too richly composed and features too many objects, the viewer will expect to be able to interact with everything. When she finds that she can't, she will realize she's hit a 'wall' in the interactive world."

In his book *The Complete Wargames Handbook,* author James F. Dunnigan cautions, "Keep in mind that a computer does what you tell it to do, not what you want it to do. Unlike people (some people, anyway), you can't just tell a computer what you want done and expect your request to be carried out. Computers require explicit instructions. These are called computer programs, or computer software. The terms 'program' and 'software' are often used interchangeably."

The Ten Geometric Design Structures

We will explore ten geometric structures in this chapter: sequential, branching, conditional branching (branching with barriers, branching with forced paths, bottlenecking, branching with optional scenes), exploratorium, parallel streaming, worlds, and multilinear.

Sequential (Linear)

Sequential structure is the basic building block of both interactive and linear media projects. User navigation follows a strictly defined procedural path—one node after another. A user cannot jump from node A to node C, for example, without having first traversed node B.

Although sequential structure is built into the design scheme of practically every new media application ever produced, it is often not talked about. That's because, for most interactive projects, linear structure is not the primary design structure used in the application; it's simply an underlying design system that keeps things moving along (see fig. 2.2).

In the early days of multimedia (late eighties to early nineties), sequential structure was used quite heavily in projects such as electronic books and multimedia novels. The Voyager Company published many of these self-label "expanded books," titles such as Douglas Adams's *Hitchhiker's Guide to the Galaxy*, Herman Melville's *Moby Dick*, and *The Complete Annotated Alice* based on the Lewis Carroll stories.

Fig. 2.2. Sequential structure

Electronic books ("e-books") helped to redefine the boundaries of the printed word. Writers and publishers were able to create works of fiction or nonfiction that their predecessors only dreamed of. Electronic books enhanced the standard text by adding elements such as images, sound, and animation.

In 1991, the first stages of the 3-D graphic novel *Sinkha* were put into production by noted Italian science-fiction illustrator Marco Patrito and his production team, Virtual Views. *Sinkha* was a labor of love that was created over a five-year period on a shoestring budget. Upon its final release, the title won the 1996 New Media Invision award for Best Electronic Book and was hailed as an idyllic mesh of art and fiction.

Sinkha stood out from every other e-book on the market because it was neither book, feature film, nor game. It was truly something different—the first 3-D multimedia novel—as its press kit proudly proclaimed. Tens of thousands of hours went into creating the title and the result is a beautifully rendered graphical environment unlike anything you have ever seen. The artwork in *Sinkha* has been compared to the quality images found in mainstream games such as *Myst* and *The Journeyman Project*.

The central story of *Sinkha* concerns the character Hyleyn, who wishes to leave home in search of adventure. She hooks up with the Sinkha, a godlike race of creatures who seduce her into their magical, synthetic environments. Hyleyn's enchanters soon become her captors and the race is on to see who will prevail—the innocent girl torn away from her family or the dark forces of the Sinkha. To advance *Sinkha*'s story, the user is required to click an icon to turn each "page." This limited user interaction triggers new pages of text, mood-altering music, and a poetic dance of photo-realistic 3-D images to appear onscreen. Since the images are basically static (no animation or QuickTime movies in this title), users are drawn into the images in a search for deeper meaning. The end result is a user experience more like browsing pictures at an exhibition rather than playing a game.

Sequential with Cul-de-Sacs

Sometimes a linear sequence of nodes can diverge into isolated nonlinear deviations—offer the user the choice to step off the procedural path into areas that in no way fulfill the critical objective of the piece. Such digressions are called cul-de-sacs—usually puzzles, games, or sidebars that explore the themes of the work, but in no way affect the outcome of the story or objective of the work.

In the real world of automobiles and pavement, a cul-de-sac branches off a major street, right? The interesting thing about a cul-de-sac is that its entrance is also its exit. This applies to interactive cul-de-sacs as well and is especially important for the software designer who's trying to help you tell an interactive narrative (To learn more about cul-de-sacs and their use in interactive stories, see chapter 7).

An interactive corporate training title, for example, might have a node that demonstrates a crucial concept. Several key words or phrases within that node may be "hot." Clicking on one of the words might send the user to another node that shows that word, along with its definition. This sidebar or footnote has no impact on the training lesson itself. It's only there to enhance the user's understanding of the key words and phrases contained in the material. Once the user has finished reading the definition, he or she has only one option—to return to the lesson (see fig. 2.3).

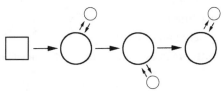

Fig. 2.3. Sequential structure with cul-de-sacs

Many children's edutainment CD-ROMs, such as Mindscape's *The Animals!* use sequential storytelling techniques—e.g., a trip to the zoo—and link them to a ton of archived data. A child can travel through the story and click on an object within a scene. This action will transport the child to a cul-de-sac—a self-contained node of information such as a video clip of a lion, a photograph of a pelican, an audio clip of a monkey, or a text description of a polar bear. Once the information has been delivered and digested by the child, she can either replay the information or return to the main body of the zoo story. In no way does this sideshow alter the multimedia application. The cul-de-sac simply enhances the user experience.

Branching

In an interactive program, branching offers the most rudimentary course of extending how users navigate throughout the program. In a typical branching structure, the user is presented with several choices or options upon arriving at certain predesignated "forks in the road." Based on which path the user chooses, the program follows a new node of content.

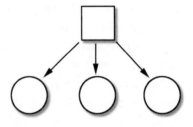

Fig. 2.4. Traditional branching structure

Branching structures are popular because they easily demonstrate the fundamental concept of interactive theory—user choice. Namely, when confronted with a path decision, the user must choose among one of several options—A, B, or C—to proceed to the corresponding node (fig. 2.4).

The danger of branching structures is that they can spiral out of control very quickly. Author Neal Stephenson refers to this type of structure as the "tree of death," where the story line keeps forking until there ends up being an unmanageable number of outcomes (see fig. 2.5).

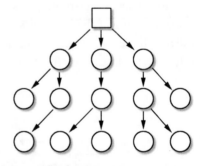

Fig. 2.5. Extended branching structure

Conditional Branching: Branching with Barriers

A subset of branching structure is conditional branching, which requires the user to abide by the rules of a predetermined condition along the branch in order to proceed through the program. Oftentimes, these conditions are puzzles or other obstacles that are slapped down in the middle of the application. The user is forced to solve the puzzle before he or she can continue (see fig. 2.6).

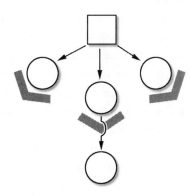

Fig. 2.6. Branching with barriers structure

"A lot of games have puzzles that are just sort of tacked or stuck into the middle of the story," notes Greg Roach. "Very often, the user wonders, What does this puzzle have to do with anything? I feel very strongly that all the obstacles to your progress, all of the problems that you are presented with to solve, need to arise organically out of character and situation."

Conditional Branching: Branching with Forced Paths

Conditional branching often limits user choice in other ways. While appearing on the surface to offer many choices and options, the program will often continue regardless of the user's actual choice. In essence, the program offers the illusion of choice without actually allowing the user to alter the program in any way. The validity of interactivity is strictly limited by the "choices" offered by the writer.

For example, let's say a branching story leads you into a seedy motel office, where the manager is standing behind a desk. Your choice is:

A. Ask manager for a room

B. Walk back outside

If you choose A, the manager gives you a key. If you choose B, the manager follows you outside and hands you a key. Notice that in both instances, the user received the key, regardless of choice. The user was forced down one "correct" path and all other choices lead to "game-overs" (see fig. 2.7).

"The use of 'game-overs' completely works against the goal of creating a perfectly seamless narrative experience," claims Douglas Gayeton. "To require the viewer to leave the application, return to the menu, then come back in at the point where the application was last saved, is akin to turning off the projector, asking the audience to get up from their seats and leave the movie theater, wait in the lobby, then go back into the theater and sit to watch the next part of the show. The entire seamlessness of the experience is lost. Instead, there should be a tangible sense of risk involved in under-

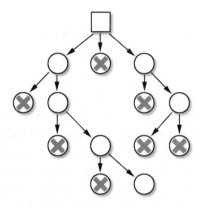

Fig. 2.7. Branching with forced path structure

taking an action, but in no way should this be done at the expense of pulling the viewer out of the experience."

A branching structure using "forced paths" or critical paths offers the end-user more options and/or more paths to choose from, but only one solution advances the story. For example, the story sequence leads you into the seedy motel office with the manager standing behind the desk. Your choice is:

A. Ask manager for a room

B. Walk back outside

C. Punch the manager in the nose

If you choose A, the manager shakes his head no. If you choose B, the office door slams shut behind you. If you choose C, the manager reluctantly offers you a key.

Conditional Branching: Bottlenecking

Another type of condition placed on branching structures (especially when the structure is used in an interactive narrative) manifests itself as "bottlenecking." Bottlenecking is when various branching nodes are brought back into the spine of the story in order to "rein everything in." This is a crucial structural procedure when you consider the exponential possibilities created by traditional branching structure (see fig. 2.8).

When the various story nodes are folded back so that they converge into a single story spine, the interactive narrative becomes more manageable. This type of design structure has been implemented in a number of popular multi-

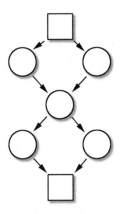

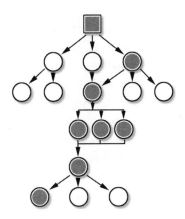

Fig. 2.8. Branching with bottlenecking structure

Fig. 2.9. Branching with optional scenes structure

media games and "interactive movies" over the past several years, including Origin's popular *Wing Commander* series.

"The *Wing Commanders* are long hallways with lots of doors that ultimately keep leading you back to the hallway and a final destination," explains Terry Borst, co-author of *Wing Commander II* and *Wing Commander IV.* "The doors are often of 'The Lady or the Tiger' variety—one's a good choice; the other isn't."

Conditional Branching: Branching with Optional Scenes

Sometimes the user gets to choose between alternative scenes that spin out from and return to the primary spine of the application—whether that spine is a story (as in an interactive narrative) or an objective (as in an informational multimedia application such as a training title). Alternative scenes are commonly found in education and training programs, where it is necessary to demonstrate numerous concepts (see fig. 2.9).

Example: Interactive Customer Service Training CD

```
Client:    Fashion Boutique, U.S.A.
Purpose:   To train employees in how to deal with customers at the cus-
           tomer service counter at a clothing store.
Setup:     You are an employee standing behind the customer service counter.
           A customer approaches your window. You greet the customer.
User:      Hello, may I help you?
```

Alternate Scene 1: Clothing Return, with Receipt

Customer: Yes, I bought this shirt for my son's birthday and I purchased the wrong size shirt by accident. I need to exchange it.

User: (Employee chooses best response.) No problem, ma'am. Do you have your receipt with you?

Customer: Yes, here it is.

Note Employee/customer encounter continues in this manner until there is a resolution.

Alternate Scene 2: Angry Customer, Credit Card Denied

Customer: The young lady over at the cash register won't ring up my purchase. She says your machine is rejecting my card. I don't know what her problem is. I just used that same credit card this morning at another store and there was nothing wrong with the card then . . .

User: (Employee chooses best response.) Sir, I'd like to help you. If I can have your credit card, I will call an account representative right away and find out what the problem is.

Customer: Damn plastic! Here's my card.

Note Employee/customer encounter continues in this manner until there is a resolution.

Alternate Scene 3: Clothing Return, without Receipt

Customer: Hi. I received this dress as a gift and I'd like to exchange it for cash, please.

User: (Employee chooses best response.) I'm sorry. We don't offer cash exchanges for our merchandise. If you have your receipt, I'd be happy to process a store credit for you.

Customer: I don't have a receipt. The dress was a gift. Can I speak with the store manager, please?

Note Employee/customer encounter continues in this manner until there is a resolution.

I think you see where this is going. The alternate scenes in the above example take the user through a range of customer service situations that a new employee might be confronted with on the job. There are only three alternate scenes shown here, but an actual training program may include dozens of scenes for the user to choose from. Depending on the program, the user might be required to successfully navigate one scene, or a series of scenes, before he or she is returned to the main spine of the program. In this case, the main spine would probably direct the user to another training module—perhaps a training scenario on how to use the cash register.

Exploratorium

Exploratoriums are empowering structures that allow the user to "pause" amid the program to explore a "world within a world." Many interactive storybook titles utilize exploratoriums—from the humorous Living Books titles, *Arthur's Birthday* and *Just Grandma and Me* to Disney's *Pocahontas Animated Storybook* and *Toy Story Animated Storybook* to simulated environments such as Imergy/ Simon and Schuster's *Star Trek Captain's Chair*.

The Living Books series of children's interactive storybook titles apply two basic design structures—sequential and exploratorium. The user activates each "page" of the story to turn each page in sequential order. The printed words from say, Marc Brown's *Arthur's Birthday* appear onscreen, along with a graphic illustration. Then the story is read aloud. The experience then pauses for the user to interact with the program. The user may click on a word from the story (clicking on the word "party" activates the soundtrack that says the word). But the main lure of user interactivity is to uncover the entertainment click-ons hidden somewhere in the background (clicking on the big blue balloon in screen ten, for example, causes the balloon to pop and spill water on Grandma's head!).

In Mercer Mayer's *Just Grandma and Me*, the first scene finds Little Critter and Grandma waiting in front of Grandma's house for the bus to arrive. While the characters are waiting, the user may use her mouse to click on an array of objects that appear onscreen. For example, clicking on the white picket fence transforms the object into an animated xylophone that the user sees and hears. Clicking on a flower causes a bumble bee to fly out from the pedals and land on Little Critter's nose. There are numerous items that sing, dance, sputter, and animate within the scene. It's up to the user to uncover them, at his or her own pace, by interacting with the environment. Time seems to stand still as kids click on everything in sight. Both mesmerizing and empowering, interactive storybooks teach users more about the backstory of the characters and the story of the world (see fig. 2.10).

Disney's *Pocahontas Animated Storybook* and *Toy Story Animated Storybook* titles are in a class by themselves. Not only do they emulate the finest qualities found in the Living Books series, but they build on their underlying structures to add even more functionality in the pieces. Both *Pocahontas* and *Toy Story* allow users to enter exploratory game environments where a child can pause the linear story in order to play a ten-minute game of "bow and arrow" or "put the toys away."

Many of the exploratory environments in *Pocahontas* use scrolling screens—an effect that allows the user to expand the play area of an exploratorium by scrolling the background a full 180 degrees—which increases the amount of possible user interaction within a given scene.

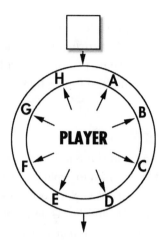

Fig. 2.10. Exploratorium structure. Letters A, B, C, D, E, F, G, and H are "hot spots" or entertainment click-ons imbedded into the program.

Toy Story has enhanced its games by allowing the user to play according to skill level, so that the game "grows" with the age of the child. This is an important feature when it's the parent shelling out the bucks to purchase the program.

Imergy/Simon and Schuster's *Star Trek Captain's Chair* is a simulated virtual tour of five starship bridges—the USS Enterprise NCC-1701 (from the original series, *Star Trek*), the USS Enterprise NCC-1701-D (*Star Trek: The Next Generation*), the USS Enterprise NCC-1701-E (*Star Trek: First Contact*), the USS Defiant NX-74205 (*Star Trek: Deep Space Nine*), and the USS Voyager NCC-74656 (*Star Trek: Voyager*).

Star Trek Captain's Chair gives the user a chance to experience the excitement of actually being onboard (and on the bridge) of a Starfleet ship. Using photo-realistic QuickTime VR (virtual reality) technology, *Captain's Chair* is an archival holosimulation that stimulates the imagination. There is no time limit or mission to accomplish. Exploration is a thrill in itself.

Parallel Streaming

Parallel streaming describes many "states" or paths that exist simultaneously at various levels within the same application. In an interactive narrative, this type of structure allows the writer to create a single linear story, while allowing the user to switch between perspectives, paths, or states. The user can then experience the same series of events from multiple points of view (see fig. 2.11).

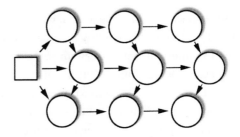

Fig. 2.11. Parallel streaming structure

A number of theatrical performances, feature films, and novels have experimented with this concept of parallel streaming. John Krizanc's environmental play *Tamara* was an early experiment in interactivity that ran for ten years in Los Angeles. In the play, the actors performed scenes in parallel throughout the many rooms of a house. Unlike a traditional performance, where each audience member experiences the play from a single vantage point—from their seats, *Tamara* audience members choose a character to follow around the house, wherever the action may take them. This unique perspective allows an audience member to experience the unfolding story in an atmosphere of isolation and voyeurism. The audience's point of view of the play is experienced through the eyes of the characters they follow. The audience cannot interact with the cast of the play (that would violate the story), but they can move around the room and move in for a closer look at the action.

The entire performance cannot be fully appreciated, therefore, without viewing the play several times from a different character's point of view. In order to reveal the higher arc of the story, multiple viewings from multilinear points of view are necessary. However, each viewing is in itself a valid and satisfying interactive narrative.

Akira Kurosawa's feature film *Rashomon* gives its audience four viewpoints of the same incident—an episode of rape and murder in a forest. The crime is reported by four witnesses, each from his or her own unique point of view. The audience must then ask itself, Who is telling the truth? The film goes on to pose an even larger question, What is truth?

Another example of parallel streaming structure is *Neurostatica*, an online multicharacter story set in a time-based environment. The project was created, written, designed, and directed by Douglas Gayeton; produced by Glenn Kaino; and illustrated by Steve Vance. The story is twenty minutes long and features ten characters and forty locations. Every thirty seconds, the story progresses. The user is able to follow individual characters or go on his or her own journey. Since time always moves forward, being in one location means missing what is happening elsewhere. This is very similar to the *Tamara* model. The user is rewarded for repeated viewings of *Neurostatica*, and, in fact, the only way to get to the *über* ending is to actually piece together "hints" from each of the ten interconnected story lines. Aside from multiple characters, the user discovers valuable plot points by interacting with the environments.

"For me, one of the most interesting things about the project is that the twenty-minute length provides two important elements to the experience," explains Gayeton. "First, it insures the dramatic semblance of three-act structure, in that each of the story lines plays out over twenty minutes, and second, it fulfills the same type of 'contract' that a sitcom makes with a viewer, in that it agrees to deliver a complete experience in a mutually agreed-upon time frame. Online experiences that have no shape, that provide the user with no sense of where they are in a story, will never work, so *Neurostatica* is valuable from the standpoint that it explores how to capture the bounded experience principles we get from television."

In October 1994, Seattle-based HyperBole Studios released its award-winning multimedia CD-ROM, *The Madness of Roland*. Touted as the "world's first interactive multimedia novel," *Roland* is one of the only interactive titles ever to be released to market that was designed to allow the reader/user to experience the story from multiple points of view (see fig. 2.12).

Fig. 2.12. Screen shot from *The Madness of Roland*. TM and Copyright of HyperBole Studios, 1994. Reprinted by permission.

The story is based on the legend of Paladin Roland, a knight in the service of Charlemagne. Users navigate the program by following one of several characters who "tell the tale" from their unique point of view, oftentimes resulting in contradictory versions of the story. *Roland* uses text, Pythonesque-digital color paintings, animation, QuickTime movies, theater-style audio recordings of the text, hypertextual links to different chapters of the saga, and an original soundtrack to transport you to the world of Charlemagne's France (see fig. 2.13).

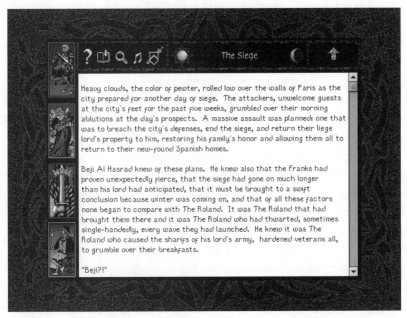

Fig. 2.13. Screen shot from *The Madness of Roland*. TM and Copyright of HyperBole Studios, 1994. Reprinted by permission.

"*Roland* was originally conceived as a stage play that would exist in the space between traditional theater, dance, opera, mime, and film," claims the project's writer/designer/director, Greg Roach. "As I began work on the stage version, it soon became apparent that very few theater companies would be able to afford to produce *Roland* as fully as I had envisioned it, with its huge sweep, spectacular sets, and dozens of characters. Fortunately for me (and *Roland*), I discovered the plastic possibilities of interactive multimedia."

The Madness of Roland was a very ambitious work at the time of its release, winning numerous awards (Best Story/Script, New Media Invision Awards, Best Interactive, QuickTime Movie Festival; Top 50 CD-ROMs, *MacUser* magazine).

Worlds

When two or more environments are interconnected by a common thread—be it a theme, goal,
mission, or story—you have the basis for a world
structure. Add to that world a series of predefined
events or tasks that the user must trigger/accom-
plish in order to move the story or mission forward and you have a design structure that works
very well with interactive media programs.

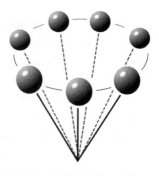

Fig. 2.14. World structure. Notice that the world is in the shape of a funnel.

In a world experience, exploring the surroundings is just as important (and fun) as completing the story or achieving an objective. This
poses a unique set of problems for the writer. If the user is free to roam the
environment at will—without the strict navigation barriers of, say, a branching structure—how can the writer construct a coherent story or objective?

Myst accomplished this by "hiding" a very linear story in a series of
"worlds" (linked locations) for users to reconstruct at their own pace. A world
design structure works well for *Myst* because the player is free to roam an en-
chanting environment in search of clues to the story. The act of exploration is
just as important as the act of discovering the narrative. Each activity has equal
merit. The player advances the story by triggering certain author-defined
events. Exploring all the worlds, uncovering all the clues, and interacting with
all the triggers leads the player to the end of the game (see fig. 2.14).

The design structure built into the interactive movie/game *Johnny Mnemonic* is a world. Writer/designer Douglas Gayeton likes to call it a sphere. Each
sphere contains multiple levels, each with its own set of "missions" to solve in
order to advance the story. And each sphere represents a separate "act" of the
story. As Gayeton explains it:

> As you enter a new experience, you have to piece together all the given ob-
> jects, the clues, and all of the information which is embedded in that story. It
> is your mission to reconstruct a plot which is a reasonable facsimile of the
> higher, arcing story that you've entered. I've made diagrams that resemble a
> sphere. The outside of the sphere has twenty, let's say it has twenty-seven
> points. The sphere mirrors life—we are simultaneously problem-solving a
> dozen things at the same time. . . .
>
> In an interactive experience, let's say you're simultaneously problem-solv-

ing nine things. And let's say you need to figure out three things to solve each of those nine things. That means that when you first come into the experience, you're not on a path, you're on the outside of a sphere. A sphere with twenty-seven points that you're exposed to. If you solve three of the correct points, it moves you into the circle one notch because you have just solved one of the nine things. Of those nine things, there's three things you have to figure for every nine—that comes to twenty-seven. Once you figure out three of those inner things, or three of the inner nine, you've just solved the first act of the story.

Another way to look at a world structure would be an overhead view, as if looking down into the center of a funnel or cone. The plot points or tasks that the user must accomplish are represented by the eight outer nodes. The eight inner nodes in the carousel represent the next set of tasks (see fig. 2.15).

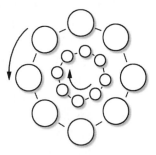

Fig. 2.15. Carousel entry into a world structure

Greg Roach, CEO and artistic director of HyperBole Studios, was asked to share his thoughts on the underlying design structure used in his latest interactive CD-ROM project, *The X-Files*. Needless to say, his description sounded a lot like a world/funnel structure:

> The narrative structure used in *The X-Files* resembles a series of linked circles (nodes). Inside a given circle, the player has complete freedom to complete a series of events or participate in a number of activities inside of that node, and do it in any order that the person may choose. Inside of a node, we have three basic classes of items:
> - *Candy* All the stuff that brings the world to life. Anything from an object sitting on a desk that you can pick up and look at or manipulate, to a character's backstory.
> - *Growing food* The things you must do to advance the story.
> - *Triggers* In our object-oriented program, when you trip a trigger, it causes a message to be sent to the game engine, which then causes subsequent "state" changes in either the environment, characters, or objects. A trigger can be a spot on the floor, a character, an object you pick up, or even something you say.

WRITING FOR INTERACTIVE MEDIA

Once you have interacted with (or accomplished) all the growing food for a node, an "act" of the story is completed. The player then seamlessly segues into the next act.

The X-Files uses a narrative segment, commonly called a "link." A link is a much shorter, restricted segment. [There are] ten nodes and five links in *The X-Files*. So while a node is a much larger, more open piece of the structure, links are smaller, more focused pieces of action that allow us to more easily focus certain story elements. Links are still highly interactive, they are simply less expansive than full-blown nodes.

The other thing [done] in terms of the overall arc of the story is to "funnel" it. In the early stages of the story, you're in the wide end of the funnel, so there is much more play when it comes to where you can go to physically and how you deal with characters in the piece. As we move forward into the story, the player gets further down into the funnel until reaching the climactic final portion or neck of the funnel. The environment at that point in time has become more constricted. There is a much more definitive channel to run through. We do this because we want to create a sense of acceleration, accomplishment, and release that is critical to a classic three-act structure, as opposed to meandering toward the end of the game.

Inside of that, we have something called multithreading. These are story elements that are added to or taken away from the narrative, based on the player's choices. In circumstances where you get into a conversation with a character, for example, the user will encounter "chained dialogues" that have a kind of branching structure. How the player chooses to traverse that chain feeds directly into those psychological *über* variables. Rather than affecting the story, chained dialogues affect the user's experience with the story.

The idea of widely variable narratives—where a player can drive the story all over the place—has significant problems. Setting aside the artistic and aesthetic issues and just considering the practical production terms, these types of interactive projects just don't work.

The X-Files has a fixed story that is experienced through a series of problems or obstacles that the player solves. And we give the player the tools to go about doing that. Very often, there are multiple ways to approach a given problem. In general, story variability comes in three different forms:

- *Psychology* Music, backstory, aesthetics, soundtrack, little telling pieces that can change the tone or flavor of a scene or a piece of information based upon these psychological variables.

- *Characters and your relations with those characters* If a character is killed and you are talking to a relative of that character about the event, his or her reaction to you will be based on your accumulated history with the program (angry, vengeful, blaming, sad, appreciative, etc.). The event can be "customized" for each player and yet the narrative event itself can stay fixed.

- *Narrative embellishments* Little pieces of action that are added to the experience or removed based upon your accumulated history with the material. These almost become tangential to the main narrative.

Multilinear or Hypermedia

Another type of design structure, known as multilinear, either encompasses every type of user path imaginable or no path at all. The World Wide Web, hypertext fiction, MUDs (multi-user domains), MOOs (multi-user object-oriented environments), and many simulations are good examples. Multilinear structure demands a different kind of involvement from its users than do puzzles, branching games, or linear narratives. That's because it is the users themselves who must traverse their own unique paths through an environment. The writer sets the boundaries and rules of interactivity, but the users must chart their own course through the material.

Simulations such as *Tank Platoon II, SimCity, Flight Unlimited,* and *Gettysburg* are ideal examples of multilinear structures put to the test. Whether you are piloting a jet fighter, driving a tank, building a virtual city, or re-creating a Civil War battle, simulated experiences cannot be predetermined by the writer/creator. Each simulation has a certain amount of randomness and spontaneity built into its "play." That's what makes them so enjoyable. No two simulations are exactly alike (see fig. 2.16).

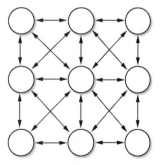

It is impossible for a writer/designer to preconceive every possible move a pilot might make in a flight simulator, or predict all the possible ways in which an armchair Darwinian might try to populate the world. When structuring a simulated environment, writers must first define all the major interactive elements in the program, then assign specific

Fig. 2.16. Multilinear or hypermedia structure

characteristics (attributes and conduct) to those elements—a rule book, so to speak. A skilled programmer can then take that rule book and create a workable space.

In *The Complete Wargames Handbook*, Dunnigan writes, "What makes a simulation such a powerful form of communication is that it is, like most events, nonlinear. A book or film is linear. The author leads you from point to point, with no deviation allowed. Simulations, games in general, and analytic history, are nonlinear. That is, you can wander all over the place and still be somewhere. Flip through a book, and you pick up pieces out of context. Make different moves in a game, and you have a context, because the game allows, even encourages, deviating from the historical events."

Hypermedia structures, in much the same way as the World Wide Web or a hypertext fiction title, allow the user to become an interactor—a facilitator of the story. While surfing the Web, the user decides which home page to start from and selects which links to follow through the electronic universe. User action determines a pathway through the material. Similarly, hypertext fictions are about the journey as much as they are about the narrative that waits to be pieced together.

"From the beginning, I referred to hypertext fictions as multiple fictions," claims hypertext guru, Michael Joyce. "Not because I wanted to steer attention away from the technology or the modality of the telling, but because my own experience reading and teaching these fictions is that they are, in some sense, almost lifelike structures."

3

What Interactive Documents Look Like

Your task as a writer is to make your position clear through the precise statement of your dominant idea, clear examples that make the basis of your idea plain, arrangement of your points so that they lead your reader along the path of your thoughts without confusion, and effective language that holds your reader's attention.

DAVID KANN

We've spent the first two chapters discussing how to plan and structure your interactive ideas. Here we take a look at the not-so-systematic process of writing documents for interactive media—be it a proposal, screenplay, or design document.

One of the most important things to keep in mind about interactive documents is that they cannot be dry and predictable. Interactive writing must *sing*. The words need to jump off the page, allowing the reader to easily envision the project as if it were already made.

David Kann emphasizes the importance of the written word in his book *The Literate Writer*, saying, "The voice you choose to express your ideas—your choice of words, the length and rhythm of your sentences, whether or not you use figurative language and words that appeal to your reader's emotions—both reflects and helps you refine your sense of your situation, your purpose, and your audience."

Readers of interactive documents are often producers working at multi-

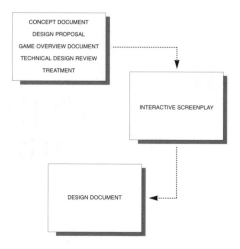

media publishing companies who are in charge of financing and overseeing the production process of an interactive property. These producers risk their jobs whenever they "green light" an interactive document, so they have every reason in the world to say no. Saying yes means someone has given his or her stamp of approval to a document the person hopes will be produced into a "winning" interactive application. If the property should eventually bomb in the marketplace, that producer's job may be on the line. Saying no is the safest course of action.

The creative atmosphere that results from such overcautious behavior can be stifling to the writer unfamiliar with dealing with such situations. The trick is to not get caught up in the "spiral of death," the much-feared industry term for a project that has stalled and is going nowhere fast. Even in situations where a writer is creating an interactive document without producer supervision— say in a small work-for-hire job or speculative work—the written document must be a powerful representation of the envisioned work. In short, the writing of interactive documents must be effective and engaging.

Effective and Engaging Writing

Interactive writers face the unenviable task of transforming written words into dynamic documents—paper-based material that summarizes every aspect of the interactive application while showcasing its best features.

"Writing should pull the user into their computer," claims writer/designer Deborah Todd. "It has to make them feel they are there, with the characters or immersed in the story, and completely involved with their interactive experience. They have to feel 'present' with it. The best compliment I have ever had about a project I worked on was when a fifteen-year-old boy wrote us and said that he felt like he was talking to his computer. This kid was immersed. We did the job of getting him into the experience, holding his attention, making it fun and meaningful, and leaving a lasting impression. When you can do that, you feel like you've made it."

Effective writing promotes a credible or believable interaction between writer and reader that simulates reality and emotionally impacts the user. Writing that engages the user holds his or her attention and empowers the person. The user is able to communicate, alter, or customize aspects of the experience, which makes them want to come back for more.

Clarity and Design Issues

Check your written document carefully for spelling errors and any other errors you can spot. Errors like misspelled words may cause a reader to stop perusing your work and reach instead for a fresh one from the "pile" that is or looks more professional. This may sound like a minor point, but many writers ignore it and send in written documents with lots of errors. Don't destroy your career opportunities at the pass. Make certain your written material is error free with all words spelled correctly. You'll be glad you checked and corrected it.

How you lay out the page is also important. Without getting too fancy, create a page layout that enhances the reading experience. Some pointers to consider:
- Make the page easy to read and pleasing to the eye
- Use bullet points, bold words, and underlines when appropriate
- Double-space rather than single-space
- Use professional-quality graphics to draw attention to key areas of text (if you can't create professional-quality graphics, don't use any!)
- Make sure the page has ample "white space" around the main body of text

The Proposal

Writers of interactive texts are commonly asked to create proposals—documents that explain, highlight, and help sell an interactive application *before* it is created. It may be almost any length, but proposals usually range from ten to twenty pages. A well-written proposal effectively conveys the central idea, premise, or message of the work. It should explain how the idea lends itself well to the interactive environment and why the idea will perform well in the marketplace.

Proposals come in many forms and are labeled with different names (depending on a writer's background). The most common names for interactive proposals are:

- Treatment
- Outline
- Concept document
- Design proposal
- Game overview document
- Technical design review

Proposals allow the creative team to review the application's key elements such as story, theme, navigation, and marketing elements early on in the development process. Proposals are commonly used to pitch interactive projects to prospective investors or publishers. If your proposal describes and shows your plan for an interactive property with powerful appeal, you are that much closer to a yes decision—and a green light to proceed.

Writer/designer Jeff Sullivan describes interactive proposals as game overview documents, characterizing them as "nontechnical overviews of the project, detailing such issues as target audience, genre, plot, characters, location, backstory, gameplay elements, description of typical play sessions, and an overview of major game design choices and their implications. In essence, this document is much like a feature film treatment but with a description of the sort of gameplay the user will participate in (story puzzles, game puzzles, et al.)"

Interactive writer/instructor Harry Youtt explains, "I don't have a name for the initial document, and its nature varies. Very frequently it is linked to a presentation that lays out the possibilities. I usually create something in Corel's Presentations or a rough, working HTML file. This differs from the pitch-presentation in that it has zeroed in on the specific project. The goal is to get the client really focused on the potentialities that the new medium really provides. The hard-copy document that I leave with the client is a printout of the presentation, perhaps with some additional notes."

According to Youtt, his proposals attempt to achieve the following:

- I want my client to realize that to maximize the impact of the new medium, the client has to begin thinking in the metaphor of the new medium, seeing the task as a function of the medium.

- I want my client to come to the realization, in motion, that the only way this project is *really* going to maximize, is when the client's mind and mine are in true alliance. This happens when the client enters the new metaphor, actually begins to coexperience the possibilities of accomplishing its task, delivering its message in the form it has commissioned me to accomplish.

- I want my client to be jarred into accepting that what this is about is not old wine in new bottles. It is a new dimension. Even though the client may *think* it knows this from previous experience, *my* experience is that our field is so new and dynamic that this eureka-realization has usually not happened yet at the time I arrive on scene.

Deborah Todd says, "Mostly, we want to get the big picture down on paper. There's a ton of brainstorming during this collaborative time—that's what the early meetings are all about, no matter how good of an idea someone thinks they have about the game. So, there's a lot of back-and-forth, calls and meetings, throwing out ideas and writing it in a cohesive document that gives a really clear overview of the thing. Sometimes it turns into a marketing piece, so it has to be really schmoozy. Other times, if you're lucky enough to work with a team that has a green light and understands what the concept is, you just do slightly enhanced bullet points. Sometimes, you just keep cranking out gameplay concept after gameplay concept, especially if the company you're working with has top management who doesn't 'get it,' or they can't agree which direction they want to go.

"I swear, for one project I worked on, we could have produced at least six CD-ROMs out of all of the gameplay we came up with. That was the title, of course, that ended up getting canceled. Go figure!

"The top three concepts I try to convey in an interactive outline are overall gameplay, character workup, and almost always some marketing."

Anatomy of an Interactive Proposal

1. Title and Title Page

Titles by themselves cannot be copyrighted. One thing that bugs some writers about working on retail titles is the fact that a publisher may, and usually does, change the title. A writer may dream up a brilliant title, only to see it changed.

The best thing about some interactive proposals is the title, which could well be the strongest selling point of the project. Work hard to get a compelling, magnetic title. One way to do this is to bounce ideas off a family member, relative, friend, and other writers.

Never underestimate the power of a strong title for a multimedia game. Readers respond to great titles. Here are a few examples:

- Total Annihilation
- Zork Grand Inquisitor
- Duke Nukem Forever
- Starship Titanic
- The Journeyman Project
- ScruTiny in the Great Round
- Quest for Glory: Dragonfire

Here are a few eye-catching titles for some interactive nonfiction titles:

- JFK Assassination: A Visual Investigation
- Cosmopolitan Virtual Makeover
- Comic Book Confidential
- Poetry in Motion
- Harvest of the Sun: Vincent van Gogh
- In the Company of Whales
- I Photograph to Remember

2. One-Line Summary/Quick Pitch

This is where writers summarize their work in twenty words or less. Imagine for a moment that you are with a small gathering of friends and associates. Somebody asks you what your interactive project is about. Quickly, without hesitation, the following words spill forth from your lips . . .

That's what the quick summary is—a quick summary of your application in one phrase or one sentence that anyone can easily comprehend. Think *TV Guide* listing. Make sure to state the preferred delivery platform (if your have one) in your quick pitch (CD-ROM, Web site, kiosk, arcade, multiplayer online game, etc.).

3. Premise

Used in narrative multimedia applications, a premise is a one-paragraph description that summarizes the interactive project and its core objective. Sometimes referred to as a summary, a premise is perhaps the most important element since it is the first major description of your project the reader will encounter.

Pretend for a moment that you are a writer toiling away at an interactive media production company. One day, your boss ushers you into her office and proclaims that the company is dramatically shifting its development strategy. Due to a cash crunch, the firm will now develop innovative applications based solely on properties in the public domain. Your responsibility is to come up with some test concepts for an interactive title based on the nursery rhyme *Jack and Jill.*

After you realize she is not joking, you stop laughing, scratch your noggin, and hark back to your childhood. You recount the once familiar tale:

Jack and Jill went up the hill to fetch a pail of water. Jack fell down and broke his crown and Jill came tumbling after.

How would you approach the task of making *Jack and Jill* interactive? Well, a writer might first pose a series of questions to help formulate a new approach to the material. Questions such as:
- What caused Jack to fall down?
- Why was Jack wearing a crown?
- What caused Jill to come tumbling after?

Or perhaps alternative situations such as:
- What if Jack and Joe went up the hill?
- What if the hill was a pyramid instead of a hill?

By posing a few simple analytical questions and altering at least one key element familiar to our story, whole new creative ideas suddenly become possible. Let's take a look:

Jack and Joe climbed up a pyramid to fetch a golden amulet. Joe tripped Jack and he fell down. Joe snatched Jack's crown, scooped up the amulet, and was never seen in the city again.

With a little more tinkering, the concept could be expanded into a full-blown adventure game concept—a *Jack and Jill* meets *Torin's Passage:*

On a day that starts like any other, young Jack learns that the world he knows is about to change forever. A mysterious warlock, known only as Mean Joe Green, puts his parents under an evil spell and snatches his father's magic crown, then vanishes into the vast labyrinth of the black pyramid. Knowing only the sound of the Jillian's voice, Jack vows to find her, force her to relinquish his father's crown, and release his parents from bondage. Thus begins an exciting adventure that will take Jack to the five inner worlds of the black pyramid—a world filled with danger and fantasy. Use your wits to help Jack solve many challenging riddles, as he discovers more about himself than he could ever have imagined.

The following formula may help you generate an interactive premise that will hook your reader:

[Project Title] is a story about [Name of Your Protagonist], a [Description of Your Protagonist] who, after [Obstacle], wants to [Outer Motivation] by [Method of Accomplishing Outer Motivation]. We will know [Protagonist] has succeeded at the end of the story when [Protagonist] has [Accomplishment That Signifies Success].

EXAMPLE: *The Journeyman Project II: Buried in Time* is a story about you—Agent 5, a likable player who, after being framed for altering the fabric of time and thrown in jail, must escape and traverse history to unravel the plot against you. We will know you have succeeded at the end of the interactive adventure when you gather all the evidence necessary to prove your innocence.

ANOTHER EXAMPLE: *Alone in the Dark* is about Edward Carnby or Edward's niece Emily (user chooses between a male or female protagonist), a slick private eye who, after the demise of eccentric artist Jeremy Hartwood, tries to find the reason behind his untimely death by searching through Hartwood's creepy old mansion. We will know Edward/Emily has succeeded when he/she defeats all the demons and pieces together the clues to the mystery.

4. Concept Overview

Most informational multimedia proposals start with an overview of the basic concept, rather than a premise. A concept overview is a summary of your idea, which tells the reader how your interactive application will be different from the thousands of interactive media projects being published each year.

5. Story Summary

In a narrative multimedia proposal, this is where you describe in further detail, the story and objective of the property and explain how the user will interact with the story. A story summary varies in length from one page to ten pages or more.

6. Character Descriptions

If your interactive project uses characters, this is where you take the time to introduce them to the reader. Try to include character traits such as personality, physical appearance, backstory, and their relationships to the rest of the characters in the project.

7. Underlying Design Structure(s) with Flowchart(s)

This is where you explain what type of underlying structure(s) you will use in your interactive project and why. Often the best way to demonstrate the flow of a program is by creating a flowchart or matrix, which are charts that demonstrate how your nodes of interaction are hyperlinked together. (Chapter 2 defines each type of interactive structure in detail.)

8. Compelling Features/Rules of Interaction

Here's where you identify special features, rules, tools, or tricks that will make your project stand out. What's so cool about your project and what special rules will the user need to follow? For example, the CD-ROM game *Bad Day on the Midway* has several unique "rules of interaction" built into the game such as allowing players the ability to jump into the various character bodies to hear their thoughts.

9. Interface Methodology

This is where you spell out how you see the user will interact with the program. Let's look at the interactive art piece, *ScruTiny in the Great Round,* produced by Calliope Media.

The main index screen is a collection of twenty-four screen images arranged in a circle. Actions are initiated by moving the cursor and clicking once on an active spot—there is no need to double-click. Each screen has two main levels, the sun level and the moon level, and many animated sequences in between. Moving a cursor to different parts of the screen will also change the mix of music, sound effects, voice, and at times graphics. There is no "correct" way to navigate through *ScruTiny.* Users explore at their own pace as they please.

10. Walkthru/Play Scenario

This is where the writer literally walks the reader through one small section of the program—explaining each sight, sound, animation, dialogue, and all other possible interactivities that a user might encounter during a play scenario. This section of your proposal is especially important because it helps bring your words to life. Walkthrus help the reader conceptualize a writer's vision.

11. Sales and Marketing Forecast

To demonstrate how confident you are that your idea will be a runaway commercial success, this is where you put your money where your mouth is. If it's a commercial application, identify your competition, explain why this project will sell, who will buy it, how much money it should make, and why. If this is a not-for-profit informational or educational project, give a passionate explanation why this project should be made.

12. Creative Team Credentials

If you have special credentials for writing an interactive application on a particular subject, state these facts up front. Mention any previously published works and toot your own horn if your track record includes any notable projects. Don't be modest here, because this part of the proposal can influence a decision to finance and/or produce your project.

If you have no previous interactive credits, then tell about any other published work you have done, including books, articles, short stories, newspaper work, columns, or whatever. Be sure to include biographies on any creative team members that you can "attach" to your project in the event the project should go into development.

What Does a Proposal Look Like?

Now that we have reviewed the critical elements that make up an interactive proposal, let's take a look at what an actual interactive proposal looks like. Keep in mind that no two proposals are exactly the same. Some writers create dense, five-page proposals that include only the essential "story" and "design" elements necessary to get their message across. Other writers will create an elaborate fifteen- to twenty-page document that contains all the essential proposal elements, plus storyboards, maps, technical specifications, a budget, and a production schedule.

UR Here is a concept document (proposal) written by Cristina Bogossian, a student at UC Irvine Extension's Digital Arts Program. Notice that she has given equal weight to the written word and the look and feel of the paper document, creating a presentation with impact.

Welcome to Earth.

As long as you know *"you are here,"* you can now get
information and directions to virtually any place you might need
or wish to go, by simply touching a button (or two...)

Where do you *need* to go today?

COPYRIGHT © 1998 BY CRISTINA BOGOSSIAN

CONTACT:
Cristina Bogossian
Post Office Box 663
Balboa, California 92661
714.574.2472
cri@aol.com

Fig. 3.1. Concept document for *UR Here* written by Cristina Bogossian. Reprinted by permission.

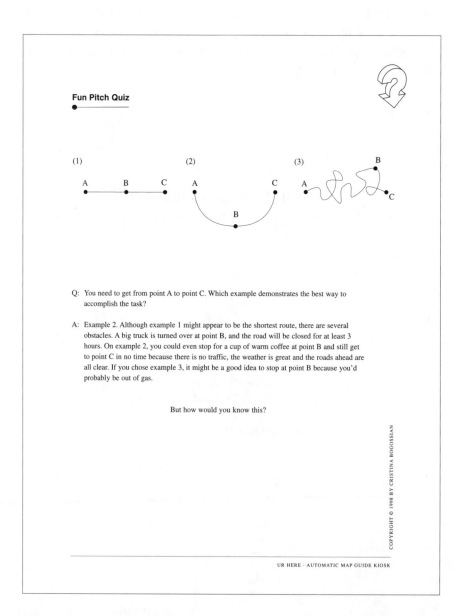

Fun Pitch Quiz

(1)

A   B   C

(2)

A   C

B

(3)

                      B

A   C

Q: You need to get from point A to point C. Which example demonstrates the best way to accomplish the task?

A: Example 2. Although example 1 might appear to be the shortest route, there are several obstacles. A big truck is turned over at point B, and the road will be closed for at least 3 hours. On example 2, you could even stop for a cup of warm coffee at point B and still get to point C in no time because there is no traffic, the weather is great and the roads ahead are all clear. If you chose example 3, it might be a good idea to stop at point B because you'd probably be out of gas.

But how would you know this?

COPYRIGHT © 1998 BY CRISTINA BOGOSSIAN

UR HERE - AUTOMATIC MAP GUIDE KIOSK

Fig. 3.2. Concept document for *UR Here* written by Cristina Bogossian. Reprinted by permission.

Premise

"*UR Here*" is an easy-to-use automatic map guide kiosk that will show the user the best way to get from point A to .... virtually anywhere they need, or simply wish to go. These extremely helpful kiosks will be conveniently located in strategic places all across the nation (such as airports, train stations, tourist attractions or even convenient stores and gas stations along major freeways), and it's designed to help the user get detailed information about specific place or destination. This would include map directions and updated information about weather conditions, traffic reports and alternative routes. And, for those in need of a more complete guide, this kiosk will also help the user locate gas stations, restroom areas and restaurants as well as other "UR Here" locations along the way. After interacting with the program, the user will have the knowledge necessary to be successful at his/her journey, whether it is just a short drive to a new business across town or an adventurous trip to another side of the coast."you'll be lost without it"

Explanation of Underlying Structure

UR Here's structure has the critical objective to give the user the information he/she is looking for. The user will, during navigation, define the path that will lead to the program's objective. This touch-screen informational kiosk has an opening screen (common point to all users) that will branch to a multi-directional flow, allowing users to make choices that will lead them to achieving their goals. The main design structure used on the program is conditional branching where the user will be given choices that will determine his/her own path (for example, "if you want a traffic report touch button A, if not touch button B"). It also uses sequential structure when the user will simply respond to pre-defined questions or tasks that will move him/her from one screen to another while following the same path (for example: "please enter your starting point", which after completed will lead to the following screen: "please enter your destination point"). The kiosk will also present loopbacks to allow user to make changes or new choices. The exit screen may or may not be different for different users, all depending on what type of information was requested.

Rules of Interaction

The opening screen displays an animated 3D logo which revolves around itself while a welcome message and instructions on how to launch the program fades in and out of the screen, each time showing the same message in one of the seven different languages available at the kiosk.

COPYRIGHT © 1998 BY CRISTINA BOGOSSIAN

UR HERE - AUTOMATIC MAP GUIDE KIOSK

Fig. 3.3. Concept document for *UR Here* written by Cristina Bogossian. Reprinted by permission.

Rules of Interaction (cont.)

The program is launched as soon as the user touches the animated logo on the center of the screen. Another screen will then appear asking the user to choose from one of the seven languages he/she would like to use to interact with the program by touching one of his/her own country's animated flag. After that, a third screen will explain the user the program's objective, rules of interaction and also instructions on how to use it (on the bottom of the screen 3 buttons will give user the option to "continue,", "quit" or "see demo"). If "continue" was selected, the user will then be asked pre-defined tasks which will lead to program's main goal. Along the way, the user will be given choices, such as "would you like an updated weather report from your destination?" and asked questions, such as "what is your starting point (leave blank to use kiosk as default)" The user will need to provide some of the required information in order to continue the navigation. At anytime, the user will be able to go back to other screens, quit the program, see the demo or get help, by touching one of the easy to recognize buttons on the bottom of the screen.

Bonus Feature

A simplified version of the yellow pages will be a helpful bonus feature of this project. A "Smart Yellow Pages™" icon will appear as a corner button on the bottom left side of the screen and at any time users will be able to access information about business and services of a specific area.

Featured Technology and Authoring Tools

The "*URHere*" kiosk will work using a "touch screen" technology and will be created using a custom interactive program made specially for this project. It will feature outstanding animated graphics and animation, a user friendly interface and will be as easy to use as an ATM machine so the user can be "on the road" at no time.

Key Market Strategies

The target market for this UR Here includes everyday drivers, adventurous travelers and basically anyone who needs to get from one point to another. Marketing strategies will include continuous use of the project's logo/symbol, which will be displayed in each of the kiosk's locations and printed in all advertising materials. These will help the public get familiarized with the new product, and will also help the user locate the kiosks by recognizing the logo. To

COPYRIGHT © 1998 BY CRISTINA BOGOSSIAN

UR HERE - AUTOMATIC MAP GUIDE KIOSK

Fig. 3.4. Concept document for *UR Here* written by Cristina Bogossian. Reprinted by permission.

present the concept of UR Here to its target market, ads will be placed on the travel section of newspapers with national circulation as well as national travel magazines.

Project Key Selling Points

Convenience. That's our project main selling point. Sure, anyone can buy a map guide in one of the many bookstores in town. But how often people get frustrated trying to unfold enormous maps with tiny and almost unreadable typestyles? Sure, there are internet web sites and computer software packages that will provide you with map information, but will anyone have computer and internet access everywhere they go? Another key selling point of this project is the driving movie featured which will be available for selected locations (such as major tourist attractions) and consists of giving the user a demo drive to his destination, emphasizing major cross streets and freeways. More? Come take a ride!

Creative Team Bios

CRISTINA BOGOSSIAN was born n Brazil and graduated in 1993 with a degree in Graphic Design. She moved to California in 1996, where she successfully completed the Certificate Program in Computers for Graphic Design and is now working for a small in-house ad agency in Orange County. She is also enrolled in the Certificate Program for Interactive Multimedia as she plans to become an expert in developing original and creative interactive multimedia software dedicated to the public use. This will be her second interactive project.

ALEXANDRE and TATIANE BORTOLUZZI are also from Brazil and have been working with computer programming for the past 10 years. Alex graduated with a Computer Science degree in 1992, and Tati received her Bachelor's Degree in Mathematics last year. They will be this project's programmers.

BRUNO BOGHOSSIAN is only 11 years old and an Internet Creative Consultant. This is his second professional project and he is researching related sites and softwares for our study and comparison.

KATHIA BOGHOSSIAN is a professional writer and research specialist. She is analysing other related software and their faults in order to make this a better and more complete project, which will also be her second.

COPYRIGHT © 1998 BY CRISTINA BOGOSSIAN

UR HERE - AUTOMATIC MAP GUIDE KIOSK

Fig. 3.5. Concept document for *UR Here* written by Cristina Bogossian. Reprinted by permission.

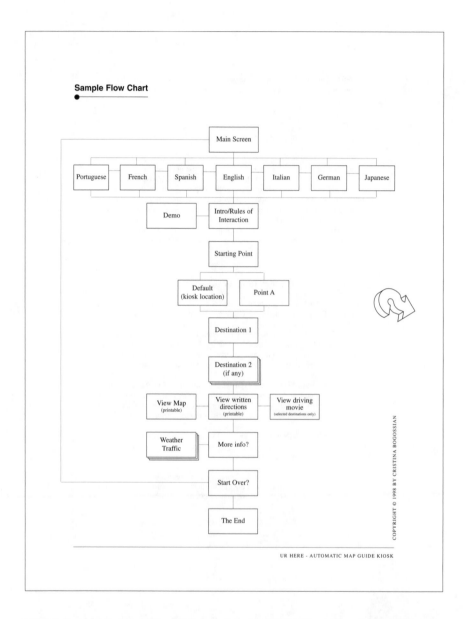

Fig. 3.6. Concept document for *UR Here* written by Cristina Bogossian. Reprinted by permission.

Fig. 3.7. Concept document for *UR Here* written by Cristina Bogossian. Reprinted by permission.

The Design Document

Filmmakers use screenplays. Builders use blueprints. Composers use a score. Interactive writers, producers, and designers use something called a "design document."

The design document is the written instrument utilized by the creative design team to assemble an interactive application. Design documents range in length from one hundred to one thousand pages or more, depending on the size and scope of the project. As is often the case in a retail or Web-based project, the design document is a work in progress. Typically, the first stage of writing a design document is to expand the interactive proposal, fleshing out the design elements, incorporating design changes as a result of technology tests and feedback from project members, and accounting for any changes to the project needs and goals.

"The goal of any major revisions in this phase is to bring the design into line with a realistic production schedule," claims Jeff Sullivan. "By this time we should know in great detail what can and can't work, what could work with further testing, and what contingency plans will be implemented if something doesn't work."

The Anatomy of a Design Document

The interactive design document is a written record that describes in detail every element crucial to bringing an interactive application to life. These documents flesh out the twelve components of an interactive proposal—title and title page, one-line summary/quick pitch, premise, concept overview, story summary, character descriptions, underlying design structure(s) with flow-chart(s), compelling features/rules of interaction, interface methodology, walk-thru/play scenario, sales and marketing forecast, and creative team credentials—and may also include the following five elements:

1. Storyboard
A storyboard is an outline of a story, scene, event, or program told in a series of sketches, with support documentation that describes all related audio, video, graphics, animation, interactivities, and navigation elements.

2. Screenplay

Interactive screenplays are stories written as a series of scenes containing characters and dramatized through actions and dialogue in a particular format. Unlike the Hollywood film industry, there is no standard page format used in the interactive business. Many new media production companies ask their writers to use proprietary software programs to write their screenplays.

Individual writers use whatever software tools they can find that will help them write more efficiently. Interactive writers use programs such as StoryVision, Microsoft Word, ClarisWorks, ScriptThing, Filemaker Pro, Inspiration, and Storyspace to help them write and organize their interactive screenplays.

But what are interactive screenplays really made of? We asked noted writer and designer Raymond Benson for his thoughts.

"For graphic adventures like *Return of the Phantom* or *Dark Seed II,* my writing style is best described as a room-by-room format. The written page looks similar to a feature film screenplay. For example, if my room was a lobby, my script would say ROOM – LOBBY.

"Next I would write everything that happens in the room as it relates to the plot. I would then write a description of the room and everything it has to have in it for the artists whose job it will be to make the room come to life visually. I describe how those room objects are used and their importance to the story. I then describe any foreground or background animation that may occur in the room—can the character run, jump, hit, etc. I describe any text that may occur on the screen . . . any narrative. I describe the music and sound effects in the room. Then I list the entrances and exits. Next, I list all the hot spots in the room and what those hot spots trigger. If there is inventory used in the game, you have to describe what those inventory objects can or cannot do—if I use this item on the doorknob, what response will I get? After all that, I list any special applications or notes to the programmers—logic puzzles, flags, all the stuff that they'll need to create." (To learn more about the interactive screenplay, see chapters 5–10 and chapter 17.)

3. Technical Specifications

Here is where you specify all the technical information that your designers and programmers will need to build your interactive masterpiece. You spell out the delivery platform(s), hardware systems requirements, software system requirements, authoring tools to be used to build the project, multiplayer capabilities, and any other unique creative elements essential to your project.

4. Production Schedule

The production schedule is a calendar of events that spells out each stage of the production process—from preproduction to delivery of the final project. A production schedule is usually created and maintained by the project manager and is used to keep the creative team in sync, budget the project, and provides the client with a thumbnail view of the overall scope and time frame of the project being produced.

5. Budget

A budget is a detailed accounting of how much your interactive project costs. Early on in the development cycle, a budget overview or a projected budget is created that estimates what the project will cost. As the project is assembled, a working budget is maintained by a member of the production team (usually the project manager). Budgets are created with spreadsheet programs such as Microsoft Excel or Movie Magic, where daily reports can be generated to keep tabs on the money being spent on the project.

Effective design documents meet three basic criteria:

- They are simple—so that the creative team understands it and knows exactly what they are to contribute to it.
- They are straightforward—so that all the creative elements fit together in a logical way. The document should be segmented and categorized so that each element is easy to find.
- They are saturated—every element that needs to be there, should be.

II.

Interactivity and Narrative

4

Homer to Cyberbard, What's the Difference?

Stories that instruct, renew, and heal provide a vital nourishment to the psyche that cannot be obtained in any other way. Stories reveal over and over again the precious and peculiar knack that humans have for triumph over travail. They provide all the vital instructions we need to live a useful, necessary, and unbounded life—a life of meaning, a life worth remembering.

CLARISSA PINKOLA ESTES, PH.D.

S torytellers, contrary to much current discussion on the subject, have a lot to learn from each other no matter what technology they use and no matter how differently an audience "interacts" with their disparate texts. Interactive texts like *Big Brother, The X-Files, Psychic Detective, Paul Is Dead, Tex Murphy: Overseer,* or *Phantasmagoria* allow the user to change plot and presentation in ways not even conceivable for older technologies. But whatever technology writers use, the stories they create are fashioned on the crucible of language. The system of language (its *langue*) stamps an unbreakable mold on all stories no matter when or how they are told.

It's also obvious that interactive texts draw many, if not most, of their characters and plots from older stories without regard to whether those tales began as fables, film, or literature. *The X-Files,* to offer a current example, is based on the hit TV series and uses digital technology to create an interactive environment that is unique and dazzling. The interactive text's writer and designer, Greg Roach, has little patience with the notion that cyberstories are animals that exist without kin to their cousins. Fox Interactive president Jon Richmond agrees, "With story-driven interactivity, we are able to capture the mysterious *X-Files* style and provide players with unique and authentic interactive experiences."

These pages are obviously intended for the writer who sees a new frontier—a writer who wants to develop stories for a medium that is digitally compressed, computer displayed, and interactive, or "participatory." The first thing you probably need to hear is, Don't buy hype. And don't be arrogant. Stories have been told in lots of ways for a long time. From tribal and religious rituals we have inherited stories that get retold in modern contexts at suburban bedsides, rural living rooms, or inner-city apartments. The older themes survive in modern media, though usually diluted or trivialized in their presentation. Even as the shells of older narratives flicker recognizably on film or television screens, newer stories rise to incorporate, compete with, or even replace their archetypal ancestors. We can see the same thing happening in interactive texts. You can't look at *Myst*, or *Paul Is Dead*, or even *Tomb Raider II* starring Lara Croft, without seeing the imprint of a narrative ancestor.

An interactive title like *Big Brother* certainly presents its story in ways that are different from its source text *1984*. It offers spatial freedoms in its presentation that are not possible in any presentation of George Orwell's story. But one of the contributions of modern narrative and structuralist study has been to demonstrate that the underlying logic that drives the interactive title and Orwell's prose, the structure that determines the pace of the story, its dramatic oppositions and surprises, the elements that make for a satisfying experience, remains the same for the digital text as for the original. The notion that technology determines narrative form is false. Human consciousness, probably language itself, determines the structure and form of what we recognize as stories.

The skald of ancient Scandinavia, the blind poet, and the tribal shaman have indeed given way to a new age of storytellers who use digital compression to tell their tales. The presentation of stories has obviously changed over the millennia, but the formal elements of narrative itself—not to mention its themes, concerns, questions, and relationship to the human psyche—do not change with the technology of its presentation.

The basis for storytelling remains constant, but the experience of an interactive, digitally presented narrative is obviously not the same as for other media. Just as a moviegoer's experience of *Midnight in the Garden of Good and Evil* is different from the experience of John Berendt's book, so a user's experience of an interactive narrative will be distinguished in its own way from prose, poetry, film, television, and so on. Too often, however, the unique aspects of interactively designed texts are used to excuse weak or trivial storytelling, stereotyped characters and so on. Every new technology finds it easier to mimic reality than to render a convincing work of fiction. Filmmakers didn't start out using celluloid to fashion stories; they were awed by the capacity of the medium to mimic the ordinary stuff of experience. They'd film trains, crowds, clouds—anything! You can hear reverberations of this early fascination for mimicking the quotidian in books written by the new generation of cyberphiles. The "holodeck," made popular in modern Star Trek episodes, is taken as the ultimate in verisimilitude. The problem is that mimicking reality, even to the finest detail, will not in itself help you write an engaging story. In fact, it may well prove a hindrance.

It's tempting—when given the capacity of the digital stage to mimic reality and to invite user interaction—to elevate those unique aspects of the digital text over the quality of stories that interactive writers actually tell and that users buy or acquire. A holodeck doesn't guarantee a good story, Janeway. Sorry. It just ain't so. This chapter is intended for writers who want to tell good stories, with good pacing, plot, and characterization *regardless* of their chosen medium. To that end, we'll be looking at the things that all stories and storytelling methods have in common, and then applying those common lessons to the creation of stories in cyberspace.

The potential for stories that can offer virtual reality and unlimited information is truly revolutionary. The underlying structure of narrative is constant, but its presentation varies enormously and nowhere can we find greater potential for variations in the way a story is presented than in digitally constructed texts. In addition, computer-generated stories can give users ways to participate in and experience narratives that are not possible in print, onstage, on TV, or with film. But if you want to make a living writing interactively, you need to recognize, up front, that most interactive texts, and by far the most lucrative, are not primarily concerned with storytelling. Right now the best-selling interactive texts (aside from pornography) are texts that use very predictable, almost modular story lines to give the user access to gaming elements, arcades, and exotic environments that dominate the text's architecture. Most interactive texts are hybrids, incorporating some kind of multiform plot with arenas that engage the user in other ways. Usually, these "other ways" comprise the dominant role in this experience.

It would be very surprising to see the technology evolve much differently. Critics note that the characters in the most popular interactive texts are stereotyped and that their concerns are determined by the circumstance of action or peril or quest, rather than any kind of literary development. The *Mortal Kombat* and *Wing Commander* series, as examples, present characters whose inner lives are static, and who change only as the action of the game/drama/puzzle demands. Writers of these hybrids, however, do not lament the profits that these mixed forms generate. And serious writers understand that the potential for digital technology to explore fiction in fresh and important ways is not diminished by present applications.

Classic thinkers insisted that good fiction must find a balance between entertainment (*dulce*) and instruction (*utile*). Right now, most digital texts can be said to amaze, confound, excite, and titillate. But the potential for interactive stories is not bound by what the market presently rewards. Cybertexts *can* create characters as complex as Lord Jim or Othello, but we ought to recognize that the logical problems encountered when trying to render such characters in multiform plots and the effort required to do it is immense.

It takes a lot of effort to integrate character and action and theme in a story that deals seriously with the human condition. It should not be hard to understand why Norman Mailer's *The Naked and the Dead*, Tolstoy's *War and Peace*, Oliver Stone's *Platoon*, or Stanley Kubrick's adaptation of *All Quiet on the Western Front* are more moving, honest, and insightful presentations of the human experience than is *Rambo*. But in the digital arena we don't yet have texts for this kind of comparison. We don't have a digital text, at present, that creates characters or landscape or psychology with the subtlety of Charlotte Brontë. We don't yet have a digital text that depicts war with anything like the honesty of Tolstoy or Hemingway. And producers of interactive texts remind us that at present there isn't much demand for these kinds of products.

In fairness, there probably has never been as much "demand" for demanding narrative in any medium as we'd like to think. Even so, I'm going to bet that some cybergenius will create a new *Iliad* whose characters evolve in ways that do not violate the program's logic and that will movingly and meaningfully illuminate aspects of the human condition.

In the meantime, interactive sci-fi stories, cop dramas, and role-playing environments already immerse their users in an experience that differs from that provided by other media. But whether you want to write *Wing Commander XXV*, or an interactive installment of *Star Wars*, you need to absorb the lessons that older venues, and older stories, have to teach. Every storyteller from the medieval bard to the modern moviemaker gives us lessons to be learned, adapted, and applied.

Interactive writers begin their projects, like anyone else, when their ideas and words get transferred to paper. Pros like Greg Roach, Douglas Gayeton, Carolyn Miller, Deborah Todd, Larry Kay, and Michael Kaplan agree that the tremendous potential of digital technology has first to be realized as words on a well-defined page. Terry Borst is a good example of someone who, writing both Hollywood screenplays and interactive stories, does not see the new technology as supplanting older storytelling technologies. The challenge for interactive writers, says Borst, is to carefully weave story and design. "I think there is little question that gaming is a more satisfactory experience when the writers and programmers are on the same page from the beginning of production."

But what makes interactive stories unique? What is it that interactive writers must understand about this new medium? Janet Murray lists four properties in her book *Hamlet on the Holodeck* that she sees as unique to digital environments. Digital environs are procedural, spatial, encyclopedic, and participatory. Digital stories, to expand, are realized only when a computer executes a series of rules (procedures) that the programmer (not the user) authors. Computers allow us to move through space in ways that video and Celluloid cannot. And it's apparent that computers supply information to the user in veritable encyclopedias of quantity and detail. Anyone who has experienced *Riven* or *Myst* or a good flight simulator knows something of this capacity.

But, most importantly, interactive technology adds the element of participation to the dramatically rendered story. Writers of interactive texts give their users choices that alter the narrative's presentation and plot. This dramatically changes the relationship between the storyteller and his audience. The user of an interactively designed story becomes an agent who, choosing among options that the writer/programmer creates or encodes, is empowered to shape the logic and presentation of a digitally determined environment. The interactive narrative gives the user challenges, decisions, and options that will steer the story, which will determine "the unities"—place, time, and incident—out of which the story (or game or puzzle or hybrid) unfolds.

The user participates in this game. But in this scenario, users aren't authors. A writer authors all the interactions that are possible for the interactive text. A user can only choose options that a writer provides. There are Web sites, of course, where masses of people interact to truly author their own narratives. This is the cyberequivalent of the campfire or the front porch and goes way back to oral traditions of storytelling. But we're concerned with an interactive writer who, either alone or with others, wants to craft a finished product for sale in the marketplace. That writer must appreciate that a user's participation distinguishes interactive narratives from stories told on mainstream mass media. Writers initially feel giddy with this freedom. Imagine being able to create multiple plots, puzzles, arcades, or environments in which users participate to shape a new experience of narrative! But most writers quickly discover that the marriage of participation to narrative brings special challenges and, sometimes, frustrations.

5

Immersion and the Seamless Experience

I look at interactive writing as theatre on the computer. I'm trying to create an emotional experience for the user. I want the user to get involved with my characters—to care about them. I want the player to discover the special world of the game. If you can immerse the user into the interactive experience like you would with a movie or a good book, where the user forgets the outside world and is lost in the computer screen, then you've succeeded.

RAYMOND BENSON

We all know what it means to be immersed in a good book or film, and how irritating it is to have that seamless experience ruptured. It doesn't matter whether the story is told at bedside or on TV, interruptions are not appreciated by audiences. Television writers accommodate the intrusions created by commercial breaks by setting up act closures or cliffhangers designed to bring the viewer back from the fridge to the tube, but it's never completely satisfying. Steven Boccho, you can bet, does not like to see his day's outtakes spliced in with ads for Calvin Klein or Chevrolet.

Interactive narratives won't, for a while at least, have to worry about commercials. But interactive writers face challenges posed by their users' participation that make Boccho's problem pale by comparison. Interactive storytellers have to accommodate the viewer/user's intrusion into the text in ways that keep the illusion of immersion intact. Michael Murtaugh has written an excellent work on this subject—"The Automatist Storytelling System"—his master's thesis at MIT Media Lab.

Murtaugh points out that the world created by the narrative and the act that produces it are necessarily distinct. The word "necessary" is important. It's common to read claims that digitized narratives blur the line between writer and user and that this is a good thing. Wrong, says Murtaugh. The line always exists, no matter how cleverly we try to disguise it. He uses the example of cinema verité, the school of filmmaking that claimed in its youth to "disappear" into the things filmed. That didn't happen of course. It couldn't happen and so the new school was forced to accept as fact that cameras, lights, and sound recorders "significantly alter" whatever is being filmed.

This is not only a necessary condition of the narrative experience, it is an essential one. A clear demarcation between the world created by the narrative and its producing agent is necessary if the viewer/user is to feel immersed in the experience of the story. With regard to a user who participates in the narrative, it's clear that some balance has to be struck between intruding into the narrative world and letting the narrative "play out." Contrary to a lot of what I have read on this subject, I doubt very seriously whether it would be a good idea in a cyberversion of *Casablanca* to stop that last dramatic scene with Bogey and Bergman, wink to the user, and say, "Okay. Click on how you'd like this to turn out."

In this regard, narrative experiences and gaming experiences offer an illuminating contrast. The narrative experience has much different requirements for satisfaction than do games, puzzles, or role-playing. That's at least partly because in those arenas, immersion isn't the point. The game is the thing and designers demand that game writers intrude on the game world at specified rates. Dubbed "clicks per minute," a gamer is told he must require a response from the user at rates of ten or twelve or more clicks every minute. This is fine for games. It kills stories.

For the user to be immersed in a cybertext, there has to be some boundary between the person and the narrative. Without this clear demarcation, a user cannot truly be immersed in the experience of the story. Murtaugh points out that a primary challenge for interactive writers and designers is how to manage a text's "interaction with the viewer without distracting them from or otherwise disrupting the narrative."

Murtaugh's remarks are intended for academic consideration, but much of what he writes is critical for writers and designers of interactive narratives. For instance, Murtaugh asks, "If viewers can change characters' actions with the wave of their hands, why should they care about the story? What indeed then is the story?"

Murtaugh goes so far as to say that if a user *chooses what happens* in a story, he or she is not likely to feel immersed in the experience that follows. Murtaugh suggests that it might be better to provide users with "handles," a species of interface that would essentially let the user select relevant materials, tone, and parameters that affect the presentation, speed, and pacing of the texts' plot(s). The user's interaction in this scheme will affect the way that the plots unfold rather than determine outcomes and events. Most interactive titles are nowhere near this sophisticated. *Wing Commander III*, written by Terry Borst and Frank DePalma (a title that won the 1996 Academy of Interactive Arts and Sciences "Cybie" for Best Writing), offers a more typical choice. From A-22, Scene 16:

```
If Mission A1 success:          If Mission A1 failure:


HOBBES                          HOBBES
Congratulations, old            I'm very sorry, old
friend.                         friend. I let you down.


BLAIR                           BLAIR
Yeah, just like old times,      Sure as hell wasn't all
eh, Hobbes?                     your fault.
```

It's important to note that since both of these choices have to be consistent with the dialogue that follows, *neither* choice leads to any change whatever in the relationship between Blair and Hobbes. In terms of character development, it doesn't matter whether Mission A1 succeeds or fails since neither outcome changes the *bonhomme* between Hobbes and his buddy Blair. Here, the user's participation doesn't enrich the story in any meaningful way. Whether Hobbes was a hero in this encounter, an inept, or a coward matters not at all. Either choice leads right back to the story's spine and this dialogue:

```
HOBBES
I must say it certainly felt good to be back out there
again. My gratitude for your trust in me is endless.


BLAIR
Forget it, Hobbes. You're back where you belong now.
```

Interactive scripts envision the illusion, at least, of a seamless narrative experience, but a seamless experience has to offer more than a choice of weapons, experiences, or outcomes. Can designers offer participation that enriches and alters a narrative experience without trivializing or rupturing the experience itself? How many interruptions will be tolerated in, say, a two-hour narrative? How will the viewer be offered those choices? How will she be alerted to the options available, told when a decision is impending? How will the interfacing devices and the commands or graphics associated with a viewer's decision intrude on the ongoing narrative's text?

Murtaugh suggests that a user should not be forced to interact simply to "get at" the story's content. A user may simply want the story to "play out" by itself, reserving the right to participate. I love the excerpt from Tinsley Galyean's doctoral dissertation—"Narrative Guidance of Interactivity"—that Murtaugh quotes to emphasize this point: "The common click-to-go-forward paradigm . . . requires that the viewer constantly push the story forward, a situation roughly analogous to listening to a narcoleptic storyteller."

Cheerleaders for cyberstories don't like to deal with these kinds of problems, and fortunately for writers the demand for texts like the *Wing Commander* series or *Riven* are not primarily predicated on story appeal. The environment, violent, sensual, and sometimes explicitly sadistic, are the draw here, not a concern over the relationship between Blair and Hobbes.

But if interactive stories do aspire to vital character and story, the balance between participation and "guided" response will have to be addressed. Already programmers are experimenting with a myriad of interface devices designed to make user choices more intuitive and less intrusive. Intelligent agents are being designed to monitor the user's choices and, in a sense, predict future choices. The agent can then be programmed to accommodate the user's predilection, or, for variety, to offer a contrary path with contrary payoffs and expectations. As Murtaugh says, the way in which writers/designers/programmers choose to guide users through narratives addresses directly the fundamental problem of interactive writing. How do you combine narrative structure and responsiveness while preserving that seamless web of immersion?

Galyean offers the metaphor of a river as a solution for balancing these opposed commitments. In a river there is a "continuous flow" in which the user "steers" or directs the current but is rarely, if ever, forced to encounter a narrative roadblock or dead end. In this paradigm, a writer guides the user's participation by dictating that trivial choices should have a minimal impact on the narrative flow, while relevant choices be allowed to significantly alter flow.

What sounds reasonable in theory is a bitch to practice. Most interactors, for instance, want multiform plots. Imagine the complexity of dictating the relevance of choices as users move from one branch into another! Or would the writer simply limit the branches to be explored so that the opportunity for these inconsistencies could be curtailed?

Janet Murray discusses the problem of immersion in her book along with the problem of "regulating arousal." If a horror movie is too frightening, Murray notes, we cover our eyes or turn away from the screen. The immersion, in this case, is broken not by a user's participation but by the ability of the medium to produce sensory overkill. Murray dissects a romantic scene from *Witness* that essentially illustrates how information is withheld from the viewer so that a sense of immersion and "clear demarcation" remains unruptured as John Book (Harrison Ford) initiates a romantic interlude with Rachel (Kelly McGillis).

It's a fine analysis. Book and Rachel are alone in a barn. A car repair triggers the radio and music. Describing the scene that follows, Murray details how the director blocks, frames, and shoots the scene. At one point, Murray observes, Rachel "is seen moving into the frame, her back to the camera. . . . This over-the-shoulder position of the camera is a standard film technique that keeps us identified with the characters while also distanced enough so that we are reminded of the presence of the other actor in the frame of the movie and of our own exclusion from it. This combination of tremendous intimacy with a clearly demarcated border maximizes our immersion in the dramatic scene."

The choices that the director makes, in other words, maximizes the viewer's immersion in the scene and allows for the greatest dramatic impact. Bingo. But left completely unstated in this analysis is the obvious fact that by choosing this particular way to film the scene, the director rejected other options. Why did he reject those options? Because other alternatives were judged inferior; they were seen to diminish rather than enhance the impact of the scene on the viewer. The director, in effect, withholds other ways of shooting this scene from the viewer. He creates a border between the narrative world and the viewer's capacity to affect it. This "clear demarcation" between director and viewer, participant and text, is necessary to achieve the great intimacy and power of this scene.

So do we give the user of the cyberversion of *Witness* access to the director's rejected options? Do we take advantage of the new technology to break the border that separates user and text? Is it really a good thing to be given total spatial freedom in a narrative experience that, to work at all, must be integrated and controlled? You can take the camera anywhere in cyberspace. You can *be* the camera, or John Book, or Rachel. You can watch the cop dance with the Amish babe in 3-D if you like. Let's say you can even have the holodeck. Is that a good thing?

Here's a bet: A digitized version of the *Witness* scene that is dependent for its presentation on a user's participation will not play as powerfully as its celluloid original. It wouldn't matter if our user was the Orson Welles of cyberdrama, he or she would still be forced to constantly intrude on the narrative. The decisions that a trained director has to make—lighting, blocking, camera, sound, and so on—would now have to be made by the user. The freedom to participate, in this case, works against immersion in the story. It prevents the arousal of desire. We have turned our agent into an editor.

It seems that even in cyberspace we may want to refuse some advantages of the medium to our user, circumscribing (to what extent? when?) the user's participation in decisions that may impact the issues of immersion and arousal. Murray skates around this basic problem. She mentions the notion of "mechanics," for instance, "the equivalent of the fade-out technique in movies. They signal that something is happening that can only take place in the viewer's or interactor's imagination." We may want to turn away at that first kiss. Or from that brutal rape. Or from that death camp. So are we being told that the interactive writer may have to restrict the user's participation in order to optimally enhance his or her experience? Can we suggest that writers/designers may want to exclude some procedure, space, or information, engaging instead the user's imagination to fill in the narrative blanks? Is it the case that along with the participatory, spatial, procedural, and encyclopedic dimensions of cyberspace, the writer may find that less is still more? I hope so.

What's Writing Got to Do with It?

A good interactive game involves you emotionally, and a great game, the game of tomorrow, the games that are starting to happen today, actually give you an emotional payoff.

HOWARD BURKONS

In the last chapters we discussed some of the challenges that distinguish interactive writing and cybertexts from other kinds of writing and media. But sooner or later you leave Philosophy 101 for the written page. Now it's time to shift gears and move on to the nuts and bolts required to write an interactive script. We have several examples of interactive scripts to display. *The X-Files* gives us some good material, along with the *Wing Commander* series, *Johnny Mnemonic*, and, finally, *Subterfuge*. Note that all these interactive scripts are designed to integrate the user's choices into one or more narrative lines, each line of which is "linear." For our purposes, a linear narrative describes a dramatized story that is structured similar to any mainstream feature film. Interactive stories use linear narratives to generate or connect related characters and situations according to a three-act structure, which, when mated to multiform plotting, can generate multiple endings.

Of course, there are certainly interactive scripts that don't do the same things as linear narratives like *The X-Files* and *Subterfuge*. Some scripts may abandon narrative altogether, or conceal narrative, or concentrate on role-playing, puzzles, and the like. We'll discuss some of these hybrids later on. However, since most paying opportunities for interactive writing involve some association with a linear plotline, the screenplays we will talk about are a good place to start.

Let's be careful at the outset not to give the impression that there is yet such a thing as a single, standardized format for interactive scripts. But it will be obvious to you that many of the lessons learned from other dramatic forums, screenwriting in particular, are naturally suited to interactive writers. The most important thing that screenplays and interactive scripts have in common is that they both tell a dramatic story—that is, a story that actors and actresses, real or animated, will perform. The key word here is that the story is *dramatic.* A dramatic story has to be *dramatized.*

Most people writing interactive screenplays are not used to writing drama, so let's talk about the "dramatic point of view." When a writer talks about the dramatic point of view, she isn't talking about a camera direction or a character's perspective. It's important to understand that dramatic scripts using dramatic elements must be told from a point of view that is different from ordinary writing and most prose. Laurence Perrine's enduring text *Literature: Structure, Sound, and Sense* says that with the dramatic point of view, "the narrator disappears into a kind of roving sound camera. The camera can go anywhere but can record only what is seen and heard. It cannot comment, interpret, or enter a character's mind." A dramatic script places the audience "in the position of a spectator at a movie or play. He sees what the characters do and hears what they say but can only infer what they think or feel and what they are like. The author is not there to explain."

Show, Don't Tell

It's crucial for the interactive writer of dramatized stories to realize that he or she not only doesn't have to "explain" what a character is thinking, feeling, or intending, but shouldn't want to. Dramatic writers do not tell—they show. Don't tell me something like, "Johnny is sitting angrily beside the bus stop." If Johnny is angry, he should show me his anger. Maybe he slams his fist into a bench. Or maybe he refuses a ride from a friend. Properly contextualized, either situation will allow the audience to feel Johnny's emotion because they participate in it.

"Genuine emotion," Perrine cautions, "like character, must be presented indirectly—must be dramatized. It cannot be produced by words that identify emotions, like angry, sad, pathetic, heartbreaking, or passionate. If a writer is to draw forth genuine emotion, he must produce a character in a situation that deserves our sympathy and must [show] us enough about the character and situation to make them real and convincing."

Truer words were never penned. Interactive scripts should not tell the user anything at all about what goes on in Jack's mind or Jill's heart. Interactive scripts should dramatize emotion; they should allow us to hear what characters say and see what they do. If you read a line like, "She shoots him an angry glance," you ought to know that you're being cheated. Glances can neither be shot nor angry.

Interactive scripts should use language to paint pictures with which a reader, viewer, director, or designer can interact. It's not that hard to do. For instance, what picture do you see here?

- "Sarah walks to the door."

Now, before that picture fades, compare it with these:

- Sarah dances to the door.
- Sarah limps to the door.
- Sarah eases to the door.
- Sarah slips to the door.
- Sarah rushes to the door.

You get the point? In "real life," we interpret emotion by what people *do*. Writers have to use verbs that engage the reader to make inferences about Sarah's feelings, state of mind, and so on. That's the kind of participation that makes characters and stories come alive. It shows me a picture of Sarah, instead of telling me who she is.

It ought to be obvious from the remarks above that technical descriptions do not engage a reader's participation. Interactive scripts should not be mired in machine language. Douglas Gayeton comments, "I've seen lots of interactive screenplays, and the one thing that impressed me was how inefficient they were. People who write interactive screenplays love to take it and throw it down on the desk so that it makes a really big, thick, heavy sound, and then say, 'this is my interactive screenplay.' And you're supposed to be impressed by that. But I'm not. Do you know that the screenplay for *Johnny Mnemonic* is 135 pages long? It's written in screenplay form. We were incredibly aggressive with how we put it together in the most economical, logical way." (See fig. 6.1)

["Johnny Mnemonic" Shooting - Blue 5/16/94] 72.

DR. SATAI (Cont'd)
... a doctor. She, my employer, has requested a gentleman you represent named Johnny. Please contact us immediately!

The message gives way to STATIC.

INT. RALFI'S OFFICE (RO-2C-WOO)

Johnny is at the wall behind him.

JOHNNY (RO-2C-M)

Johnny moves back to POSITION #1.

INT. RALFI'S OFFICE (RO-2D-WOO)

Johnny stares at the corner of RALFI'S DESK. There's lots of crap here, but one useful thing: a weird kind of MAGNIFYING GLASS called a ...

TRANS-VU

It takes the odd patterns (encryption code) on the fax from RO-2A and translates them. There's a KNOB/DIAL on the handle of the Trans-VU. As you turn it, the glass shows different encryption codes/languages. Also in this shot is a PHOTOGRAPH of RALFI with PRETTY and YOMOMMA. It's a weird, somewhat kinky portrait ...

JOHNNY (RO-2D-U)

Johnny takes the TRANS-VU and puts it in his pocket.

<u>RALFI'S OFFICE - EXPLORE MODE</u>
POSITION #3: SEATED ON RALFI'S SOFA

INT. RALFI'S OFFICE (RO-3A-WOO)

Johnny looks up at an HDTV set on the counter in front of him.

JOHNNY (RO-3A-U1)

If RO-3D-U1=T, he takes the MINI CD-ROM labeled "MEMORY BACK-UP out of his pocket and places it into a WIRELESS CD-ROM READER on the COFFEE TABLE. The disc is a backup of Johnny's memories which were wiped out when he had his implants installed. What we see on the HDTV ...

WEIRD, DREAMLIKE FOOTAGE OF CHILDHOOD, ETC. (RO-AV-2)

Johnny is transfixed by images of a YOUNG BOY playing with a sprinkler on a sun-drenched backyard lawn. The young boy looks a lot like Johnny ...

Fig. 6.1. Sample page from the interactive screenplay *Johnny Mnemonic,* written by John Platten and Douglas Gayeton. Courtesy of Sony Imagesoft. Reprinted by permission.

The graphics and description necessary to complete even one action scene have to be summarized quickly and vividly in these kinds of scripts. If you want to write pages of description, write novels. Interactive screenplays can't be as easily and accessibly read as an ordinary screenplay, but they must capture, entertain, or provoke a reader who wants to participate in a dramatized story. It's up to the writer to know what distinguishes a dramatic story from a story that allows its writer to editorialize about, comment upon, or telegraph his characters' interior lives. The interactive scripter, like the feature film screenwriter, should originate and organize dramatic elements into a work of fiction that shows but does not tell.

Nuts and Bolts: What Does It Look Like?

Although it is true that many interactive scripts tend to look a lot like teleplays or film scripts, it's also true that many interactive products never get scripted at all. Interactive narratives can originate on storyboards, books, or come straight off a producer's notes. The sample page from *Johnny Mnemonic* is fairly typical of the mainstream screen document for multimedia products you'll see in the market today.

If we look for similarities of function and structure, we'll see right away that there are many similarities between the straightforward movie script (or linear narrative) and interactive screenplays. Both scripts identify characters, provide dialogue and direction, and describe activity. Both scripts segregate the story into separate locations and separate times (see fig. 6.2).

What you should *not* do when looking at screenplays or interactive scripts is get hung up on things that your reader could care less about. We're concerned with what scripts share in common, not what makes *The X-Files* look a little differently than *Wing Commander IV.*

Let's examine the parts of an interactive script. The example that follows is a screenplay excerpt from the science-fiction interactive adventure *Subterfuge,* written by Darryl Wimberley. For identification purposes, each line of the screenplay below has been numbered from 1 to 21.

Line 1: Transition
Transitions are used to indicate how the user gets from one scene to the next (we are leaving this place and time and are going someplace else). They can be very helpful for clarification purposes if used in the right context in an interactive screenplay.

                              TIMMONS
              Where you going? Don't you want
              to drive?

INT. GRAVITY CAR - NIGHT

Bowman sits in the driver's seat and is confronted with an
amazing array of displays—all of them projected onto the
windshield. Beyond lies the salt flat—dark and featureless.
He puts on a safety harness.

                              TIMMONS
              Just about everything is automatic—
              you really can't screw it up.

Bowman reaches out for a largish knob and twists it. The car
collapses to the ground. WHAM!

                              TIMMONS
              Unless you turn off the field.

Timmons reaches over and twists in the opposite direction. The
car rises. He flips a switch next to it over and locks it down.

                              TIMMONS
              Accelerator is where you expect it;
              so are the brakes. Turns are automatically
              banked—the computers calculate the proper
              angle considering your airspeed and the
              radius of the turn you request with the
              wheel.

                              BOWMAN
              Altitude?

                              TIMMONS
              The only tricky part. You can't crash
              it, at least now the I've enabled the
              interlocks. The car will not allow you
              to crash into anything—ground, another
              vehicle, whatever. Just like a plane—
              push in the wheel to dive, pull back
              to climb. Let's turn on the lights.

He flicks a switch. Deep blue runway lights stretch into the
distance along the desert floor.

**Fig. 6.2. Sample page from the feature film screenplay *Burning Sky*, written by Jon Labrie.
Reprinted by permission.**

```
1.   FADE IN:

2.   INT. SPACE FREIGHTER - NIGHT (FR-2A-AUTO)

3.   Jupiter's famous Red Spot glowers like a troll's angry eye

4.   against the backdrop of an indigo sky as seen though a portal

5.   in the freighter's ceiling.

6.

7.   A spartan, almost military interior accommodates two recently

8.   engaged lovers. JAKE STRYKER lounges his two hundred pounds,

9.   spent and naked, beside a striking, well-toned beauty. SANDY

10.  AIMES traps one of Jake's legs between her own. Long legs has

11.  Sandy. Powerful. A mane of chestnut hair falls thick over

12.  shoulders still wet with sweat. Jake leans past her, taps a

13.  cigarette from its pack.

14.                      SANDY

15.          Surgeon General says those things

16.          will kill ya.

17.  IF Jake flicks open his Zippo, THEN a blue flame appears. He lights

18.  the tip of his cigarette and—

19.  A BLINDING WHITE HOT LIGHT EXPLOSION ENVELOPS THE FREIGHTER,

20.  FOLLOWED BY THE ROAR OF A POWERFUL EXPLOSION, SENDING SHIP

21.  FRAGMENTS AND HUMAN BODIES THROUGH THE AIR LIKE RAG DOLLS.
```

Fig. 6.3. Elements of an interactive screenplay excerpted from *Subterfuge*

The four most common transitions are "fade in" (an image materializes from a black screen), "fade out" (the screen image disappears into darkness), "cut to" (the scene image abruptly jumps from one shot to another), and "dissolve to" (a screen image fuses from one scene into another).

Line 2: Slugline with Address
A "slugline" is an indicator that allows interactive producers and designers to consolidate scenes sharing the same locale. In fig. 6.3, "INT. SPACE FREIGHTER - NIGHT" is the slugline. Also called slugs, they provide tags by which scenes can be numbered, categorized, or sorted in any of a myriad of useful ways. Sluglines tell the reader whether a scene is located inside or outside, where that scene is taking place, and whether it is day or night.

In the above example, the "address" immediately follows the slugline (FR-

2A-AUTO). The address is a notation that tells the programming team where in the scene the user is and what the user is able to do there. What do the symbols signify? "FR" stands for the scene location—in this case, it's a space freighter. "2A" tells us where in that location we are—say the cockpit. "AUTO," which stands for automatic mode, states what the user can do in that location—in this case, nothing.

Lines 3–8: Scene Description

Directly below the slugline is something deceptively simple—the scene description. Many writers have a terrible time setting up a scene. They either write far too much detail, write the wrong sort of detail, or else they leave out something essential. What we need here are some criteria for establishing the scene.

There are only a few details that are essential to any scene. You have to identify those details, integrate and heighten them, and make them come alive. And you have to do it quickly. It's no accident that the best writers are also the briefest. A detail isn't essential unless it's absolutely necessary to establish or advance the narrative. If a detail is essential, it must be described. If a detail is not essential, it should not be described at all. In our example from *Subterfuge,* lines 3–5 demonstrate that even the most complicated setups and interactions do not take much space on the page. So how can you ensure a similar brevity, clarity, and power?

You can start by recognizing that there are basically only four things which you ever need to describe when you're establishing a scene: Period and Place, People and Props. Everything in the universe comes under these headings—just think of it as a writer's version of air, earth, fire, and water.

It's important to note that Period and Place, People and Props get established immediately beneath the slug. Do not introduce dramatic elements at your whim. For an example of how this works, take a look at the opening setup for *Subterfuge.* The environ is somewhat complex. There are multiple situations and information to digest and characters to introduce. But the writing is crisp and rapid. It doesn't linger or delay. This is essential for any writer, but especially for the writer of interactive texts.

Lines 8–13: Character Description

Even writers who can quickly and vividly establish period, place, and props sometimes falter when it comes to people. The same guidelines apply to establishing character as to scenes and action. You should not overwrite. You should include only those details that are essential to the narrative.

Some common things to avoid:

- Don't describe your heroine as twenty-three years old. An exact age isn't an essential detail for any character and can create problems in the real world for casting. You need to find other ways to suggest that a character is an infant, adolescent, in midlife, thirtysomething, and so on. Notice that the characters in *Subterfuge* are not given specific ages. We nevertheless have a good sense of the characters' relative ages, mostly as a result of what they do in their introductory scenes.
- When your character is doing something, you should be careful to use present-tense construction. Just as with scene description, use active verbs instead of passive ones. (Sandy *traps* Jake's legs, versus Sandy *is trapping* Jake's legs.) If you can link verbs and adjectives together quickly and vividly, that's great, but do not overdescribe a character's appearance or activities. Finally, when you're "writing character," learn to use the dramatic point of view.

We spoke earlier about how important it is for writers of dramatic stories to understand and use the dramatic point of view, to show instead of tell. Interactive writers tend to be weak in this regard. One strategy shared by many interactive documents is that they do not tell the reader about the characters' histories or their inner lives.

The best writers rarely use words that describe emotion or intent; words like "angry" or "angrily," "sad" or "sadly," and "afraid" or "fearfully" are words that tell us things that ought to be shown. Good writers show us characters' inner lives by providing the reader with dialogue and action. We hear what the characters say, we see what they do; this dramatized presentation allows the reader to participate in the story, to interact, if you will, with the text. If the interaction is well crafted, fictive characters emerge from the page as living people.

Interactive scripters should always remember that the word "drama" derives from the Greek, meaning "to do," not "to be." Aristotle went so far, in this regard, as to assert that plot and character cannot be separated. For him, what we do and what we say are all that is possible. Freud would disagree, of course. But then Freud was a terrible dramatist.

Make up some questions about *Subterfuge*'s Jake and Sandy; questions about their interior lives. Is she prudish, for instance? Is he a stickler for detail? Would we call this couple aristocratic or working-class? Do Jake and Sandy like each other? Love each other? Is something hung up in their relationship?

If you take a minute, you'll realize that you can give pretty good answers to all the questions posed above. That should be interesting to you because none of the questions are even posed, much less answered directly in the script. What does happen is that the scene invites you to see a series of images and to overhear a conversation; your own built-in storyteller kicks in to do the rest. You are truly interacting with the text here. You are making guesses, imagining consequences, and, whether you know it or not, your mind is, to quote James Cameron, "plotting a curve," an extrapolated series of incident and possibility that you rightly expect to arrive at some destination.

The great thing about the narrative experience is that it doesn't matter whether your guesses are right or not. It's the story's journey that gives the most pleasure to a reader, not its destination. The only thing we require of a narrative's destination is that it be honest—that is, consistent with the hints and inferences and logic plotted long before.

Lines 15–16: Dialogue

A dramatist has two basic tools with which to engage the reader. He can show us what people do and he can allow us to overhear what they say. When a reader is given these dramatic elements, a whole universe of interaction, participation, and complexity is possible. Scenes and action can show us what people do. Dialogue, if it's good, should show us what they are really saying. Good dialogue reveals character, motivation, and tone in a way that keeps the reader making inferences, making guesses.

Dialogue direction occurs when immediately in parentheses beneath the character's name, the writer tells the reader how to interpret the line (as in the word "sarcastically" in the example below).

JOHN
(sarcastically)
I'm sure you'd never run out on me, Mary.

A couple of obvious problems arise with most dialogue direction; if the scene is well written, direction won't be necessary, and if the scene is badly written, dialogue direction won't help. If we don't know John and Mary's characters well enough to judge whether Mary would "run out" on John, then the scene needs more work, more preparation. Dialogue direction isn't a shortcut that works in this situation.

Beginning writers direct dialogue all the time. It's a way to tell instead of show. Experienced writers rarely feel the need to coach the reader's response to dialogue. Good writers understand that the best dialogue, like the best scene description, shows instead of tells. Bad dialogue leaves a lot less scope for the reader's imagination. For example, have you ever heard soap opera, excuse me, daytime drama dialogue? Let's try some:

"What is it, Suzy?"

"I don't know it—it's terrible."

"It's Bret."

"Yes. We were so in love last summer, you know, when he was at the pool and I had that job warming the suntan lotion in the microwave. But then Betsy came along—"

"Betsy the Bitch."

"The same."

"Yes, and there it went, Gary! Bret, the job, the lotion, the tan—even the microwave went bad. I am soooo depressed!"

"It pains me to see you this way, Suzy."

"Yes, but what can I—what can we—do about it, Gary?"

So, Bret's jilted Suzy for Betsy the Bitch. Suzy's lost her guy, her job, and her tan. Gary's moving in for the score. Suzy's ready to be the scoreboard. Is there anything left to the imagination in the parody offered above? Are there any issues, emotions, or motivations not told about these transparently thin characters? Notice words like "pain," "depressed," which tell us the characters feelings instead of showing them. The parody points out a serious deficit with daytime dialogue. It specifically does not show. It always tells.

Contrast the soap with another boy-girl situation. This one comes from literature, Hemingway's *Hills Like White Elephants*. With only the barest of information regarding place and setting, I want you to see how much you know and, more importantly, how much more you feel about the two people engaged in the dialogue. The place is Spain. A railroad track separates the station's cantina from the long, white hills that stretch across the valley of the Ebro. We'll leap into the middle of the scene:

"They're lovely hills," she said. "They don't really look like white elephants. I just meant the coloring of their skin through the trees."

"Should we have another drink?"

"All right."

"The beer's nice and cool," the man said.

"It's lovely," the girl said.

"It's really an awfully simple operation, Jig," the man said. "It's not really an operation at all."

The girl looked at the ground the table legs rested on.

"I know you wouldn't mind it, Jig. It's really not anything. It's just to let the air in."

The girl did not say anything.

"I'll go with you and I'll stay with you all the time. They just let the air in and then it's all perfectly natural."

"Then what will we do afterward?"

"We'll be fine afterward. Just like we were before."

Question one: What is the operation they're talking about? Why the reference to white elephants? When we call something a white elephant, do we imply that it's valuable or cheap? precious or worthless? Some other questions: Are this man and woman married? Is the man really concerned for the woman's welfare? Are they going to be "fine afterward"? Were they really okay before? What's the point of a scene description like "she looked at the ground the table legs rested on"?

You should be able to see by now that Hemingway's dialogue shows instead of tells. The feelings of the story's characters, their intentions, motivations, even facts crucial to understanding their relationship are all presented indirectly. Anyone can be a passive recipient of soap opera information. Not so with dramatic dialogue. Dramatic dialogue requires the reader to interpret what she hears and sees, to make inferences, choices, and decisions. A reader engaged dramatically feels emotions precisely because he's not told what to feel. The experience produced is honest, it's genuine. The only thing that soap opera dialogue produces (and in fairness the only thing it's meant to produce) is sentiment and saccharine.

It would be fatal to give the impression that all dialogue should read like Hemingway's. It's important to realize that dialogue has to fit the tone and intent of your story. A sci-fi script like *Subterfuge* isn't going to explore a man's manipulation of women in the same way as does *Hills Like White Elephants*. But any writer can enrich her characters' lives by applying the tools that Hemingway's story provides. Any story can profit from the lessons that good dialogue teaches.

If interactive stories are to compete in the marketplace with interactive games or pornography, their writers are going to have to create characters with depth and complexity sufficient to sustain as much as a couple of hours of participation. If interactive writers go into this competition thinking that bells and whistles, or tits and ass, will replace the well-wrought tale or the overheard conversation, we'll only be seeing soap opera and science fiction for the short length of time it takes their producers to go broke.

Lines 17–18: Conditional Statement

A conditional statement explains a condition that needs to happen at some point in the program in order for the user to proceed. A conditional statement means that something happens only if something else happens first. It is used to convey user choice in an interactive document.

Conditional statements bookend conditional words such as "IF," "THEN," and "GOTO." When the term "if" is used in a sentence, a condition is created. For example, IF Jack and Jill go up the hill, THEN several things may happen:

1. Jack falls down and breaks his crown and Jill comes tumbling after.

or

2. Jack pushes Jill over the edge and proclaims himself King of the Hill.

or

3. Jack collapses and dies of heatstroke and Jill lives happily ever after with Humpty Dumpty.

The three options above are called decision branches. In the Jack and Jill interactive example, the user reaches a point where a decision must be made. Once that choice is made, a condition is met. The program will GOTO option one or GOTO option two or GOTO option three. If the user makes no choice or if the program automatically makes the choice for the user after a period of time, an intelligent agent built into the program's code may produce a standard action. This is called a "DEFAULT."

Lines 19–21: Action Description

Once a scene is established, it obviously doesn't stop. New characters and action change the scene's initial conditions. A script's action should be described as briefly and vividly as are its initiating scenes. Whether it's the most complicated sci-fi environ you can envision or the simplest fistfight, a scene's action should not take up a lot of space on the page.

A BLINDING WHITE HOT LIGHT EXPLOSION ENVELOPS THE FREIGHTER, FOLLOWED BY THE ROAR OF A POWERFUL EXPLOSION, SENDING SHIP FRAGMENTS AND HUMAN BODIES THROUGH THE AIR LIKE RAG DOLLS.

Interactive writers don't have a virtual reality closet for pitching stories to their prospective producers. They're stuck with words on paper. Writers must therefore use language to engage a reader's imagination and participation so that the reader sees the action come to life in his imagination.

So How Do I Know If It's Good?

So far we've talked about how to select details for your scene, how and where to introduce your scene. Now, let's talk about what makes a scene enjoyable to read.

You make a scene come alive with language. We've talked a bit (and we'll talk more) about how to make language dramatic, how to show versus tell. But beyond reflecting the dramatic point of view, your language must also be clear, vivid, and fast. As an exercise, require yourself to establish all your scenes with six lines or less. That's six lines—not six sentences. Some other tips: Work on a vocabulary of active verbs. Get rid of passive verbs like "is," and "are." When you describe a scene, combine active verbs with details that are as concrete as possible. "Stacy is tired," doesn't paint the same picture as, "Stacy collapses beside the handrail." "Sarah is studying," isn't nearly so compelling as, "Sarah buries her head in a stack of textbooks." You see the difference? Active verbs and concrete detail make for the kind of language that's a pleasure to read.

Don't be overwhelmed by technology as you digest the coming pages. Don't be arrogant, either. Children today own CD-ROMs loaded with fairytales whose roots go back thousands of years. It takes more than a computer to transport that little one to another world. It takes imagination. And it takes a story.

Language, Spines, and Cul-de-Sacs

There is a reason why 95 percent of the interactive titles out there suck. They suck because they have nothing to do with what an emotionally engaging story is. Nothing. Five years from now somebody will say, You mean they used to do interactivity without three-act structure? Three-act structure is not some kind of recent Hollywood conceit. This is something that was refined in the body of dramatic literature over the past three thousand years. Three-act structure is a way to dramatically create an emotionally resonating experience. The fact that most interactive stories lack a three-act structure points to the fact that they're not made by storytellers. They're made by technologists.

DOUGLAS GAYETON

Stories need a spine—a strong linear narrative made up of action, dialogue, theme, and metaphor—that holds the story together. But before we start developing spines for interactive scripts, we need to realize that terms like "spine" or "paradigm" or "three-act breakdown" are really only specialized vocabulary which describes structures common to all stories.

The fairy tale/nursery rhyme/narrative *Who Killed Cock Robin?* has at its simple core all the potential of a modern mystery/thriller. More importantly, *Cock Robin* should remind us that all stories, all language, all writing, or signifying systems of any sort share the same structural basis. Please note that I'm not saying stories are structurally similar at their roots; I'm saying they are structurally identical.

Suspicions of the sort asserted above have been around for a long time. Among the first to suspect were probably linguists. For instance, if a linguist in the 1800s were interested in the etiology of the word "darling," he would probably trace the word back through time, through Middle English and then Old English or perhaps even further. From its meaning in years past, he would reconstruct its modern usage. The recovery of the word's genesis and "meaning" would be intimately bound up with its daily use and its history.

But what if "darling" were to be viewed from a perspective outside history? What if, after all, history were not the prime determinant of a word's meaning, or better, what if a word's "meaning" were not as important as the mechanism by which it "signified"? Language viewed this way becomes the product of a system that can be viewed synchronically, apart from history, like the cross section of an orange. Would the word "darling" then be seen as an evolution of daily use or as the product of a structure within which the sound of the word was of secondary importance to the system out of which the phoneme was produced?

In 1916, Ferdinand de Saussure rocked the philological cage when he made just such an assertion. De Saussure's work asserts that language can be viewed as a system of signs (langue) that generate signification regardless of an individual word's history or use. A word's meaning is arbitrary, in this view, but its signification is always and everywhere determined. This structural approach to signs and signifying led to all sorts of inquiry. Two figures who came out of this activity seem to be especially relevant for interactive writers and designers.

Vladimir Propp is familiar to academics as the Russian formalist who used structuralist views of language to dissect the morphology of folktales. Folktales used to be thought of as very static, disconnected stories, peculiar artifacts of the particular culture in which they arose. Propp demonstrated quite the opposite. He showed that stories from Stone Age Europe to modern Brazil can be explained by a finite number of functions, a function being defined as "an act of a character formed from the point of view of its significance for the course of action." Applying linguistic theory and methodology to folktales, Propp found that tales originating from, say, eighteenth-century Russia or fifth-century China could be reduced to the same functional and structural constituents. Propp developed a relatively small number of functions that accounted for an astounding variety of character, incident, intervention, and jeopardy.

This functional approach to fables can obviously be applied (and has been) to narratives of all kinds. Claude Lévi-Strauss, popular among structuralists, is known for applying functionally based views of language to studies of myth. His analysis of myths, very similar to Propp's work with folktales, reveals structures whose details can be substituted in an almost modular way with no detriment to their function.

Anything can be "deconstructed" as a system of signifiers. Myths, fairytales, bullfights, fashion design—all become texts for study in Lévi-Strauss's view, and each of these "texts," as Robert Con Davis notes (in his anthology *Contemporary Literary Criticism*), "is modeled on a flexible version of a narrative sequence, a kind of storytelling."

Persons working in artificial intelligence are laboring to come up with digital representations of qualitative information. If this kind of technology-based story unit can be mated to the modular categories uncovered by Propp and Lévi-Strauss, it is possible to imagine a powerful storytelling tool—one that would allow a user making relatively small numbers of intrusions to generate an enormous variety of narratives. But don't let me sound too flippant with regard to that proposal! There will still be an enormous amount of work involved to set up these modular functions, coordinate them, and then devise agents and interfaces that will allow the user to remain immersed while participating in the text.

The structuralist buzz has gotten way out of hand in academia. But its first insights are important for interactive writers and designers because thinkers like Propp and Lévi-Strauss remind us that technology, even in its most exotic form, can never be more than an extension of language. A new signifier on the block. It's important for interactive storytellers to know, therefore, that there is no scheme, design, or pattern that can be divined for interactive narrative that is not also a structural sibling to all the narratives that have or will exist. All stories share a common genesis in language, and language, Fredric Jameson reminds us, is a prison within whose walls all discussion and discourse, all stories, must take place.

It's easy to forget that every time a new technology is brought to the task of telling stories, its proponents declare boldly that *narrative itself* will radically change in the new, technological wake. The users of new technologies all want somehow to be thought of as unique. Film theorist Dudley Andrew was writing in the mid-seventies about film's infatuation with itself, when he observed: "If modern cinema is somehow new, as every critic has suggested, its newness lies not in some mystical absence of a storyteller, or reduction of spectacle, or ascendency of 'film-writing,' or any other formula of new freedom which has been advanced. . . . Our stories get told in comprehensible ways, our acting has a rule behind it, the sets we use have a purposeful look, and the camera work which delivers all this to us moves meaningfully within the world it photographs."

Andrew was interested in the specific rules that governed the cinematic system of signifying. He was interested in the subcodes, the grammar, by which an audience understood that, say, a "DISSOLVE" signified a move in time or place from one scene to another. He was also interested in the larger picture, the narrative structure that film had finally come to recognize in common with old-fashioned storytellers and storytelling methods of the past.

Interactive writers, and I suppose critics, need to review this very recent history of cinema. By understanding the deconstruction that Andrew and others have undertaken for film and literature, new-technology writers can incorporate the "codes," the structures that have been seen to inform our storytelling past, while working to develop or recognize the unfamiliar subcodes that interactive narrative will definitely contribute to the narrative future.

But we must start by understanding that stories—whether told on movie screens or computer monitors—are functionally and structurally identical. When someone claims to have found a "new" structure that explains a film's appeal, the person isn't being accurate. That's not to say that structural approaches to narrative aren't useful. They're extremely useful, even essential. Later on, we'll detail the three-act structure. We'll talk about hinges and plot points. But the "three-act structure," the "paradigm," the "hinge," or the "plot point" aren't new and aren't unique to film or any other medium. These are just words that describe the structures out of which all stories are generated. They've been around for as long as stories have existed and, contrary to postmodernist claims, they *do* have beginnings, middles, and ends.

What we need to do now is to develop a structural approach to interactive stories that will help a designer develop procedures that will keep our plot(s) coordinated and well crafted. The underlying structure for an interactive story is its spine—and a spine is a linear narrative. If you're still not sure what a linear narrative is, go rent a tape, see a movie, or watch a sitcom. Finished? All right, you just watched a linear narrative.

The spine for an interactive screenplay, then, should look and read almost exactly like a standard screenplay. The qualification "almost" is, however, important. The standard movie script doesn't contemplate choice. The interactive script is largely concerned with choice. The choices that a viewer gets are not enumerated along the spine, however. (Can you imagine reading multiple versions of thirty or so scenes, back-to-back for, say, three hundred pages?)

It's absolutely crucial to understand that you cannot generate interesting or engaging options for your user unless you have a first-rate spine. Ironically, too, the more interesting and complex your spine, the more important it will become to develop user choices that do not violate your story's logic. Interactive writers must deliver an honest, linear narrative that nevertheless gives any number of chances for the viewer to interact. Software folks use these kinds of designs to build what they call an "engine." Think of an engine as the chassis of a car. All the software gets strapped onto the chassis and integrated with it. This engine will help a software designer and programmer write instructions for a computer that will invite a viewer to make choices while preserving the linear narrative and the pleasure provided by the narrative.

The linear story's structure can provide part of what we need to write an interactive script. But it's not enough. We want to tell dramatic stories that will be viewed over some multimedia technology and that will allow the viewer to affect the narrative's presentation. To do that, we have to find a way to leave the spine and come back to the spine in way that won't violate the story's logic.

We need a structure, in other words, that will allow the viewer to interact with the text, while preserving the satisfaction that comes with an honest ending. Enter the cul-de-sac. Creating a cul-de-sac for an interactive screenplay would consist in single or multiple scenes, command-directed to fit the viewer's specific choice or randomized so that even if a viewer made exactly the same decisions on multiple viewings, the story would, randomly, vary. The scenes written for all cul-de-sacs represent alternate versions of a scene already present in the script's spine. These alternate scenes will appear in either an attached and cross-referenced appendix or immediately following the interactive indicator in the script.

How Cul-de-Sacs Work

There are two things that have to happen for a worthwhile story to come of this engine. First, as with any successful feature film, you must have a tight and compelling linear narrative—the spine has to work. The second thing that has to work are the cul-de-sacs, the paths by which you invite the user to influence the text.

It's easier to show how a cul-de-sac can work than it is to describe a cul-de-sac's operation in the abstract. Let's take an early scene from the screenplay for *Subterfuge:*

INT. RESEARCH FACILITY - NIGHT
A sphere glows white hot in its plasma cage. Sandy Aimes pads across a catwalk which spans the entire interior. A lot has apparently changed.

"SECURITY TERRA-SQL," Sandy's uniform declares. And Jake's nowhere in sight. Sandy unlimbers a flashlight from her belt. And takes a private elevator to—

INT. EXECUTIVE VAULT - NIGHT
An executive suite tastefully decorated with antique furniture featuring a chromeplated vault on the far wall. A computer screen replaces lock and key. A coded card gives Aimes access to the keyboard; she TAPS a digital code onto the computer's screen.

EXT. RESEARCH FACILITY - NIGHT
A teardropped TOYOTA MOTORS up to the steel fence; "TERRA-SQL," the van's one-way windshield mirrors the sign. The passengers remain, unseen, behind. A uniformed GUARD waves them through without inspection.

The van spills a pair of THUGS into the shadows. Railguns and lasers rest casually in holsters that, in an earlier age, might have restrained rifles and handguns. A third man climbs out; "THE BUTCHER" squeezes ape-sized shoulders and legs from the van's interior. A chain secures his leather vest. A scar creases his face from jaw to ear.

> BUTCHER
>> How much time?

> THUG
>> Fifteen minutes to find her. Ten or so more
>> till shift change at the gate.

The Butcher unsheathes a knife. No laser or railgun here.

> BUTCHER
>> Let's go.

INT. EXECUTIVE SUITE/VAULT - NIGHT
Sandy Aimes adjusts a camera already snugged onto a microfilm viewer, projects the film onto the vault's wall. They're blueprints. Hundreds of 'em. The camera catches the prints one by one. SNICK-SNICK. SNICK-SNICK. Almost done. Sandy doesn't see the shadow at her feet. But she feels the barrel at her back! Sandy whirls, kicks—A boot catches one of the Butcher's THUGS full in the groin! Aimes goes for her own gun—But The Butcher's too quick. Sandy's railgun goes spinning across the floor. And then The Butcher collects her camera.

> BUTCHER
>> Dirty pictures, Sandy?

                              SANDY
          See for yourself.

                              BUTCHER
          I don't think so.
A single fist CRUSHES THE CAMERA to junk.

                              BUTCHER
          I'm gonna have some fun with you, Sandy.
          But first I got a question.
The ape leans into Sandy's face.

                              BUTCHER
          Who you workin' for?

INT. METRO LAS VEGAS - NIGHT
Corroded grates and cable tangle with the leavings of a Twenty-Second
Century sewer. Electric CIRCUITS SPIT like snakes. Sparks drift like
fireflies in the gloom. A Senior Security GUARD (DANNY) and his PARTNER
edge along behind handheld lamps. Scarred helmets wink rank and service
above uniforms hung with flak vests and other, well-used hardware. A
steady DRIP-DRIP OF WATER and waste keeps time with the CLICK-CLICK OF A
GEIGER COUNTER.

                              GUARD
          Couple of leaks.

                              PARTNER
          Hot?

                              GUARD
          A little.

                              PARTNER
          Let's make this quick.
The senior man SILENCES his GEIGER COUNTER, pulls a direction-finder from
a zippered cache, BEEP. . . . BEEP. . . . No promise there. He turns to face
a steel paneled tunnel of sagging cable. BEEP-BEEP.

                              GUARD
          Down there.

                              PARTNER
          Hell of a place for a beeper.

                              GUARD
                   Like you said. Let's make this quick.
The uniformed men SLUDGE TOWARD the signal. BEEP-BEEP.

                              PARTNER
                   See anything?

                              GUARD
                   No.

                              PARTNER
                   I don't like it.
No reply.

                              PARTNER
                   Let's get out of here.

                              GUARD
                   What about the beeper?

                              PARTNER
                   Screw the beeper.
But the finder insists; BEEP-BEEP . . . BEEP-BEEP . . .
                              GUARD
                   We're right on top of it.

                              PARTNER
                   I don't see anything.
The Partner takes another step—INTO A PITCH-BLACK HOLE!!

                              PARTNER
                   DANNY!
A sure hand snatches him upright.

                              GUARD
                   Easy. You're okay.
The Guards find themselves in a steel cavern. The lamps display a spider's
web of corroded cable. And then—

                              PARTNER
                   My God.
A nightmare. Twenty yards away a woman arches half-stripped and half-
impaled over a steel pike. It's Sandy Aimes. Tortured legs, back, and
neck tremble with the effort to maintain a bridge above the spear which

already teases her spine. Hands and feet bleed through wire garrotes which spread-eagle Sandy above certain death. A DISTRESS BEEPER WHIMPERS alongside.

>   SANDY
>   C . . . ! Ca . . .

>   GUARD
>   METRO SECURITY I HANG ON!
>   (to Partner)
>   MOVE!
> The Guards stagger toward the pinioned woman.

>   SANDY
>   Can't . . . Hold it!

>   GUARD
>   HELL YOU CAN'T! WE'RE RIGHT HERE!
> SHORTED CABLES bar the way, Deadly as cobras, The Guards bat them aside.
> BEEP-BEEP! BEEP-BEEP!

>   SANDY
>   K . . . K . . .Kay!

>   PARTNER
>   HANG ON LADY!

>   SANDY
>   Nine!

>   GUARD
>   HANG ON!!

>   SANDY
>   Oh, God, JAKE!!
> And that's it. Legs, neck and back collapse. SHE PLUNGES TO THE PIKE which
> waits below. The shaft blooms through Sandy's chest like a rose. BEEP
> BEEP! BEEP BEEP! BEEP BEEP!!!!

So, what just happened in this sequence? A guard and his partner receive a signal from a distress beeper. Turns out we have already met the brutally murdered victim whom the guards have discovered; Sandy Aimes was the lover of Jake Stryker, the story's protagonist. Jake begins the story as a hotshot rocket-jock, only to be found, a few years after splitting up with Sandy, an alcoholic, working the loading docks on a space station above the earth.

The story follows an exterior line of development—Who killed Sandy Aimes?—with an interior line of development: a man who's pissed his career away finds purpose and meaning as he struggles to clear the reputation of his dead lover. The cops, you see, tell Jake that Sandy was killed because she was stealing technology from her employer and double-crossed her thieving partners. Jake doesn't buy that version of Sandy's death. He drops down from orbit to discover the truth.

This is a straightforward genre. The environment is not what will account for the story's appeal, nor all the sci-fi fun that you can build into the story. What appeals about this story is the way that the exterior events function in relation to Jake's interior story. Soooo . . . how can we make such a story interactive?

When the guards finally discover Sandy's body, only three things have to be true. She must die. She must utter the words or sounds— "K . . . K . . . Kay" and "Nine" before she dies. We, the audience cannot be certain about whether Sandy is a thief or not. Functionally speaking, these are the only narrative requirements that Sandy fulfills in this particular sequence. A cul-de-sac simply provides alternate ways to depict Sandy's death, pique the audience's interest, and provide the clue Kay-Nine, our "rosebud" for the story.

The spine provides the initial and end conditions of this sequence, which cannot change. It provides a tone, though, which can change. Sandy's death, in the spine, is cruel and horrible and graphic. We can change that tone, and even concrete actions associated with the sequence, so long as we don't change the narratively essential information that the spine presents. What is presented in the spine's version? Well, we know that Sandy has taken something. We meet the Butcher and his goons. We hear the Butcher's dialogue with Sandy and we infer, rightly, that the Butcher is responsible for Sandy's horrible death. That's the way the spine plays out this portion of the linear narrative. But the spine only provides one way to see this story. We can imagine any number of ways, for instance, to dramatize Sandy acquiring the photographed blueprints that she's later accused of stealing. There are any number of ways for the Butcher to find Sandy and kill her. I'm going to play out a couple of alternate versions in the cul-de-sacs that follow. These alternate versions don't have to be taken as final or complete by any means, but they'll certainly do for purposes of illustrating the cul-de-sac's function. We will see, at the end of this short exercise, how to provide choices to the user without cheating the user.

For brevity's sake, I'm going to summarize these cul-de-sacs:

Cul-de-Sac #1

Sandy breaks into the Terra Sol vault, makes her photos, gets to her apartment and reviews the prints. The Butcher breaks into her apartment. The dialogue between the Butcher and Sandy remains basically the same. CUT TO: A building SUPE raps at Sandy's door demanding rent. He kicks the door open. There's Sandy, near death. The building Supe, in this case, hears Sandy's dying words, "K . . . Kay . . . Nine."

Cul-de-Sac #2

Sandy isn't seen stealing the prints at all. Instead, she's to make a secret meeting with a person, unnamed. We wouldn't even see the prints in this scenario, until Sandy shows them to her contact. We wouldn't see Sandy's contact. We wouldn't know if the person Sandy's meeting is a thief, a broker, or the FBI. The dialogue would focus only on how Sandy was able to get into the plant and how she was able to get the prints out. Nothing else. Remember, the cul-de-sac cannot violate any dimension, external or internal, of the linear story that follows. Everything must fit, including the characters' inner lives and the story's action.

What we would know at the end of this second cul-de-sac is that the contact betrays Sandy. Enter the Butcher. CUT TO: Sandy's found dead on the street. A street person rifling through her pockets would throw out some matchbooks looking for cash. Sandy's last words come as cops rush to the scene, chasing off the ghoul who's robbing Jake Stryker's dying, onetime lover. A cop picks up the matchbook. "K-NINE? This your address, lady? Hang on, now!" "K . . . KKK . . . Kay-Nine!" Sandy seems to affirm. And then dies.

You see how this works? You have a lot of latitude in your cul-de-sacs. But the cul-de-sac cannot in any way violate the logic already established in your spine. Sandy Aimes must steal some blueprints. We cannot know, beyond The Butcher and his goons, who Sandy's killers are. We cannot create dialogue which confirms that Sandy is a thief (that would be cheating the story's conclusion), but we also cannot create dialogue that unequivocally absolves Sandy. If we did that, Jake Stryker would have a much smaller dramatic obstacle to overcome in his search for the truth. The cul-de-sac must rejoin the spine without changing it. Sandy must die. And we must get the clue—Kay-Nine—into the story in a way that does not cheat. These are aspects of the exterior story that must not change.

But notice that the character's inner dynamic has to be preserved as well. A spine's initial and end conditions apply as equally to character relationships, emotions, intentions, and so on as it does to the exterior devices of action and evidence. So remember: When you build a cul-de-sac, the initial conditions of action and character cannot change. The end conditions must remain exactly the same. Otherwise your alternate scene(s) and your user's choices will violate the linear narrative that provides the backbone of your story.

It's important to reiterate that the cul-de-sacs above represent choices that will be presented to the interactive user. The exact design of the interface allowing that choice will have a lot to do with how satisfying the interactive narrative will be. But pay attention here: it would be just as wrong for the writer to specify the interface for the user's options as it is for a screenwriter to tell a director how to use camera, lights, or edits. Make the story vivid. Make your images, movement, and transitions vivid, and, obviously, the language as well. If you do that successfully, there will still be a ton of creative work left for graphic designers, programmers, editors, directors, performers, etc.

We've done a good bit of work here, but knowing what a spine does and knowing how to keep your separate story paths compatible will not guarantee a good story. Providing a design for an interactive engine doesn't help you originate a worthwhile narrative. In fact, there isn't any kind of how-to method that can guarantee you anything.

Next we're going to break down the structural requirements that exist for well-written stories. This is work you have to do unless you'd like to reinvent the wheel every time you sit down to compose a narrative. Once you understand that stories aren't structurally arbitrary, you'll be a long way toward developing consistent stories and becoming a reliable critic of yourself. It's essential work in this regard, but don't kid yourself—it's not enough. I know I can help you a lot in these coming pages—maybe even a hell of a lot—but ultimately, you will have to become your own reader and your own teacher. Only then can you really begin to write.

What Is an Interactive Story?

Literature is the true recorder of history; it provides the context for life. Latin American magical realism would segue easily from literature to the interactive world. The movement is beyond surreal. It presents a very clear picture of the evolution, history, and politics of the region. You can deal with all of these issues in a creative way, yet get the point across in a totally entertaining way. You can move diagonally into people's consciousness with that kind of wordplay.

MICHELE EM

Here's a thought. All stories from all sources are in some sense interactive. Even on paper there is an interaction between the book and its user. Speaking with regard to film, James Cameron puts it this way: "When you watch a movie where you don't know what's going to happen next, your brain works in an interactive way with the information that you're currently being given and tries to plot the trajectory . . . that's why I love the word plot, because your mind is plotting a curve. Is it this guy, or is it that guy? Is he gonna do this, or is he gonna do that?"

As we've discussed, interactive scripts should not (and probably cannot) give total control to the viewer. A good interactive script should find some middle ground, some balance between button-pushing and total passivity. An interactive design must also give the viewer the choice to limit choice.

Recall for a moment the bedtime story. If you don't have children, dig deep to your own childhood. Your mother or father tells you a story—say, Robin Hood. If your parent spins a really good yarn, you are Robin Hood; you snuggle

101

beneath the covers without a peep. In this narrative, you do not intrude. You are immersed completely. Your choice is to make no choice.

More often, though, just as Robin Hood is about to launch his unfailing arrow through the heart of the Black Knight, you might say, "No, Daddy, he knocks him off the horse. He knocks him off and then he ties him up and then he makes him do good to all the people he hurt." At that moment, your mother or father, as the storyteller, must do something interesting—he or she must interact with your input. The story must be changed to correspond with your participation. That means the story must be interrupted. The storyteller must break, however briefly, the seamless narrative immersion.

Something else ought to be equally obvious: a child doesn't mind the interruption. Children don't mind a certain break of the narrative flow provided their contribution gets worked into an honest ending. Everything changes once the Black Knight is allowed to survive Robin's arrow (for one thing, the child has guaranteed him- or herself a sequel). The most important thing that changes, though, is the relationship between the storyteller and his or her audience.

Only in fairly modern times have audiences been denied the authority to in some way participate in the text. The bedtime story and its antecedents offer a participatory model. By encouraging a child to intrude and then accepting the brief rupture of immersion that follows, the child becomes cocreator of the story with the storyteller. Interactive scripts offer users choices, but not creation. And digital technology has not yet provided an interface more seamless or protean than the spoken fable. Or the bedtime story.

But we aren't kids, I can just hear somebody in tight slacks saying, We're way past bedtime stories. *Whoa.* In the first place, we definitely are not past bedtime stories as any movie from *E.T.* to *Friday the Thirteenth Part VIII* ought to variously demonstrate. It seems likely that in our narrative past we not only tolerated interruptions of our stories, we demanded them. Greek dramas now seen by passive audiences in silent theaters were once religious rites in which audiences, well versed in the narratives performed, did not think of themselves as "spectators" at all, but as participants in their ritually told stories. Early Greek dramas, in fact, did not even have a chorus. It's interesting that once the "chorus" left the seats for the stage it became an extension of the writer's voice. Once that happened, the audience became more modern in their response to the playwright's selection and interpretation of detail. A modern vestige of the older rites can still be seen at a Catholic mass. The liturgy is a story. It is, however, a carefully designed story that demands controlled interruption in the form of responses, prayers, and even requests from the faithful audience to their chief storyteller, the priest.

But even if this kind of interruption can be made enjoyable in an interactive narrative, can an honest ending be made compatible with a user's intrusion? How many characters, after all, can rob from the rich and give to the poor? And what finally happens to that Black Knight? Can interactive scripts give the user significant narrative options while preserving the logical consistencies necessary for a satisfying plot? Yes, they can. But those scripts must start with the realization that stories, whether told at bedsides, in amphitheaters, or on computer terminals, incorporate linear narrative(s) as part of their architecture. Linear narrative, familiar to the "passive" moviegoer, often becomes the spine for the interactive writer.

The Linear Narrative of Science

We're interested in working definitions, not ontology. And I probably ought to remind you that we're dealing with narrative interactivity here; hybrids and games and so on have additional structural imperatives that we'll discuss later. But with regard to story, interactive writers can learn a lot from literature.

Back in the mid-forties, a couple of excellent writers wrote a book called *Understanding Fiction,* which described a story as a work of fiction that "broadens our experience and increases our knowledge of the possibilities of the self. Fiction is a vital image of life in motion. It is an *imaginative enactment* of life—and, as such, it is an extension of our own lives." These words by Robert Penn Warren and Cleanth Brooks came out of a critical movement whose adherents came to be called the New Critics or New Humanists. Warren and Brooks had the advantage of approaching literature from the writer's perspective. Among the many things that distinguish their book from contemporary critical works is that *Understanding Fiction* actually helps you understand fiction.

It's an old saw that good writers must be good readers. The problem is, many writer wanna-bes don't read and, worse, don't know how to read. There are bound to be folks, for instance, who, poring over Hemingway's dialogue in chapter 6, did not see that the man is trying to pressure the woman into an abortion that she does not want. Such a person needs to work on reading before they tackle writing.

And it's not always easy to know what to read. You can ingest lots of material at State U. or Ivy League or Film School that won't help you write at all. Unlike a lot of present approaches to literature that take an ideological or structuralist/deconstructionist approach to the systems that *surround* the story, *Understanding Fiction* keeps the story as the center of its concern. Warren and Brooks insist that readers can improve their experience of stories by knowing something about how stories work. The writers do something else that is positively an anathema to contemporary scholarship; they insist that stories, to *be* stories, must be meaningful.

What does it mean to be meaningful? It means that stories must ultimately have something to do with the big questions, what Faulkner called "the verities of the soul." Sound heavy? It doesn't have to be. Just think a moment—everything you read or see in a story involves directly or indirectly "some comment on values in human nature and conduct," to quote Warren and Brooks. The notion that you can have a value-neutral story is untrue. It's also untrue that stories have to propagandize, take a moral position, or even have a "moral" in the usual sense of the word. But good stories always involve people whose conflicts ultimately show us something about human nature or the human condition that is inseparable from the codes by which we evaluate behavior, accomplishment, heroism, cowardice—the whole spectrum of human activity.

"In the game world the moral physics is very slight," says Janet Murray. "In a story the moral physics must be more substantial and lifelike." It's important to realize that an audience's stake in a story rises enormously when human values are at the heart of the conflict. Remember Alan Ladd's performance in *Shane?* Would we care as much about Shane's final shoot-out if his past were squeaky clean, or if he had no compunction about killing? How about *Casablanca?* Would we care as much about Rick and Ilsa's final scene if the story had not been set against the backdrop of World War II, or if Ilsa had not been married at a time when marriage still counted to a man of courage and principle? Or take a look at the interactive *Johnny Mnemonic*. Would our concern for Johnny be as deep if he were not struggling to find worth and dignity against a system that we are to perceive as an embodiment of tyranny and evil?

It's no accident that Steven Spielberg got critical raves for *Schindler's List* and not for *Jurassic Park*, or that *Phantasmagoria*, for all its faults, is taken more seriously by persons with high aspirations for interactive texts than *Wing Commander IV*. What the interactive *X-Files* and the celluloid *Schindler's List* have most importantly in common is that their central characters are morally compromised agents placed in jeopardy simply because of their stand on a morally grounded principle.

In the interactive version of *The X-Files,* you are the star. You play Craig Willmore, a junior field agent with the Seattle bureau of the FBI; a man wet behind the ears, innocent, and a reluctant hero. In Spielberg's film, Schindler is a con man, a kind of Ivan Boesky bent on profit before he confronts the horrors of Jewish extermination. Schindler's sacrifice to save Jews from extermination is meaningful. Willmore's sacrifice, totally fictive, totally divorced from anything like the Holocaust, is also meaningful. The FBI agent pursues a quest while investigating the disappearance of Mulder and Scully. That quest ends with Willmore (i.e., you) cracking the case and redeeming his own integrity.

Stories are not games. And for now, we're not going to deconstruct hybrids like *Paul Is Dead, Myst,* or *Mario Brothers* that use story lines only as backpacks for digressions to games, arenas, or exhibitionism. Nor are we in this section going to extend our structural analysis to MUDs (multi-user domains) nor to live-action role-playing scenarios. We'll cover these venues later and show how they still incorporate, to a limited degree, linear narrative structure. But for now, let's start by saying you've been hired to develop a story with a cast of characters set in the near future whose jeopardy hinges on a moral decision regarding the use of a particular technology. Do you see the modular nature of this task? A near-infinite variety of incident, character, violence, sensuality can be captured in the general assignment outlined above. But you have to be specific. And the first thing you have to do is come up with a linear narrative, a spine for your interactive drama.

The experience unique to narrative is not the same thing as the experience rendered by combat or roller-coaster rides. Story writers, I hope you can see, have a lot more to do than string together a series of obstacles for some character seeking an objective. That's only the barest scratch on the surface of what a story should accomplish. An interactive script may offer dizzying chase scenes and fights, great erotica and environment, but if those exterior events don't have something to do with the characters' insides, the story will fall flat.

Now, does this mean good stories always have to aim for high art? Do we have to always base our stories on some historic injustice, or have at their heart some weighty concern? Of course not. Go rent *Indiana Jones and the Temple of Doom* or pop in the CD-ROM game *Starship Titanic.* Do you see high art coming out of the opening scenes of either of these? Good stories don't have to be "heavy." They don't have to center on Hitlers or Gandhis. There's only one thing that a story *has* to do. It has to be honest.

An Honest Story: Satisfaction? Or Betrayal?

Interactive stories have to work to remain honest. James Cameron sees integrity as important for all stories, regardless of their source. "Good movies work in a way that engages you in this process," the film director says. "You are creating alternatives in your mind, laying them up against what really happens. Then you have a sense of satisfaction or betrayal."

Satisfaction or betrayal. Not a bad way to judge whether a narrative plays fair or cheats. *I'm Your Man* was a (by now ancient) film released and billed as "interactive." The filmmakers provided a means for the audience to vote on various outcomes spun out by the movie's mystery plot. The problem was, a single, unified narrative could not support three conclusions. Multiple conclusions can't be sustained for single-lined narratives unless they are contrived or unless the "evidence" supplied in earlier scenes is ignored or amended.

A variation on the multiple ending is the "trick" ending. One of the best known of American writers is also the most dishonest. Robert Penn Warren and Cleanth Brooks were among the first to take on O. Henry for his "surprise" endings. In *The Furnished Room*, for example, O. Henry paints the picture of a distraught young man searching for his (apparently) estranged lover. Finding a room for the evening, the young man is tortured by the smell of his love's perfume. The scent fills the room, driving him mad, and the young gent rushes to the landlady. Had his lover recently occupied the apartment? No, he's told. The lady was never there. The lady was never there and so the reader is left to conclude reasonably that the perfume was never there, either. Our distraught, young man only imagined the perfume; he was probably unbalanced, an implication that seems affirmed when the young man himself commits suicide.

But in the story's final lines, we find out from the landlady herself that the young man's lover had been there. In fact, she too had earlier committed suicide in the apartment. The perfume was definitely in the room, therefore, and the young man had smelled it. Now, it's not a problem at all that the landlady deceives the young man. There is always a problem, however, when the author deceives the reader.

When a writer is said to have resorted to a "deus ex machina" (as in O. Henry's *The Furnished Room*), we understand that his or her story has contrived a conclusion that depends on the just-found piece of evidence or the providential intervention of some element totally unsupported by the plot. The term is from the Greek theater and means "god in the machine." In many early dramas, a god would literally descend to the stage and sort everything out at the end. It refers to both the idea that playwrights would resort to such tricks rather than fix the story themselves and the notion of information or decisions being delivered automatically without human intervention.

We're familiar with these kinds of endings. They aren't satisfying. We know at some level that the author of the text isn't playing fair and sins of this kind, whether by commission or omission, bring to their audiences the immediate and bitter taste of betrayal.

"What happens next" must in an honest story bear a consistent and logical relationship with *all* that has happened before. You run into writers who claim not to have worked out their screenplays' conclusions: "I never know how it's going to end! I just . . . *explore!*" To which Syd Field, author of *Screenplay*, replies in words I cannot improve: "Bullshit." Field goes on to say that "the ending is the first thing you must know before you begin writing." I think Field is right. It's fine to explore, but if a screenwriter explores for a hundred pages without a destination, the likely result is either a weak resolution or, worse, a dishonest one.

The writer of an honest story makes a contract with his or her reader: "I will give you everything you need to appreciate this story, to revel in its nuances and to anticipate its outcome. Everything I do will be done for the purpose of advancing action and dialogue to a particular conclusion that must be consistent with everything that has gone before." But what about interactive narratives? Should they work for consistent plots? Should they integrate an entire narrative work to support a final destination? And should they be subject to the same judgments of satisfaction or betrayal as linear stories? Should they, in other words, be honest?

Yes, they should.

Interactive writers need to understand that beginnings are inevitably tied up with ends. This isn't to say that an ending can't be ambiguous or varied or multiple. Jorge Luis Borges's fiction revels in parallel or unresolved narrative lines that refuse to give the reader a comfortable sense of arrival. Alain Resnais consciously follows Borges's example in his film *Providence,* which renders different points of view and different resolutions of a single narrative complication. The interactive CD-ROM game *Psychic Detective* offers an interactive twist on this familiar theme.

There is a difference between a narrative that is *solved* and one that is *resolved.* Later on, we'll talk about that distinction. But if you want to avoid cheating your user, get rid of the idea that you can "just start writing." Take some time before your start to define, at least for yourself, how the thing is supposed to end. This is a crucial preparation, even if you're only committed to a single story line. When things start to multiply, believe me, it gets to be imperative.

Multiform Plots

Many interactive scripts generate linear plots that weave in and out of each other's causally constructed universe. In *Hamlet on the Holodeck*, Janet Murray compares multiple and single plot lines: "A linear story has to end in some one place: the last shot of a movie is never a split screen. But a multi-threaded story can offer many voices at once without giving any one of them the last word."

Murray's paean glosses over a problem that plagues interactive writers. It's obviously true to observe that a "multi-threaded" story offers multiple voices. But it would be wrong to infer that users experience these voices "at once." Multiple voices, perspectives, etcetera cannot be experienced simultaneously. An interactive text offers options that a user experiences sequentially. The user can be given tons of control over this sequencing, but she experiences the text one choice at a time. This basic fact of interactive life creates real problems for interactive storytellers.

Users feel cheated when multiple versions or voices in a narrative line contradict each other. Users experience satisfaction to the extent that their choices result in an honest ending or endings. This requires interactive writers to mate each voice and choice to its own logic track, or, more likely, to recognize that all voices and all perspectives are not possible. In the real world of interactive writing, some voices and choices can only exist if others are made impossible.

"Since plot is a function of causality," says Murray, "it is crucial to reinforce the sense that the interactor's choices have led to the events of the story." True enough. An interactor needs to have the "sense" of creation. But this sense is illusory. For sophisticated users, it's no more than the willing suspension of disbelief. Seasoned users know that a good design cannot allow them to choose options that generate presentation or plot lines that don't make sense. Whatever sense of freedom the user feels results from choices made by the writer and designer. A user can't be allowed total freedom because the person is bound to choose an option that will be inconsistent, even wildly inconsistent, with choices previously made.

Interactive writers have to appreciate that every voice in their texts, every nuance and interaction, must be consistent with every interaction that precedes and every option that follows in the story world. That requires you to reconcile beginnings with ends even if you decide not to present a particular resolution in the text. Even if you decide to leave a plot line's final frame completely up in the air, or to make it ambiguous, postmodernist, *whatever,* you can't write the first interaction until you know where that interaction leads and how it affects the other narrative lines of the story.

Murray clearly understands that when crafting multiple plot lines, limits have to be put on a user's freedom even if the goal of the writer is only to have his or her various stories make sense. But the specifics offered as a solution to this problem are not convincing. Murray and others, as an example, point to artificial intelligence researcher Marvin Minsky and his conception of "frames" as a way to generate and coordinate multidirectional plots.

Summarized with apologies to Minsky, frames are units of conceptual generalities that have, as subsets, particular attributes associated with the generic. Sounds like Propp's morphology, doesn't it? Saloon hall girls, to use Murray's example, might be the defining category of a particular frame. But connected to that frame like Legos are the physical, thematic, or other attributes assigned to the generic. Music will come from a player piano, in this frame—not from Miles Davis. And dance hall girls will come in all varieties from scantily dressed to prostitutes. At a more general level, frames can be constructed to accommodate themes, genre conventions, mood, and so on.

But here again I find a claim that, as a writer, I know is simplistic. "A frame-based authoring system would allow a writer to enter each element in its generic and particular forms and would keep track of the connections between them." No, it won't. Even a detailed knowledge of how to build frames doesn't guarantee that the writer or designer will not fail at some juncture to anticipate one of the thousands or tens of thousands of ways in which a user's selection of blond hair, blue eyes, or a handgun violates some other necessity of the plot line specified by some other aspect of a connected frame. Easy to say it'll work. Hard to do.

I'm sure that Minsky and other artificial intelligence researchers would acknowledge that the frame is only an organizing tool that depends on endless parameters and extremely complex procedures designed, ultimately, to prevent a user from making decisions that lead to nonsense. The logic behind each interactive plot line that a writer generates has to be accounted for in any design, even those with advanced intelligent agents or frames. Comes with the territory.

Multiple characters and narrative lines offer a tremendous vista for the writer's imagination. But it's equally your responsibility, as an interactive writer, to figure out ways to let your user participate without creating inconsistencies in your story lines. It's a fun job, but it's also very demanding. Interactive writer Michael Kaplan can hardly be said to be a curmudgeon when it comes to new technologies. But taking on an interactive project led Kaplan to this assessment: "The real challenge with interactive writing is to make the player feel like every choice they make is critical . . . but as a writer, if I don't steer you [the user] to a common point of reference, I'm going to loose my mind trying to write an honest interactive story."

Kaplan's experience ought to convince writers working interactively that you can't create a story where a user has significant participation unless some voice that you create for a user's participation generates consequences that mandate the exclusion of others. Every interaction, whether we writers like it or not, creates conditions or facts or tone in a story that cannot be consistent with every other interaction. This is true whether you want a "closed" or "open" ending for the various lines of logic that each interaction generates, whether you're aiming for *Indiana Jones* or *The Labyrinth*.

God, Three Acts, and the Spine

I look at interactive writing as theatre on the computer. I'm trying to create an emotional experience for the user. I want the user to get involved with my characters—to care about them. I want the player to discover the special world of the game. If you can immerse the user into the interactive experience like you would with a movie or a good book, where the user forgets the outside world and is lost in the computer screen, then you've succeeded.

RAYMOND BENSON

All stories have a beginning, a middle, and an end. Peruse the library or the advertisements for interactive and screenwriting seminars and you'll find endless amplifications on that observation. Much of this material will relate in one way or another to the story's central narrative structure. We're going to call that linear, central structure "the spine."

An interactive story functions the same as a movie, a myth, a novel, or stage play. There are structural commonalities underpinning these forms that interactive writers can appropriate. You can find any number of books, for instance, that specifically address the structure of the well-written screenplay. Most of these books analyze the feature film's structure as if it sprang into existence from the nature of the medium itself to thrill us in ways never before discovered. This implication bears the twin disadvantages of being both arrogant and untrue.

Stage plays, in particular the modern three-act play, have had a direct impact on the development of what's somewhat parochially called "the Hollywood narrative," and continue to set the tone for most interactive narratives. Screenwriters and interactive scripters shouldn't be too afraid, or too lazy, to learn from the stage. If we read plays with any rigor, or see an opera, or recall our bedtime stories, it will be clear that the three-act structure, the existence of hinges, turning points, reversals, plot points, etc., are not something God invented for the silver screen. You don't see literature's contribution to screenwriting mentioned often enough in books for screenwriters. The debt is clearly there.

The three-act structure certainly didn't originate with movies. The three-act structure didn't even originate with the first plays. The notion of a beginning, a larger middle, and a concluding "chunk" of staged narrative gradually evolved from the rigid five-act formula that Horace dictated for Roman writers. Moving from that classic dictum came the capricious "act-breaks" of the Elizabethans. Finally, over the years, a common pattern emerged from these and newer works and stories on stage and screen came to be broken for specific reasons, at specific junctures, and at specific times in what we moderns call the three-act structure.

There's an irony, now, that screenwriters may have revived the three-act's favor among playwrights. Very modern playwrights chafed under the "restrictions" of the three-act "formula." A simple story was not sophisticated enough for these avant tastes so for a while we were reading experiments that in the main produced witty or angst-ridden dialogue and very unsatisfactory stories. Beads without a bracelet.

David Mamet, a Tony-winning playwright and award-winning screenwriter, remarked once that screenplays forced him to go back and learn how to tell a story. It's not an accident that plays like *Miss Saigon* or revivals like *Phantom of the Opera*, both examples of drama firmly scripted to the demands of three acts, have resurged to enjoy not only commercial but critical appeal.

Interactive scripts that in some way incorporate a linear story follow the same three-act structure common to plays as diverse as *King Lear* and *Ten Little Indians*. Applying a three-act structural analysis to the spine of an interactive narrative can be very useful. Such an analysis can help you become conscious of what structural elements must be in a coherent story, what order and proportion these elements must exist in, and what function they serve in the narrative. Interactive writers not only have to know where narrative functions must occur, they must also know when such functions occur in a satisfying story.

Syd Field is familiar to screenwriters as the author of several popular books on how to write screenplays. His application of the three-act paradigm to film shows that virtually all commercially released films follow a predictable and repeating structure. It took awhile for screenwriters to discover that movies have three acts and somebody's always claiming to have "found another way." My advice to new writers is, Don't waste your time reinventing the wheel. Syd Field doesn't claim that his books are the end-all for screenwriters, but his observations regarding plots and plot points are true. They work. They're useful. And they're so taken for granted that it's common now to see books that self-consciously follow Field's structure, their writers hoping, if published, to have a prose work that can readily be translated into a dramatic medium. Interactive writers, interestingly, can see this phenomenon when they buy books from the *Myst* and *Riven* series that fit snugly into the three-act shoe.

Interactive writers, screenwriters, and certainly writers like David Mamet know that playwrighting gives us a ubiquitous structure that can be used to initiate, develop, and pace dramatic conflict. This is what we're calling the interactive script's spine. It's not enough to know that certain functions have to happen in the spine. Dramatic events have to be plotted to occur at certain times and be arranged in certain proportions. Playwrighters speak of "pyramids" and "dramatic arcs" when they analyze their craft. It's not an accident that most narrative's have a larger second act than a first or third act. It's not an accident that first and third acts for many plays seem roughly proportional. The beginning of a story, and its end, should not occupy the viewer's attention longer than its middle.

Beginnings—Page One

A tight play, like a good interactive script or screenplay, has to be honest. If you'd like to make sure that happens, recall my advice: know your ending. You can't have an honest beginning until you know how the narrative will finish.

Once you have your ending, you can connect it to the very first seconds/interactions of your story. We can see something, here, that is common to all good drama, be it onscreen or onstage. Good stories provide some kind of trigger that gets the story going quickly; a precipitating incident that serves to introduce the main characters and place them in immediate conflict. How are we introduced to Macbeth? How are we introduced to Darth Vader? Or, for a variation on this approach, take a look at the opening for *Wing Commander III.*

Series O—A prologue . . .
MIDGAME: KILRATHI IMPERIAL THRONE ROOM - EMPEROR, THRAKHATH, ANGEL - 01THREM
A LARGE, GOTHIC, CATHEDRAL OF HELL: IN THE SHADOWS ALONG THE WALLS,
CONFEDERATION PILOTS ARE HUNG LIKE PIECES OF MEAT. BEATEN AND NEAR DEATH,
THEY CRY OUT IN PAIN AS KILRATHI SOLDIERS ROAM AMONG THEM, INFLICTING
FURTHER TORTURE WITH STRANGE, HIDEOUS WEAPONS THAT COMBINE THE PRIMITIVE
WITH THE HIGH-TECH. BLOOD DRIPS FROM THE TERRANS' WOUNDS.
A CROWD OF KILRATHI PART, AS THE EMPEROR AND PRINCE THRAKHATH ENTER. THE
EMPEROR TAKES HIS PLACE ON THE THRONE.

                    EMPEROR
          The enemy has struck at the heart
          of our Empire. A puny contingent
          of their soldiers has been
          captured here on Kilrah.
CRIES OF SHOCK AND ANGER FROM THE KILRATHI THRONG. THE EMPEROR SILENCES
THEM WITH A WAVE OF HIS PAW AND SIGNALS THRAKHATH TO BEGIN.

                    THRAKHATH
          This incursion was an act of
          desperation.
HE GESTURES TO THE TERRAN PILOTS STRUNG UP ALONG THE WALLS.

                    THRAKHATH
          The hairless apes now flail
          about, knowing they are beaten.
          They have failed their race
          utterly.
A GROWLING CHEER GOES UP. THE BLOODLUST BOILS UP IN EVERY KILRATHI PRESENT
(QUITE LITERALLY, IT'S THE LIONS VS. THE CHRISTIANS).

                    THRAKHATH
          There will be no interrogation.
THE ROOM EXPLODES IN GROWLS OF SATISFACTION. THRAKHATH TURNS TO THE
EMPEROR.

                    EMPEROR
          Do what you will with them.
THRAKHATH GESTURES DISDAINFULLY AT THE PRISONERS.

                    THRAKHATH
          Disintegration.
MOANS AND HISSES OF DISAPPOINTMENT.

                    THRAKHATH
            Silence. My brethren, they are
            not warriors, but offal.
WITH A FLICK OF HIS PAW, THRAKHATH SIGNALS AN EXECUTIONER WHO KEYS IN A
CODE AT A CONSOLE.
THE SHACKLES RESTRAINING THE CONFED PILOTS ARE WIRED AND —
IN A RAGING SURGE OF VOLTAGE AND BLINDING FLAMES THEY ARE REDUCED TO
LITTLE PILES OF ASH . . .IT AIN'T PRETTY . . .

                    THRAKHATH
            Only one among them is worthy of
            being treated as a warrior. The
            one they call 'Angel.'
ON THAT CUE, ANOTHER DISHEVELED AND BLOODIED HUMAN PILOT IS ESCORTED INTO
THE THRONE ROOM BY A HEAVILY-ARMED HONOR GUARD, AND THE BLOODLUST RISES
UP IN THE KILRATHI AGAIN.
THE PILOT IS COLONEL JEANNETTE DEVEREAUX—CALLSIGN: ANGEL. AROUND 30, SHE
IS PETITE. THE WAR HAS NOT TAKEN ITS TOLL ON HER BEAUTIFUL BELGIAN
FEATURES. BUT SHE WEARS HER DEFIANCE LIKE A SHIELD.
THE KILRATHI CAN BARELY BE KEPT AT BAY: FOR A SECOND, IT SEEMS SHE'LL BE
TORN TO PIECES RIGHT IN FRONT OF US.
THRAKHATH APPROACHES, AND ANGEL LOOKS AT HIM WITH DISDAIN AS SHE
STRUGGLES AGAINST HER CONSTRAINTS.

                    THRAKHATH
            Still defiant, Colonel Devereaux?
            If we were to offer co-existence
            with your kind, would you not
            accept it?

                    ANGEL
            The Kilrathi do not co-exist.

                    THRAKHATH
            No. And now that the tide has
            turned in this war, your defiance
            is a pathetic and useless
            gesture.

                    ANGEL
            You bore me, monsieur.
            Disintegrate me so I may join my
            comrades . . .
THRAKHATH REGARDS HER WITH AN EVIL GRIN.

<pre>
                          THRAKHATH
              Disintegration is not for you...
HISSES AND CATCALLS FROM THE SURROUNDING THRONG, WHO ARE LOOKING FOR A
KILL . . .

                          THRAKHATH
              Your fate will be different . . .
ANGEL REPLIES BY SPITTING IN HIS FACE. THRAKHATH GROWLS AND TURNS TO THE
THRONG.

                          THRAKHATH
              The human cannot appreciate the
              honor I am about to bestow her.
              She is not only a great
              warrior . . .
              (beat)
              . . .but her lair-mate is The
              Heart of the Tiger.

THRAKHATH TURNS BACK AND MOVES IN ON ANGEL WITH DEATH IN HIS EYES—AS THE
BLOODTHIRSTY CRIES FROM THE CROWD REACH A CRESCENDO . . .
DISSOLVE TO:
</pre>

What happens to Angel? We want to know. And we want to know her relationship to the characters who follow in the next few pages. Notice that the "seriousness" of the story has nothing to do with how it starts. *Macbeth* may offer introspection and terror; *Wing Commander III* may offer science-fiction escape, but structurally both *Macbeth* and *Wing Commander* provide a trigger right away that does the following:

1. Initiates the major conflicts that will fuel the story
2. Introduces the main character(s) around whom the conflict will complicate
3. Sets up the ongoing intentions and objectives for the major character(s) in the story

Notice that a story can't set up anything ongoing in the story unless the initial "trigger" is synchronized with the story's conclusion. The trigger, like anything else, has to be honest. What are some triggers we can learn from? Take *Macbeth*. Poor Mac's just back from a furious battle and already his lady is planting the seeds of ambition that (at the play's first major reversal) sees Macbeth kill his cousin before he has a chance to complete his evening prayer.

How about Hamlet? The prince is called onstage to encounter the ghost of his father. The Greeks really kicked things off: recall Oedipus killing his own father over a disputed right-of-way! The trigger for MGM's interactive online series *Paul Is Dead* is a homicide.

The trigger doesn't always have to involve the story's protagonist. Frequently, in fact, in opera, movies, and onstage, a trigger is more effective when it introduces the antagonist instead of the good guy. Let's face it, Darth Vader's more interesting than Luke Skywalker. And isn't Thrakhath somebody you'd love to have home for dinner?

The Trigger to Minute Ten

All the stories we've talked about start quickly to establish conflict that can be experienced from the dramatic point of view. The triggers occur in the same relative portions and, relatively, at the same time within each narrative. The trigger for *Wing Commander III* serves the same function for its story as does the trigger for *Macbeth*. They are structurally identical.

It's important to note where the trigger occurs and how long it takes to pay off. A good story can't take twenty minutes to start. In interactive or feature scripts, you need to be sure your user doesn't get sidetracked so badly in the first interactions that he or she misses the trigger for the ongoing narrative. Triggers like the ones cited above "set up" future conflicts while "paying off" an immediate conflict. The trigger must do its job within the first eight or ten minutes of your story's beginning. It's interesting to me that a page of interactive text, as a page of screenplay script, works out on average to a minute a page. Alternate scenes, for interactive writers, need to be thought of as alternate pages, not additional pages, since only one option at a time plays out on the screen.

In *Wing Commander III*, characters and conflicts are introduced actively and quickly. There are a few immediate payoffs (the capture of Angel, followed in storytime immediately by Colonel Blair and General Taggart viewing the wreckage of her ship, the *T.C.S. Concordia*) that set up future plot possibilities. With Angel's fate in doubt, Blair and his comrades have a personal stake in their war against the Kilrathi. Blair, in particular, has a dramatically motivated reason to pursue "the truth."

This business about a character's motivation is important. Too often writers try to make situations prompt activity. It's better when the character's motivation provides the logic that makes action either necessary or believable.

The trick is to create dramatic situations where the external events of the story and the inner life of the character work hand in hand. It starts from the first seconds of your story. It starts with the trigger.

Reversals—Act One, Act Two

Now that we've started our story with a trigger, are there other elements common to dramatic stories that can help the interactive writer? And do these other elements also occur at set places and times within the narrative?

Playwrights often speak of "reversals" within a dramatic story. There are many small reversals within a narrative, even within a given scene. But writers have known for a long time that there are two major reversals that always occur, and occur at particular times, in the first two acts of a three-act drama. A third, smaller reversal is frequently seen in the third act as well.

The first two reversals of a linear narrative are the most important for writers of any narrative to understand. As the term implies, the narrative is in some sense reversed, sending the story in a new direction. These reversals consist in dramatic situations or incidents—sometimes called hinges, linch pins, or act-breaks—that abruptly and fundamentally change the story's direction in a way not readily apparent from what has preceded that moment in the narrative. Such a reversal takes place roughly a quarter of the way through the story (just before the end of act one), and occurs once again around three-quarters of the way through the narrative at the conclusion of act two. It's important to understand that the idea of dividing something into "acts" is not arbitrary here. The three-act structure, and its many variants, are all ways for generalizing about what kind of things happen in a story and, more importantly, when they happen. In screenplays and in interactive scripts, major shifts in the story are called a variety of names. Syd Field's books dub them "plot points" for screenplays; the term could as easily apply for interactive scripts.

A caution probably needs to be made here. You can easily get the message reading Field's work that he has discovered a magic structure and created a vocabulary unique to film. However, the pattern described by a three-act analysis fits stories of all kinds. This applies to stories written before acts of any kind were a subject of study and even to plays that were written before acts were in any kind of standard use. Let's take a look at a few stories penned in the sixteenth century and compare them with a couple of stories filmed in the twentieth to see if that's the case.

Romeo and Juliet, for instance, is not a play divided into three acts.

Shakespeare didn't even write his early plays into acts. The plays' divisions, when they came, were fairly arbitrary. What is interesting, though, is comparing Shakespeare's narrative structure with, in particular, modern screenplays. We find that Shakespearean plays and Hollywood movies are structurally identical. In fact, both Shakespeare and Hollywood produce stories that conform to the three-act paradigm.

It's startling at first to discover that a centuries-old play arranges the same dramatic elements at the same time within its structure as does the commercial screenplay, but if we look at Shakespeare's *Romeo and Juliet* (and if we care to rent one of the film versions, both of which adapt the play!), we'll see that this is the case. *Romeo and Juliet* has a beginning, a middle, and an end that incorporate the same trigger, two major reversals, complication, and climax that Field describes for feature film screenplays.

Start with the play's first scenes. Romeo isn't introduced as a lover here. He's introduced as the son of the Montague family, a young man caught in the midst of a brutal dispute that threatens civil war. But something happens that completely changes Romeo's relationship to his own family and to the hated Capulets. That something "triggers" the rest of the story.

Romeo essentially crashes a party. Juliet's father, the head of the Capulet clan, gives the party in his daughter's honor. It's there that Romeo loses his heart to the daughter of his father's mortal enemy. Happens that fast. Once the conflict is initiated, there are only two possibilities. Either Romeo will capture Juliet's affection or he won't. The first act presents a problem that seems without solution. Romeo can't even see this girl, let alone court her.

It's worth noting here that good dramatic stories must involve some cost to the participants. In the case of tragedies, something painful must be exacted from the characters in a story. In comedies, the stakes are artificial and complicated, but they're assented to as "real." Writers use words like "jeopardy" or "stakes" to describe this dramatic requirement. Well, take a look at *Romeo and Juliet*. What's "at stake"? Bitter hatred? Powerful families in deadlock? Torn loyalties? The dogs of war? All opposed to young love.

Most of the first act sees Romeo thwarted. Romeo cannot approach his love without risking his own death. But then something changes this circumstance. The story's first major reversal takes place on Juliet's balcony. Romeo climbs to his love and wins her heart. Notice that this scene changes the inner lives of the two young people as well as the outer circumstances of their story. Notice too that the lovers' first tryst occurs roughly a quarter of the way through the play. The impediments and conflicts of the previous scenes pay off with a small epiphany here. But that would not, in itself, be enough to qualify this moment as a major reversal. Recall that a three-act structure supports only two major reversals. Something Field misses in his analysis is the fact that the first linchpin in the narrative, illustrated here by the balcony scene in *Romeo and Juliet*, doesn't simply reverse the outer direction of the story, it reverses the inner lives of the characters as well.

It's the dimension of inner change that I see most neglected in discussions of screenplay structure. Outside events are only worthwhile when they affect a character's head and heart. At the beginning of Shakespeare's play, for instance, Romeo isn't in love with anyone. He certainly isn't expecting to fall in love with a Capulet. Juliet never expected to fall in love at all. The play's hinge must reverse not only the external events of the story, it must also change either our sense of the characters' inner lives, or the characters' own perception of their inner lives. The inner story, in other words, must reverse synchronously with the outer story or you won't have a satisfying hinge.

What works for plays works even more formulaically onscreen and it doesn't matter whether the story is intended as a "serious" work or something done "just to entertain." It's not enough for Luke Skywalker's home to be destroyed by Darth Vader. Luke must learn at the same time that his father was a famous Jedi knight. He must fall heir to a quest. That's a reversal.

At the other end of the dramatic spectrum is *Schindler's List*. It isn't enough for Oskar Schindler's workers to be routed from their ghetto homes into a Nazi labor camp. It isn't enough for Herr Schindler to witness the beginnings of the pogrom against the Jews. Schindler's inner life must reverse along with the reverses that he (and we) can see and, in fact, that's exactly what happens.

Viewing the ghetto's liquidation, Schindler feels empathy for the first time for a group of people whom, till that point, he has regarded as chattel. The moment occurs just about a quarter of the way through Spielberg's four-hour drama. It occurs just before the end of what would be the first act. The movie's director allows a mote of color to intrude onto this particular piece of his black-and-white horror—almost like a bookmarker to keep the spot. The color comes with a little girl, a small child in a red coat, who wanders through the carnage. Schindler sees her. His wife implores him to go, but he cannot. He must stay. He stays and he looks and he is never the same. Talk about a change in circumstance. Talk about a change in a character's inner life. Talk about jeopardy, stakes, the big questions. This is a major reversal. Look where, and when, it occurs.

Is this an accident? Does every story have this kind of structure? Look at

Casablanca. When does Ilsa stroll into Rick's gin joint? What about *Titanic*? Plot point one occurs when young Jack Dawson keeps high-society Rose from committing suicide by jumping over the doomed ship's side. By saving Rose, Jack gets a grudging invitation to join the wealthy young American and her upper-strata entanglements for dinner. The incident occurs just about a quarter of the way through Cameron's long narrative.

Now let's look at an interactive script to see if the same paradigm holds. In *Wing Commander III,* Blair having the opportunity to rescue Flint is a major plot point. He's moved on from Angel to Flint and Rachel (a woman he bonds with soon after). A classic act-two plot point is when the Behemoth blows up.

Not all interactive scripts loan themselves to this analysis. But remember that in this section we are talking about interactive scripts that incorporate a *linear narrative.* A large portion of mainstream interactive scripts fall into this category. We're also talking about some proven moneymakers, too, which, if nothing else, ought to give you some incentive to take the notion of plot points seriously.

Note that interactive scripts may provide more than one option for their major plot points. That's great! But keep in mind that every option given for plot points one and two must reverse the narrative and should have some consequence for the character's inner lives. All options that are major plot points have to occur at the same relative time and position as do plot points in noninteractive narratives if the interactive script is expected to produce a satisfying rhythm and pace.

A successful story has a hinge before the end of act one and again before the end of act two. The first act's reversal sends the viewer into a series of complications and obstacles that reverse the first direction of the story. The first reversal functions like firewood for the story's midsection. It initiates the serious conflicts that will account for the lion's share of the characters' inner story.

The Second Reversal—Second Act

It's not arbitrary that the story's middle turns out to be a lot longer than its beginning or end. The complications that multiply in the story have to be paced and have to account for several levels of conflict. But the second act must end sometime. If it is to end satisfactorily, the story cannot simply declare victory. There's more work to be done. One last twist, one more major reversal needs to take place before the end of the second act.

Look again at *Romeo and Juliet*. The second act sees the lovers overcome the obstacles that kept them apart. They make love. They even marry. They seem to have found a niche between their families' hatred that is safe. What's left to do in the story?

What's left is murder. Mercutio, appropriately named, is lured into a duel with a Capulet and is killed. Romeo, defending his kinsman's honor, slays the slayer and is banished. Exile during this perilous period is worse than death. And even worse than being cut off from hearth and home, this second reversal cuts Romeo off from Juliet. It changes, once again, the characters' inner story, and it brings closure to the narrative by setting up the third and final act. The second reversal changes the story's exterior events and the characters' inner lives along lines that are congruent with the story's final resolution. That's the function of the second hinge.

Schindler's List is a much longer narrative, but proportionately its reverses occur in the same place and serve the same function as the reversals in *Romeo and Juliet*. Recall that the movie's first reversal (Schindler witnesses the liquidation of the ghetto) triggers a big change in the exterior events of the German's life and circumstance. Subsequent to the ghetto's liquidation, Schindler goes from having his own workers under his own control to having prison laborers placed under the command of a brutal Nazi commandant. That's the outer reversal. But there's also the inner story; the first hinge changes forever the way Schindler feels about his Jewish workers. He cannot be indifferent anymore, he cannot place profit solely above his feelings for the people he has helped to enslave.

The story's first reversal sets up its second. We see that small red-coated girl once more. We see her, in fact, about three-quarters of the way through the story. But this time the child is stretched on a pyre of blackened bodies that blots out the heavens. Schindler is there, trying to feign disinterest, or, more accurately, trying to feign self-interest. The first hinge changed the way Schindler felt. This second, brutal hinge compels the German war profiteer to action. The story reverses one last time. Schindler literally buys his workers from the Nazis. He moves them, protects them, saves them. The businessman who before has wanted nothing more than to be known as a great industrialist works feverishly, now, to create a plant that produces nothing.

Resolution, Catharsis, and Act Three

The third act brings a new stability out of the chaos begun and stirred in the first and second acts. Schindler defeats racism, genocide, and death. Rose survives the sinking of the Titanic to escape from her gilded cage and become a free and passionate woman. The interactive character, Adrienne, in *Phantasmagoria* may, depending on a user's participation, uncover the clues and gather the objects she needs to save her husband from the evil that holds him in its ever-tightening grip, or be crushed herself.

The first two acts pay off with a final reversal and climax in the last act of drama. Field offers an analysis of the final reversal that occurs in the third act, a final surprise for the audience. Without reproducing that work here, let me just ask you to rent *Presumed Innocent*. When does Rusty Sabich (Harrison Ford) finally discover the murder weapon? When does he, and when by extension do we, finally know the story's murderer?

Once the audience has participated in and experienced these kinds of revelations, there is a need for some moment, however qualified or temporary, of stability. A place where we know nothing else is to be revealed. Nothing else will change. A good story has to allow some vestige of catharsis. The Greeks viewed catharsis as a kind of healing. In less serious films, catharsis is unequivocal. The bad guy is defeated. All is well. *Star Wars*'s soap-opera catharsis comes when Princess Lea confers honors of war upon her heroes.

Schindler's List offers a more sobering, more meaningful kind of catharsis. A handful of stones on Oskar Schindler's tomb reminds us of the many who survived and of the masses who did not. In *Titanic*, Rose escapes the clutches of her rich American fiancé. But she loses the love of her life.

In all these dramas, whether serious or slight, we can see a pattern that shouldn't need a lot of specialized vocabulary to understand. All the stories exhibit structural elements that are identical in placement and function. Those elements do the same things. They occur in the same place. In each case, x marks the spot:

ACT 1		ACT 2		ACT 3	
BEGINNING		COMPLICATIONS		RESOLUTION	
_____ x _____	x _ I _____	_____ x _ II _____		x _ III _____	
TRIGGER	HINGE 1	HINGE 2		CLIMAX	CATHARSIS

The first reversal (hinge 1) occurs just before a quarter of the way through the story. The second reversal breaks shy of the three-quarter mark. For a two-hour drama, the first reversal should occur 25–30 minutes into the story, while the second reversal (hinge 2) needs to play out sometime around the eighty-minute mark. At a minute per page, the first hinge should appear in a well-written script somewhere around page twenty-five. The second hinge should break around page eighty.

Don't get hung up thinking these pages or times have to be exact! On the other hand the times and pages provided are useful targets; they indicate the relative place along the story's timeline in which various narrative elements invariably occur. Interactive scripts that incorporate linear narratives may take hours and hours to play out. Many of these longer formats will, in this case, proceed episodically, using digital space to create a series of linked narratives. Those individual episodes need to incorporate plot points and reversals just as stand-alone narratives.

Whether you're working on a two-hour script or a ten-hour interactive text, you need to know what plot points are, and be able to build your narrative(s) around them. The first major reversal in a 120-minute length interactive narrative will not come an hour into the story! It's going to be somewhere around the 25-minute mark. Similarly, the second hinge for a two-hour script should break sometime before the 90-minute mark.

Whether its *Star Wars* or Shakespeare, *Die Hard* or *Schindler's List*, we see the three-act structure repeat. The same elements accomplishing the same functions occur at the same relative times in these varied story forms. The three-act structure can also be applied to a great deal of prose. Those novels and short stories that tell a linear story follow the same dramatic structure seen in plays or film. This structural identity accounts for one of the reasons why some novels (especially genre works) translate easily to film, while others (like Joyce's *Ulysses*) do not. But that's a separate line of inquiry. For now, I hope you'll be helped by composing your interactive scripts in terms of the three-act structure.

The analysis given here isn't exhaustive by any means. But it will provide you with a good skeleton on which to build your story, a good way to critique your own work. Let's reiterate the elements charted along our schematic. The elements we discussed are as follows:

- The precipitating incident, or trigger
- Two reversals or hinges before the final act (remember where they need to occur, at approximately 25 percent, and again at 75 percent into your timeline)
- A final reversal in act three is a great way to set up the climax, which peaks close to the story's end
- A moment of catharsis for the audience

We've talked about the engine that will allow a user to intrude into your story. We've talked about cul-de-sacs and spines and, most of all, we've discussed stories in terms of their structure. Structural approaches can help us see what stories have in common, but they can't help us see what makes stories special, what makes one story better or worse than another. A great film and a bad one, after all, share the same narrative structure! Structuralist methodology not only doesn't have much to say about a narrative's quality or "meaning," it denies any ontology for the terms.

A deconstructionist may have a great deal of trouble finding a basis upon which to say that anything is absolutely good or absolutely bad, but an audience will not. Siskel and Ebert won't either. So what does distinguish a satisfying story from one that ultimately betrays its audience?

If pressed to pick a single characteristic that distinguishes good stories from bad ones, or average stories from great ones, I would probably say something like this: It seems to me that good and great stories largely distinguish themselves by the extent to which their characters claim our empathy and attention. The characters whose stories we relive and whose lines we recite have in some sense come to life. That sense of life can't be realized without an honest story whose stakes root in the human condition. The human condition can't be made interesting apart from some sense of meaning and value.

In the next chapter, we'll look at a selection of films and interactive texts whose characters grip us tightly. While the concept of the three-act structure is useful in analyzing these stories, a good story will always have elements that can't be explained solely in terms of structure and significance, or form and function. We'll be looking for a thread that will help us understand how truly great stories, whether interactive or filmed, bring their characters to life. Once you've followed that thread yourself, you'll have a place, at least, from which to breathe life into your own world of make-believe.

10

Performing Character

Characters are going to change or stagnate based on your actions; they are going to live or die. You're Rick in Casablanca: You have to decide who gets to use the letters of transit, or whether to let the woman win at the roulette table. If the world created is rich enough and textured enough, interacting with this world is going to emotionally engage you.

TERRY BORST

A narrative's outside events are always a vehicle for a story that goes on inside the heart. Whether it's Oskar Schindler's story, or Rose's and Jack's, or Tarzan's, it's the inner story's stakes that make the exterior threats, jeopardy, car chases, or comedy satisfying for the audience. It's not an accident that the inner story receives so much attention from analysts of fiction, for it's here that critics and writers alike contemplate the ways in which storytellers create "character."

For Aristotle, the development of character was totally determined by the exterior action of the plot. In that sense, I suppose, Aristotle was a true dramatist. It's definitely true that dramatic works, like the interactive screenplay, must find ways to *show* character instead of *telling* us who the characters are, what they feel, what motivates their actions, and so on.

Plot has been called the logic of human motivation. Dramatic stories, and that certainly includes interactively rendered dramas, cannot separate the development of plot from the presentation of character. We know people, in

127

drama, by what they say and do. If a writer editorializes, if he or she tells me that this line of dialogue is "sarcastic," or that the character glances "fearfully" toward a fictive partner, then I'm going to know that some work necessary to compelling characterization has not been done.

Warren and Brooks call the kind of characterization that goes on in movies and interactive scripts indirect. Review *Subterfuge*'s opening pages. You infer or imagine the character's emotions, intentions, and inner lives as you read these pages. You create a subtext with the writer as you plot the future circumstances of the introduced lovers and as you imagine their inner lives. Nothing in the text tells you whether your inferences, guesses, and imagination will be the same as the writer's. The only information you're given in a movie house is what a camera or audiotape can record. Your computer ought to be similarly circumspect in allowing access to its characters' inner lives.

An interactive script should not tell what a character *is*. I read things all the time that say something like, Wouldn't it be nice to click on and find out more about Hamlet's fears and desires? Or see who Ophelia really wants to sleep with! These same people, by the way, complain that the characters they most frequently encounter in their interactive critiques lack depth and life.

Game designer Jeffrey Sullivan says that, "We are limited to the depth of stories you can tell interactively. While some adventure and role-playing games allow the player to 'manipulate' a character's emotions by setting the current emotional state like a setting on a dial, this is also very primitive and unrealistic (for example, you could change a character from angry to happy in a blink of an eye—an unrealistic change for all but the most bipolar of individuals). The use of emotional 'settings' for characters also violates the 'show, don't tell' rule of drama."

Well, guess what? You can't have it both ways. An interactive text that wants its users to feel something about its characters should not tell the user anything about the character's inner life. And the more complex a character becomes, the less advisable it is to have an option that offers shortcuts of revelation. Soap operas have magazines that do this kind of thing. Is it any accident that soap-opera information is only interesting for soap-opera characters?

Complex and interesting characters have to be revealed, not explained. Interactive writers should show what a character says and does. Information regarding the character's feelings, intentions, motivation, or understanding should not be supplied directly by the writer. They should be inferred by the reader/viewer/user from dramatized clues that are presented in the text. Dialogue and action are still the primary scalpels with which a writer bares his or her character's inner story. But there's something else needed, too. Something we usually take for granted. That something is "context."

Context

Let's conduct a little thought experiment. No paper required. Only honesty and time. Supposing I tell you that a man has just viciously slapped a boy at a street corner? What do you feel about that man? Is he tall in your mind's eye or short? Blond-haired or dark? Unpleasant or handsome? How about the boy? What images come immediately to mind? And how do you interpret the events reported? What's the situation that we infer from this first report? What's going on?

Take a moment and make up a short description of your first impressions, how you feel about that man slapping a child, what you think the man's background is, how he looks, and so on. Finished? All right, now I'm going to give you the same situation—a man viciously slaps a boy—but with one additional fact: the boy had a gun in the man's stomach and was trying to kill him. Now, is the picture the same? Are your thoughts, feelings, and interpretation the same?

You get the point. Without knowing the context of an external action, it's impossible to create a character's inner life. And don't protest that the reader can figure it out after the fact. No. It's not up to the reader to provide essential information for the scene's characterization. That's your job. Remember those coloring books you had when you were younger—the ones where you connect the dots? You have to provide the dots so that the viewer can correctly fill them in. Bad writers cheat at this process. Good writers don't.

Context and Ethics—Questions of Value

A story's historical or cultural context can't exist without a concomitant ethical context. *Schindler's List* doesn't compel audiences simply because it presents pictures of organized violence against Polish Jews. The film staples those pictures with a challenge. It's the same challenge that forces itself on the film's protagonist and the challenge is, Is what you see "right"?

Is it right to slaughter Jews? Is it right for a young girl to be trapped into a marriage she detests? Should Frodo keep the Ring? Any story, whether based on fact or fancy, cannot provide circumstantial context without moral context. Even the most trite of stories cannot exist without some kind of ethical dimension. Remember our thought experiment—the man who slapped the boy? It isn't just that a moral context allows us to experience the scene differently (once we know that the boy is a robber trying to kill the man), it's that, apart from a moral context, we can't experience the scene at all.

What holds true for this simple experiment becomes even more important for more complex narrative works. Whether it's Romeo and Juliet, or Jack and Rose, or Blair and Angel, we feel empathy for fictive characters not just because of their external circumstances, but because their circumstances force a choice that reflects either directly or indirectly on human values. Structural analyses can do a great deal to help us understand how stories work, but if we decide that the ethical component of a character is somehow passé or peripheral, we will miss what is essential for the character (and the audience) to experience any kind of genuine drama at all.

Interactive writers need to understand that drama works by placing characters in situations of conflict, and that conflict can't consist solely in the cyber-equivalent of car chases. Conflict doesn't occur automatically when a man is pitted against another man or against nature or aliens or any combination of external antagonists. The deepest experience of conflict comes when an audience sees a character pitted against himself, against his own demons, his own vices, his own insecurities. We hold our loved one's hands when Rick puts Ilsa on that plane. We hold our breaths when Rose chooses Jack over his socialite antagonist. We ache to see Winston escape the ever-present eye of Big Brother. Why do we respond to these characters, and not others, in this way? Why this depth of feeling? Two reasons ultimately dominate: (1) these characters are doing what's right, and (2) it costs them.

Context, Climax, and Cost

The climax of almost any story, paper thin or profound, sees the protagonist make some kind of choice. If that choice is to be compelling, it has to involve some question of right and wrong. A story's ethical dimension, in fact, is what makes dramatic "cost" possible. Why does Rick agonize over Ilsa? What makes Oskar Schindler "get involved"? Why do we hesitate to click on the "Mission Fails" option when Colonel Christopher Blair leads the fight? None of these core questions about character can be answered unless we recognize that fictive characters are beings bound more closely to codes of value and ethics than are the people we experience in "real" life.

Resolution versus Solution

A story's climax is often thought of as the narrative's last major experience of dramatic conflict or action. The story's outer conflicts are resolved with some sort of "closure" at the climax while, at the same time, some inner conflict is resolved. But note the word "resolved." The most compelling climaxes do not "solve" their characters' problems. The best stories do not usually let their protagonists off the hook.

Titanic offers an obvious example: Rose survives at the cost of losing Jack. In *Casablanca*, Rick loses the love of his life and is almost certainly going to be tagged as a member of the Resistance. This isn't to say that sappy endings can't produce memorable characters. How many times have we watched *It's a Wonderful Life* or *Star Wars*? But I would say that even these stories leave some aspect of their narratives unresolved; their heroes do not triumph unscathed. Whether it's *The X-Files, Gabriel Knight: The Beast Within, The Dark Eye, Phantasmagoria,* or *Schindler's List,* the most compelling stories force their characters to pay a cost for whatever "stability" the narrative finally achieves.

Outer Story and Inner Story

Once we understand that a character's most important conflict is personal and relates to the character's sense of what is right and wrong, it's easier to see that one of the major functions of the story's circumstance and action is to provide the arena within which those values get tested. It takes a great deal of work, however, to allow a character's values to emerge naturally from the story's circumstance and environment. Interactive texts are still very weak in this regard. That's one reason why, when looking for examples of well-integrated character, it's hard to use interactive titles.

There is absolutely no reason why an interactive character should not aspire to the same complexity and nuances of motivation as typify the best characterizations in literature or stage or film. For that to happen, interactive writers must understand that the deeper a conflict is seated in a character's heart, the more important it is to go about dramatizing the resulting conflict indirectly. Characters don't gain empathy if they're used for either prescription or propaganda.

The Facts, Please

Writers need to make sure their outer stories are in balance with their inner stories. It takes a lot of time to research, understand, and create a believable period and place, people and props out of which character can come alive.

Schindler's List provides an excellent example of a filmed story based on a heavily researched novel that spends a great deal of imagery and imagination re-creating the context of an unfamiliar period and place, people and props. The story also provides an ethical conflict that pits the lead character's deepest ambitions against what he knows to be "right." The outer story and the inner story are well researched and balanced. We can't appreciate Oskar Schindler's inner dilemma unless his outer circumstances are made both clear and vivid. The lesson to take from this example: Do some research! The best writers in any medium know their story's environment, people, and history. Interactive scripters should require no less of themselves in this regard than do playwrights, screenwriters, and novelists.

Personal Experience

One way many writers seek to avoid the tedious business of reading and research is to look for the story and characters that come out of their "personal experience." Beginning writers are often told to "write from your experience." Personal experience is touted in studios, seminars, and bistros as the bedrock for building successful character.

Even if we confine ourselves to the silver screen, we can see that this proposition doesn't hold much water. I'd say, for instance, that Jack and Rose were fairly compelling characters in *Titanic*. Was the screenwriter a hundred-year-old survivor of that famous tragedy? Was James Cameron? What about the film's actors and actresses? Or let's pick a text that's had varied presentations. Did Orwell have to go to a time machine to write *1984*? Did the actors who performed for the filmed adaptation of his novel or for its newest interactive reiteration have a personal experience of the futuristic hell in which they participated? It's pretty obvious that none of these people had any personal experience of the stories they created. And yet, all these texts present gripping and compelling stories with unforgettable characters. How is this possible? It would seem there has to be another way to build character besides "being there," otherwise films like *Titanic* and interactive titles like *Big Brother* or *Wing Commander* could never be made.

Thomas Wolfe was criticized a few years back when he downplayed personal experience as the basis for great fiction. Wolfe's contention, basically, is that personal experience needs to be united with knowledge and social context if stories and characters of substance are to emerge. Wolfe offered the advice that writers who'd like to write something worthwhile should copy some of the habits and techniques of journalists.

The journalistic impulse can be made to serve fiction well. The payback for your story can be enormous. Wolfe offers an anecdote about Émile Zola. Zola was appalled by the conditions that coal miners of his period endured and was determined to write a novel that would expose those conditions. Zola wasn't a coal miner. He had no personal experience of the labor, no personal connection with the men and women who did the labor, nor anything else connected with coal mining. But he didn't back away from the story. And he didn't settle for a general, or thirdhand account of the coal miners' existence. He did some research. Émile Zola, posing as a mining inspector, rode down a series of shafts to a mine's dark belly.

Most of what Zola saw were things he expected. The smells I'm sure were new and distinct. Perhaps he even felt a tightness in his chest, a touch of claustrophobia. Those would have been the things a lesser writer might have seized on. But Zola was concerned with the *dramatic context* of the miner's situation. He was looking for facts that showed their plight without telling.

At the bottom of the mine, Wolfe relays the story, Zola saw a pony hauling up a cart of coal. It occurred to the writer that this animal is much larger than a man. The elevators were very small. How was the pony lowered from the surface? Zola asked one of the supervisors how they'd managed to transport the animal. He got a look of incomprehension in reply. The beast had not been transported, Zola was told. But then, How did the beast get down here? The beast has always been down here, came the reply. The beast was born here. As were his parents. All the beasts you see—all these ponies bred for fresh air and sunshine and wide fields—were born from their mothers and their mothers' mothers in this pit. Zola was devastated by the casual cruelty of what he had learned. And so the pony, discovered serendipitously in a single afternoon's journalistic research, became the image for every man, woman, and child condemned to labor and die below the sun in the anthracite bowels of the earth.

The lesson here is straightforward: If you want to build a sheet-metal worker for a character, you need to learn something about sheet metal, about the shops, the unions, the fans, the noise, the cut fingers, the blueprints. Out of that context, if you're fortunate, will emerge an image that shows but does not tell. Recall Herr Schindler there on his horse, on the hill, overlooking the ghetto. A little girl wanders through the carnage. A little girl in a red coat. It is context that allows us to experience evil and innocence side by side in this scene. It's the accumulation of facts, as well as action and dialogue, that allows us to interact, to experience something powerful about the Jewish situation and about Oskar Schindler.

Facts are necessary to provide a context that allows us to be shown and not told some character's inner story. It's easy to see that a story set in the past or in an unfamiliar culture requires a journalist's nose. But it wouldn't hurt to also take a journalistic attitude toward those things with which we think we're familiar. Most of us have quite a bit to learn about the things we think we know. Personal experience without some research can run a bit thin. Write from your personal experience, certainly, I would urge any writer, but don't write *about* it.

The Thread

Recall, please, that you always have an outer story that we can hear and see and an inner story about which we make inferences and guesses. The inner story can prompt a question as simple as, Who Done It? Who Killed Cock Robin? But more often the inner story will pose questions about motivation, intention, and feeling. Most of all, the inner story has to do with what the character needs.

Most things you hear about character borrow terms that actors and actresses use with reckless abandon. An actress "discovering" a character might be challenged to find a "thread" (sometimes also and confusingly, for our purposes, called a "spine") for her interpretation of a story's character. When directors or performers talk about the thread of a story, they are almost always concerned with the thing that gives a character's development both continuity and meaning. It's almost Aquinian to hear discussions in this regard, as if the performer is stripping away all that is "accidental" about a character in order to reach what's essential.

Writers frequently say that the key to discovering character is to identify the single need that runs from the story's beginning to its end. That core need is said to be the thread to which everything connects. For instance, Syd Field provides an analysis of *Dog Day Afternoon* in which the one need of Sonny Wortzik (Al Pacino) in the story is to get money for his lover's sex-change operation. That dramatic need, Field tells us, triggers everything else.

The problem is, Field describes Sonny's dramatic need in terms of things that can be seen—the outer story. It might be useful to think of the exterior things that a character strives for as objectives, or goals, rather than as "needs." A need, for our purposes, is something that goes on inside the character. A goal is something the character pursues in the outer story and identifying that goal will not always lead to the thread of continuity that we're trying to find in character development. Some stories present goals that change. Other stories present multiple goals. There are films like *Dog Day Afternoon* that provide a protagonist with a single goal on page one that never changes in the course of the entire narrative. Other stories, however, just don't fit that pattern.

A character's goal can change. What he needs on the outside is subject to context and opportunity. A character's core need, however, remains constant in a narrative. How does a character grow? See if this is useful: A character grows as the relationship between his goal(s) and his core need changes.

Most analyses of character concentrate on either the goal or the need. I just don't think this is useful. A character certainly must have a goal in the story; Sonny's goal in *Dog Day Afternoon* is to get money for his lover's operation. But Sonny's *need* probably has something to do with a raging need for love, or for companionship, or even dominance, that is revealed and dramatized as he pursues the story's visible goal.

Because a character's goal can change, the driving goal of the story may not even be present at a story's inception. And what if a character pursues more than one goal in a story? How do we know which goal is the thread? How do we establish priorities among goals that may arise in the story? It's here that narrative reversals offer an important clue as to how goals and needs get integrated in a story.

Reversals, Goals, and Needs

A character can't have a core and a story can't have a thread unless the writer provides it. The writer can't provide that thread if he or she doesn't recognize what a thread is and how it functions within the narrative. Recall that a three-act story has two major reversals that occur just before the end of the first and second acts. One of the reasons these hinges are so important is that they initiate or complicate goals for the protagonist's pursuit. Major reversals one and two also force a protagonist to either fulfill his or her core need or sacrifice that which he or she has most desired throughout the story.

There aren't many interactive titles that illustrate this well, so let's take a look at a couple of screenplays to discover their characters' threads and see if they exhibit the same patterns. We'll see if, structurally, the threads are the same. I want to use characters from a couple of films I know you can rent. So let's take Rocky Balboa from Sylvester Stallone's *Rocky* and Oskar Schindler from *Schindler's List* as examples for our examination.

What kind of goal can a major reversal initiate and how does it relate to a character's core need? First of all, notice that we're talking about a particular kind of character—a protagonist. This character, or occasional duo, is central to the story. To understand how hinges work for these characters, we first have to see that a protagonist's goal and need get developed simultaneously.

Consider the film *Rocky*. At the top of the third act, Rocky tells his lover that if he can "go the distance" he'll know he's not "just another bum" from the neighborhood. That dialogue spells out Rocky's goal—to go the distance, i.e., fifteen rounds with Apollo Creed—and it gives us a strong sense of Rocky's core need; that is, to attain some measure of self-worth and self-respect. We can't characterize Rocky's core need without some kind of moral context; Rocky's notion of self-worth is very much rooted in moral judgment. A leg breaker for a local loan shark and a hood, Rocky is called a "creep" in the movie, a "leg breaker," a "waste of life." Rocky doesn't want to be known that way.

Rocky's road to self-respect is linked to his goal, but it's important to know that "going the distance" wasn't a goal at the story's beginning. Even when Rocky begins training to fight Apollo, he isn't thinking of going the distance. He expects, in fact, to get his "face kicked in." And Rocky isn't facing his core need squarely at the story's beginning either. He could never make himself so vulnerable in the story's early pages. So what turns Rocky's story, and life, around? It turns out that Rocky Balboa gets a chance right before the end of act one to fight world-champion Apollo Creed. This is the narrative's first major reversal. It provides Rocky with a basis for a goal that will help fulfill his core need. It reverses the external direction of the narrative and it provides a 180-degree turn for Rocky's inner growth.

But Rocky doesn't change all at once. At first the chance to fight Apollo seems only to drive Rocky's feelings of rage and inadequacy. Gradually, however, that changes. A crusty trainer and a young woman provide much of the vehicle for that change. By the end of act two, Rocky charges up an endless flight of steps an ebullient man. We've reached Rocky's second major reversal. The hinge here doesn't reverse what happens in the outer story. It signifies instead a sea change in Rocky Balboa's heart and provides a defining moment for choice. Rocky chooses to acknowledge his core need and to fulfill it; he chooses the possibility for self-respect over a life of leg-breaking and despair. The ordeal that the boxer endures in his pursuit of self-respect is almost a confession, an expiation for what had been "a waste of life."

We started out looking for a thread. This story's thread can't really be defined as just the outside story, nor as just Rocky's core need. The story's thread has to do with the (loaded term!) dialectic that exists between Rocky's twin pursuits of goal and need. Keep that in mind and see the pattern: An outer goal helps a character to fulfill a core need. The character pays heavy costs when he chooses to fulfill that need. A moral context operates to endorse, absolve, or complicate the character's choice. And what does the character choose?

To Fulfill or to Sacrifice

Rocky's determination to go the distance with Creed helps the boxer achieve a sense of self-worth. Rocky's dramatic choice is to either pay a cost for self-respect or go back to being a leg breaker. In this sense, Rocky's character is similar to Rose's in *Titanic*. Rose isn't simply pursuing passion in her story. Rose's core need, frightening for her to acknowledge, even to herself, is the burning desire to be free—from artificial restraint, from hypocrisy, from an arranged marriage. Her romance with Jack provides the outer story, the exterior context necessary to play out Rose's deeper, inner ambition. Forced to choose between fulfillment and subjugation, Rose follows her inner voice. The story exacts its terrible price.

Rocky's road to self-respect is a template for Rose's. Rocky chooses to "go the distance" because pursuing that goal helps him fulfill his core need. Rocky's need for self-respect is endorsed by the moral code within which the story works. Rocky's need is "good"; his pursuit of goals that answer that need are noble and "good." What happens, though, if the goal you pursue for an entire story and a need you have struggled to satiate turn out to be evil?

Oskar Schindler provides an example of a character whose core need comes into conflict with his sense of right and wrong. The protagonist of *Schindler's List*, for all his pretense, has feelings of inadequacy as deeply ingrained as Rocky Balboa. In a telling moment with his wife, Schindler proudly declares that whereas his father had never more than 35 employees in his life, he now has 350. It doesn't bother him in the least that his "employees" are slave labor, that they are Jews who will not even receive the minimal wages Nazi law ironically requires Schindler to pay. His "goal," from the first scene when he's courting Nazi officers, is to build a magnificent manufacturing facility. The war gives Schindler this opportunity, the Jews provide him with labor, and he's more than happy, early in the story, to make hay while the sun shines.

Schindler's drive to build his war plant provides the outer story for *Schindler's List* just as Rocky's training regimen provides the outer story for Stallone's film. But there is an important difference between the two narratives. The difference is, Rocky's core need gets *fulfilled;* Schindler's core need gets *sacrificed.*

What inner need can we see in the character of Oskar Schindler? I heard Liam Neeson remark in an interview that, even after portraying Schindler so brilliantly, the actor still regarded the German as something of an enigma. Schindler after all was not a particularly nice guy. He was a womanizer. He had no compunctions about breaking the law, lying, bribing. He seemed, in fact, to be very comfortable with the sleazy side of human nature. He showed no compassion or pity for anyone. And yet, it was this man who gave away his fortune and risked his life to save 1,100 Jewish people while many "good" people watched passively as Jews were slaughtered by the millions.

I think ultimately Schindler is moved to act because he has a certain moral code that cannot be squared with what he most wants for himself. What he wants most is, simply, to be known. The core need to have respect from his competitors and party, to be publicly acknowledged as successful and important, drives everything that he does. However, a desire for money does not describe Schindler's core need. He wouldn't care to be the richest man in the world if that wealth carried with it the penalty of anonymity. Money, for Schindler, is only a means to an end. Throughout most of the film, he seems to be thinking, If only I can establish this manufacturing facility, if only I can amass this fortune, then everybody will know who Oskar Schindler is! Everyone will know!

All through Spielberg's story we're given hints of how important it is for Schindler to be known. He wants to walk into any restaurant in Germany and Poland and have everyone know that he is a lover, a player, a big shot. . . .

But not a butcher. By the time Schindler does become well known at nightclubs, casinos, and restaurants of quality, a couple of things have happened that taint his trophy. First, he sees that his Nazi party is exterminating Jewish men, women, and children by the trainload. Second, Schindler discovers, probably to his irritation, that he has a conscience. He turns out to be, against all odds, a truly righteous man. A righteous man is not a perfect man. A righteous man doesn't have to aspire to either humility or anonymity. A righteous man is simply a man who sees what is right and tries to do it. A righteous man may give up what is most dear to himself in the face of a more compelling need for others.

Schindler comes to see that his exterior goal—made literally concrete in the story's manufacturing facility—is inimical with the image, the "presentation" for which he wants to be remembered. Schindler would love to be known as a wealthy manufacturer. He wouldn't even mind, in another war, being known as a wealthy munitions manufacturer. But he does not want to be well known as a killer of helpless men, women, and children.

The major reversals we discussed earlier function the same way in Oskar Schindler's story as they do for Rocky Balboa's. The first reversal occurs when Oskar watches as a German commandant routs the Jews from their Polish ghetto. He sees the red-coated girl winding her way through a mass of people marked for labor or death. Witnessing the ghetto's liquidation forces him for the first time to realize that the laborers upon whose shoulders his profits depend are not chattel but are living people with pain and fear and children. That's a problem for him, an unanticipated variable in his formula to become well known. A prick to his conscience.

But Schindler doesn't give up his dream for fame right away. It takes another couple of hours before the Jewish Holocaust becomes vivid and close enough to persuade him to give up his core need. The second act is almost finished before the German war profiteer fully accepts responsibility for his role in the final solution. It takes a final straw to make Schindler see that his celebrity, and his audience, are hideous.

The second hinge provides that straw. Where the story's first hinge prompts Schindler to recognize the terrible wrong that is being committed against his Jewish employees, the story's second major reversal provides the straw that prods him to act. He stands, hat in hand, next to a mountain of burning human beings. He sees, with us, the body of a blond-haired little girl stretched limp and dead as a doll in her tiny red coat. In the very next scene, we see Schindler plotting to buy his Jewish employees from their Nazi commandant.

The story's first hinge provides a moment of recognition. The second hinge provides the impetus to act. In order to act, Schindler first must make a stark choice between what he knows is right and what he knows is wrong. That choice has to carry with it some consequence; it has to cost him something. And it does. His obsession—to be recognized, admired, acclaimed—has to be sacrificed for a more compelling need, someone else's desperate need. He cannot be well known anymore. The man who used to have a fortune spends it all to save his Jewish workers. That is not the kind of decision that, in the Germany of World War II, would get you invited to many restaurants.

The conflict between what Schindler wants and what he knows is right produces the thread that holds his story together. A story cannot create interesting characters without this kind of continuity and conflict. Conflict comes in a variety of ways and through many characters in *Schindler's List*. But the main conflict, the thread, comes as we watch Oskar Schindler struggle to choose between his need for recognition and his recognition of what is right.

Schindler establishes a munitions plant near the story's end in his own hometown. Hometown boy made good. The plant was operational for seven months, the film tells us, and was a model of nonproduction. There's a nice irony here as Schindler's manufacturing facility becomes a vehicle for his own salvation as well as for "his" Jews. An even nicer irony plays out when Schindler, never well known during the war, becomes very well and widely known for reasons he could not have imagined.

Bad Guys

It's easy enough to see how the pattern of goal, need, and choice pulls an audience into empathy with Rocky Balboa or Oskar Schindler. But what about a truly evil character? How can the pattern apply to the bad guys?

It's interesting to me that, in earlier eras frequently regarded as uptight, you could find many more powerful and interesting protagonists who were, without question, evil. It shouldn't be a surprise, if we can be honest with ourselves for even a fraction of a moment, that evil characters fascinate us at least as much as heroes. Mark Twain was not an aberrant creature when he chose, "Heaven for climate," and "Hell for conversation." The truth is, a character's probity has nothing to do with whether we, the audience, like him or not. Shakespeare's *Richard III* is about as thoroughly evil a character as has ever been created. He is a man-killer, a child-killer! A totally ruthless, savage creature. And yet, by the story's end, when Richard, facing countless foes on a bloody field, cries, "A horse! A horse! My kingdom for a horse!" there is not anyone in the audience who would not gladly give Richard what is necessary to fulfill his need.

Most people who have trouble analyzing the relationship between human values and fiction mistake the purpose of a story's moral context. A moral context does not exist to prescribe behavior. It doesn't exist to proscribe behavior, either. A story's moral context exists to make its characters compelling and complicated. Fiction is the one place in our lives where we can value a person's competency over his morality. Think of Orson Welles in *Citizen Kane* for a moment. We watch the character set against stronger and stronger obstacles. Would we be interested if he caved in? If he admitted defeat? But for Kane to prevail, he must do things that are wrong. We don't mind Kane doing things that are wrong so long as he prevails. Kane does prevail, of course. He defeats his political enemies and makes enemies of those closest to him. In the course of the story, Kane becomes a monster. If he didn't become a monster, we wouldn't be interested!

Competency outweighs morality in competition for an audience's empathy. We admire Oskar Schindler for the risks he takes to save his employees. We admire Richard III equally for the risks he takes to hoard his throne. Whatever happened to the Richards of stories past? Modern cinema and interactive story/ game/arenas have no compunction at all about killing a couple of hundred people. We don't mind reveling in slow motion over a woman's rape or torture. We love to follow serial killers, so long as they're safely in second place. But modern stories almost never have as their protagonists characters who are truly evil.

Evil characters in modern cinema tend to be either drug addicts or foils. In interactive texts, they're Kilrathi or some similarly dehumanized antagonist. *The Bad Lieutenant* offers an example of the addict; it's hard to say whether Harvey Keitel's character is bad or, merely, ill. In *The Silence of the Lambs*, Hannibal Lecter provides a character truly and refreshingly evil. But Hannibal is not the lead in this story; he's a foil for Clarice Starling, the vulnerable innocent.

Hollywood is obsessed with creating characters an audience will like. Studio developers are notorious for writing into an otherwise interesting character some tinge of good. Actors happily go along, saying things like, "My character doesn't wake up wanting to be bad." Oh, really? Well, let's look at some real-life bad guys. Stalin, for instance, used to order executions over breakfast. Attila the Hun said his greatest pleasure consisted in seeing the eyes of his enemy as the Mongol took the victim's land, raped his women, and killed his children. Would you rather take examples from make-believe? How about the Alex DeLarge from *A Clockwork Orange*? Or *Blue Velvet*'s Frank Booth? Who can forget Nurse Ratched from *One Flew over the Cuckoo's Nest*? And Little Bill Daggett in *Unforgiven*. These guys don't have any problem getting an audience. Do you really think they start their days thinking up ways to be nice?

Producers and agents and performers make a huge mistake when they assume that audiences cannot like a character doing bad things unless that character's behavior is somehow expiated or excused. "I'm okay, you're okay" works fine for transactional analysis, but it's a poor substitute, in drama, for evil.

Evil, especially when left undiluted, has fascinated audiences over the centuries. The word needs to get out that bad men and bad women make fantastic protagonists. A story's moral context doesn't exist to say that heroic choices (Schindler's) must appeal to us more than evil choices (Macbeth's, Richard III's, Citizen Kane's, etc.). Evil characters pursue outer goals that serve corrupt needs. It's the costs they incur along the way and the skill with which they overcome obstacle and adversity that make bad guys interesting. What we value as an audience is not that a character be good, but that he be competent. Jimmy Cagney's famous line in *The Public Enemy*, "Top o' the world, Ma!" didn't come from a guy who gave a damn about his mother.

Interactive texts are still rudimentary in this regard. Their characters, too, often ruled to the procedural logic of multiple plot lines, are frequently generic, stereotyped templates, made to easily fit in with divergent lines of action and incident. Noted game designer Jeffrey Sullivan claims that "Many games use stereotypical characters for a variety of reasons. The most charitable explanation is that some games are dealing with deep archetypical themes like good versus evil or reality versus fantasy, and the designers didn't want complex, exception-to-the-rule characters blurring the fundamental theme. The less charitable answers are that: (1) many games are created by people with very little dramatic storytelling ability, and stereotypes are the best they can do, and (2) many games are created under the theory that story and character are afterthoughts to be slapped onto the engine after you've tweaked the frame rate up as high as it can go."

Recall for a moment the earlier "Mission Fail, Mission Succeed" sample from *Wing Commander III*. That kind of thing, happily, is not typical for all character interactions. The sample that follows is not Henry James, but it does show that the writers for the *Wing Commander* series know how to "show" a character in development. In the following scene (from *Wing Commander III*), the development involves Colonel Blair and Flint, his female subordinate and the heir apparent to replace Angel as his romantic interest. News of Confederate losses to rabid Kilrathi attacks climax with Angel's brutal execution. The combined shock of losing more men and the special woman in his life drives Blair to the bottle. We are given two choices for Blair's dialogue with Flint. This dialogue takes two paths depending on whether Flint's morale is to go "UP" or "morale DOWN." From that crude category comes this interesting option. In the script, options related to Flint's morale are displayed side-by-side on the script's page, as was the case with the Mission Succeeds/Fails options. But for purpose of analysis, I'm going to render the options at L-7 vertically so that you can only digest (as a user would) one option at a time. Blair's got his bottle—

FLINT BANGS A FUSELAGE.

> FLINT
>
>Is that the way you face your problems?

> BLAIR
>
>Look, I need this like—

> FLINT
>
>'You have to fly with your head,
>not your heart.' Those words ring a
>bell?

Flint's morale UP:

> BLAIR
>
>(beat; grins)
>You take good notes, Lieutenant.
>(beat)
>You think we can avoid a
>scramble long enough for me to
>get a cup of coffee?

SHE SMILES BACK AT HIM AND SHRUGS.

> FLINT
>
>The Kilrathi don't usually download
>their schedule in advance.
>(beat)
>I'm sorry about Angel. Everyone on
>board is. We know she was someone
>quite special.

> BLAIR
>
>Yeah . . . That she was . . .

Notice that the dialogue here is not direct, that is, there is not a hint of direct talk about Flint's feelings for Blair, nor Blair's for Flint. This is a transitional moment for these two characters. He's vulnerable. She knows her squadron desperately needs a confident and competent commander. Notice that the lieutenant chooses to challenge her colonel, rather than to at first console him. This, in itself, is good psychology and good writing.

Notice, too, that the passage disguises its real purpose (to initiate a romance between Blair and Flint) by directing itself to the other woman, now slain, who has been "special" in the colonel's life. The dialogue seems to be about sobering up Blair so that he can effectively fly. Flint's dialogue seems to be about consoling her commander over Angel's loss.

This forms the latent text of the scene, and gives Flint an outer goal to pursue. Flint knows why Blair is down. And she's smart enough, in this option, to know that she can't broach Angel's death too quickly or directly. She gauges Blair's ability to accept consolation only after she appeals to his sense of duty and honor. That's what's "on top" of this dialogue. But there is a river of sexual subtext running not far beneath. Remember the distinction between outer goal and inner need? Flint's outer goal here is to get her C.O. off the bottle. Her inner need is to be intimate with Blair, to replace Angel as "something special."

So where are the two characters at the end of this scene? Well, clearly, Colonel Blair has allowed his vulnerability to be seen and challenged by this attractive junior officer. His response to Flint's challenge at the top of the scene markedly contrasts the scene's conclusion. What starts as, "Look, I need this like—"ends by jacking Flint's morale way up with, "Yeah . . . That she was." By the time the "Morale UP" option has played out, there is more than a rapprochement between Flint and her commander. There is, in recalling Angel's romantic link with Blair, and in Blair's acknowledgment to his lieutenant of the special pain caused by Angel's death, the clear portent for a future relationship between this very much alive, extremely good-looking pilot and Colonel C. Blair. In pursuing her outer goal, Lieutenant Flint is well on her way to filling a much deeper and completely unstated need.

Colonel Blair in this option allows his inner need to be revealed; he needs a relationship to replace what he had with Angel. The colonel doesn't yet see a possibility to fill this need. And his duty, which always brackets his outer goal, is to win the war. The outer goal here, ostensibly so hostile to what Blair needs inside, is actually its catalyst, the staple, in fact, of all wartime romance.

I'm not trying to say that this scene is a brilliant example of characterization. It is, after all, a science-fiction story/game, not *War and Peace*. The stakes can't be the same; the Kilrathi are not, when all is said and done, Napoleon. But stories have to be critiqued first on the basis of what they aim to achieve. The *Wing Commander* series can be favorably compared with most sci-fi series, whether interactively titled or *Babylon 5*. *Wing Commander III* offers a good text for interactive writers to study. Very few interactive narratives even attempt the kind of indirect, dramatic revelation of character common to this story.

Its writers understand that exterior events, to be interesting, have to tie to some other, deeper, and mostly unstated core need.

If the scene above plays out the option that raises Flint's morale/rewards her outer goal/fills her inner need, what would have to happen for Flint's morale to falter and her inner need to be thwarted? Well, let's see. I'm going to reproduce the same lead-in dialogue as for the "morale UP" option and, unlike the necessary split-scene arrangement of the original script, I'm going to keep the follow-on dialogue seamless, just as a user would experience if he or she chose "Flint's morale DOWN" as the interfaced option. Blair's hitting the bottle, remember—

```
FLINT BANGS A FUSELAGE.

                    FLINT
          Is that the way you face your
          problems?

                    BLAIR
          Look, I need this like—

                    FLINT
          'You have to fly with your head,
          not your heart.' Those words ring a
          bell?

                    BLAIR
          You have no call to lecture me.

                    FLINT
          Listen, I'm sorry about Angel. We
          all are but—

                    BLAIR
          You want to lodge a formal complaint
          regarding your commanding officer,
          Lieutenant, I suggest you do so.
          Otherwise, back off.

                    FLINT
                    (icy)
          Yes. Sir.
```

It's not hard to see the difference between these two scenes, is it? Blair's not nearly as receptive to Flint's challenge in this option and Flint delves too quickly to the real source of Blair's despair. Blair doesn't feel safe enough yet with this good-looking lieutenant to risk showing any vulnerability. Flint's attempt to raise Blair's spirits, far from closing the distance between herself and her superior, backfires to increase it. The scene ends with the colonel firmly reminding the lieutenant of her place. Flint's outer goal fails and as it does, so does the potential for fulfilling her inner, unstated need. An obstacle to intimacy has been placed by Blair squarely in Flint's path.

This scene in some ways works better for me than the first option. Why? Because romances, to be interesting, have to overcome obstacles. Romeo and Juliet had to overcome outside adversaries. The same is true for the *Titanic's* Jack and Rose. Flint and Blair's situation is more realistic and mature; it's the past and past demons that are the real barrier to their intimate involvement, not the Kilrathi or elaborately choreographed battle scenes.

We can see that in both the scenes above there is a tension between inner needs and outer goals. It's well done. Let me end with a small *non sequitur* regarding show versus tell. Take another look at the last line of dialogue in the second scene. Flint's reply to Blair at the scene's conclusion is, "Yes. Sir." Do we really need to be told in the parenthesized direction immediately above that her rejoinder is "icy"?

You get the idea. If you look at thousands of stories of all kinds across all cultures, a tension between outer goal and inner need will repeat again and again. Whether it's Oskar Schindler or Colonel Christopher Blair, successful characterization occurs when an outer and inner story drive a character to a moment of choice. Goal and desire meet. The character must then act to take what he most needs, or to sacrifice it. And to be effective, this dance should be shown, not explained.

You can't account for a story's satisfaction by looking at any of these elements in isolation, naturally. The outer story and the inner story are complementary. You can't satisfy an audience unless you have goals and needs set into some kind of dramatic conflict. You can't have conflict without choice. You can't have interesting choices unless there's some kind of meaningful cost involved. You need to show, not tell. It's a seamless whole for which storytellers strive. Nothing else will last.

What to Do and How to Do It

I'd like to bring this home by giving you ways to make the preceding chapters useful for your work. What should you do with the discussion above, for instance? What should you do with the chapters on structure, spine, mechanics, character development, and the rest? What should you take from a *Wing Commander III, Titanic,* and *Schindler's List?*

What you should take from all these analyses is a pattern, a paradigm, to replicate. But I'll clue you in: knowing what works in good stories doesn't mean you'll be able to originate good material yourself. It wouldn't be honest to tell you that. What I can tell you, though, is that these patterns can help you critique yourself. If you look at one of your own stories and can't clearly identify an opening trigger, a hinge at acts one and two, a climax, and catharsis, you don't have a good story.

Similarly, if you look at your own work and you don't see the kind of tension between inner need and outer goal that we've outlined above, you probably aren't going to have characters who command much empathy from an audience. If you find yourself telling instead of showing, something in your story or dialogue needs work.

And so on. We could do a lot more work here. I hope that's obvious. We could move from general patterns of story and character to sequences and scenes. We could spend a ton of time just talking about the scenes in act two, how those scenes, in a sense, reverse the priorities of acts one and three. We could analyze dialogue, transitions, etc. But I think it's important to start with the big pieces first.

There's a lot to digest in these last chapters. A lot to apply. Now, for something concrete to do:

1. Do some homework. Go out and rent a half-dozen or so very good films and interactive titles. Break them down scene by scene. If the films or interactive narratives are based on novels or plays, break those stories down scene by scene. Then pull back and look at the big picture. Do you see precipitating incidents early in the story? Major reversals a quarter and again three-quarters of the way through the story? How about the characters? Do they have goals that either help or hinder the fulfillment of what's inside their hearts? See if the patterns we have analyzed hold up.

2. Apply the work to your own stories.

As a writer, you have to be able to recognize patterns in the works you see or read and you have to apply those patterns to your own work. A hint to this process: instead of imagining yourself as writing a story, imagine yourself performing it. I recently talked with an actor/casting director who said that the best actors/actresses think a lot like writers and the best writers think a lot like the best performers. This strikes me as an important observation. Interactive designers and producers generally don't think in terms of human performance—but they should.

Many writers have no idea how hard and seriously an honest performer works to discover his or her character and find the thread that makes that character come alive. I think it's very possible that the best performers go about discovering their characters in much the same way that good writers create them. Performers have to research period and place, people and props just as writers do. They have to internalize the story's context and they cannot (!), as any actor will tell you, *be* anything. An actor or actress can only find something to *do*.

There are no common denominators for how performers do this work. Every extreme exists. You may have heard the anecdote that took place on the set of *Marathon Man*. Dustin Hoffman plays an abducted man horribly tortured by a Nazi portrayed by Sir Laurence Olivier. Hoffman stayed up all night, so the story goes. He ran himself literally ragged the whole night before the morning's shoot. He drank pots of coffee. He didn't sleep, didn't bathe. He came in the next morning wired, exhausted, and looking like a wreck. "My God what's happened to you?" Sir Laurence is said to have inquired. Hoffman explained to the older man, proudly, how he'd prepared for the scene.

Apparently, Sir Laurence's reaction wasn't what Hoffman expected. After listening patiently to the ordeal through which the younger man had put himself, Olivier just shook his head and said something like, "My boy, why don't you just learn to act?"

It's a nice story. But the truth is, both men were prepared for their scenes. Hoffman's "method" was perfectly suited to his own sensibilities and to the character he wanted to capture. Olivier's cool, clinical approach was perfectly suited to his classical training and to the cynical, cold-blooded Nazi he portrayed in the story.

Interactive writers probably need to fall somewhere between Dustin Hoffman and Sir Laurence Olivier. If you can throw in some Tom Wolfe, that'd be fine. But whatever you do, building character will require a lot more than a summary of attributes. It will not be furthered by asides and arcades which give us tidbits about the characters histories, subtext, etc. It requires work to portray even the simplest inner life believably. The writer-thinking-as-a-performer will realize that each scene must have a ministory, a minigoal for the performers, some outcome that does more than provide exposition. It should also become obvious for the "performing writer" that individual scenes can't be convincingly portrayed unless the writer provides some thread that holds the scenes together, some overall tension that exists continually between a character's goal(s) and need.

Finally, writers and performers have a similar imperative to commit to a story. You can't write a story half-enthusiastically and expect the story "to play." As a performer, you can't "play" a scene halfway. The corollary to commitment is risk. Writers of all stripes have to take risks to create interesting characters (imagine Oskar Schindler as a do-gooding Catholic and plot what consequences that characterization would have for his story). Performers must place themselves at risk to play a character convincingly.

An effective writer understands what good stories do to make their characters come alive. By now, you should be able to see patterns, faces in the clouds, that you can use to create and critique your own work. Think of yourself as a performer. When you've done your homework and you're ready to write, don't be embarrassed to cast yourself in the roles you create. Don't be afraid to "do" Lieutenant Flint or Joan of Arc. Commit yourself. Take a risk. See what happens.

11

Toward an Interactive Aesthetic

Interactive entertainment will prove to be a very rich area for pushing the envelope in terms of spurring new techniques and sub-genres. And that's important because the cross-fertilization of traditional entertainment and interactive design is going to build the medium—and the industry—by forcing us to find better ways of entertaining.

LARRY TUCH

Why is it important for interactive writers to create stories of quality? Why does it matter?

In the short run, producers of interactive stories don't have to worry a lot about the quality of their products. They will have novelty as a stimulus to sales. The hybrids—games, puzzles, MUDs, LARPs, the Web-sited storytellers—not to mention the information/research applications of cybertexts, tell us clearly that narration is only one aspect of what people find interesting in the interactive world.

Every new technology goes through this kind of variegation and experimentation. People forget that when film first came along, its users weren't interested in anything like a quality story. Film wasn't used to tell stories at all. A camera could shoot virtually anything and, at first, people would pay to see the result.

The same thing will initially be true for interactive storytellers. The first interactive producer to get a product on the shelf is almost bound to attract attention. Any kind of interactive story, whether it's *Wing Commander III* or *Deep Throat 3D*, will initially spark interest. But interest in the new technology will eventually invite its comparison with other storytelling forms. That comparison at present shows an enormous gap between the quality of interactive stories and the quality of stories provided on average by film, videotape, or the tube. This gap will be narrowed. But the jury's out on whether that evolution will bring consumers to narrative-based interactive drama. Right now it seems that consumers are more interested in narrative hybrids where the story is *not*, at least primarily, "the thing."

Janet Murray concludes her book by saying, "It seems to me quite possible that a future digital Homer will arise who combines literary ambition, a connection with a wide audience, and computational expertise. But for now we have to listen very, very carefully to hear, amid the cacophony of cyberspace, the first fumbling chords of the awakening bard." For someone who's touted as a superenthusiast for the medium, this is very faint praise. But I think any other assessment of the interactive world would be dishonest. Anyone looking critically at the present mix of interactive narratives has to see a potential not equaled by performance.

Interactive producers may conclude that storytelling with interfaced participation is not nearly so satisfying for users as narrative piggybacks for games, puzzles, or the "reconstructed" text. We don't know, yet, how those preferences will evolve. But we do know that if interactive producers are going to tell stories, the narratives they produce must match or exceed the quality of their audience-seeking competitors. For that reason, if for no other, interactive writers are going to have to be concerned with the quality of the stories they tell as well as the quality of its presentation.

The biggest thing that interactive writers have to overcome on their road to achieving quality interactive stories is the notion that because their technology is "different," their narratives will be judged differently—by implication, less rigorously or by different rules—from stories spawned by the archaic technologies. Interactive writers should learn and absorb everything they can from other storytelling media. The past few pages give you a decent start in that regard.

A second, almost equally large obstacle for interactive writers and producers has to do with their assessment of the professional skills required to perform stories, stage stories, create light and sound for stories, direct stories— ad infinitum. There is a sort of naïveté (or perhaps arrogance) among a few interactive folk that amazes me in this regard, a notion that actors and actresses, directors and editors fulfill functions that with a little exposure can be accomplished by any user granted spatial freedom.

It's very, very difficult to reach the quality of dramatic presentation that even an average feature film or television episode routinely achieves. Recall Murray's analysis of that short, romantic scene from *Witness*; an enormous and voraciously competitive film industry has only produced a few people who consistently turn out quality scenes like this one. Interactive producers, despite the tools their technology makes available, haven't produced a scene as compelling as the one Murray cites from *Witness*.

The least important difference in quality between interactively produced stories and filmed ones can be traced to technology. Digital imagery produces a feeling of depth and texture that is only now coming to be comparable with the imagery produced by chemical emulsion. A computer screen, even smaller than a TV screen, cannot use the same aesthetic that John Ford used in *Stagecoach*. Interactive producers need to understand that composition, lighting, editing, and so on change with the size and aspect ratio of the viewing surface. Ingmar Bergman once described film as the landscape of the human face. It would be educational for the interactive designer to see how Bergman's filmed stories like *The Seventh Seal* or *Cries and Whispers* differ from his televised series *Scenes from a Marriage.*

Other technological gaps between digital imagery and film are more obvious but also more easy to fill. Full motion will come to digital imagery very quickly. Even the modeling of a human face, once a futuristic fantasy, is now under way. Virtual reality technologies seem to offer the final challenge to film as a simulacrum of narrative activity. VR, in fact, is frequently taken for granted as the aesthetic destination of the new storytelling technologies. Most fans of interactive technology point heavily to the computer's ability to mimic "reality" as a basis for its appeal. Film initially made the claim for its special status based on its ability to represent "reality." But the experience of audiences over the last fifty years or so has shown that, once again, a technology's ability to re-create reality may not be at the heart of its aesthetic appeal.

Once again, interactive writers and producers may be able to learn something from the cinema. That "something" relocates the notion of aesthetics from the technology producing the story to the human being who receives the story. It's pretty obvious that seeing a film is a different experience for the person receiving the story onscreen than the experience that comes when that same person reads the story in a novel. The phenomenologies of film and prose are not the same. Rudolf Arnheim, an early German theorist, says that photography lies at the base of film's special appeal. Verisimilitude, the ways in which moving pictures can copy reality, becomes, for Arnheim, the thing that distinguishes the movie experience from the novel (pardon the pun) experience. Other folks, like the Brazilian André Bazin, had a slightly different and, to me, more interesting view. Bazin writes that filmed drama (I would include all representational drama) has an "asymptotic" relationship with reality. An asymptote is a curve that comes closer and closer to a fixed line without ever actually touching it. It's a nice way for Bazin to suggest that the slight differences between the filmed world and reality account for film's appeal. In reality, for instance, we can't manipulate time, we don't "cut" from scene to scene. We can't select, edit, or present imagery in the quotidian world in the ways that make movies larger-than-life. We can mimic almost to perfection the sounds that the real world provides. We can mimic movement and color to the point of verisimilitude. And with the computer we are freed from spatial limitations.

But most of the time we don't want total freedom. Most of the time we want some limit on verisimilitude. *Schindler's List* caused a bit of a stir when released because it abjured color film for black and white. The story's location in time and culture only partly accounted for that decision. Janusz Kaminski, the film's Oscar-winning cinematographer, spoke in an NBC interview about how excited he was to have the chance to work in the more primitive black-and-white film stock. Among other things, Kaminski asserted that color film can "distract" audiences, can call the audience's attention away from where it "ought to be." Kaminski insisted that the audience's attention ought to be on the faces of the people affected by the story. And many filmmakers agree with Kaminski that black-and-white film explores the "landscape of the human face" more powerfully than is possible with colored stock.

Kaminski's discussion of film stock needs to be understood in terms of a general aesthetic. Whether it's *Schindler's List* or *Titanic* or *Wing Commander,* writers, directors, and designers should not try to reproduce the real world; they should instead seek to exploit the gaps between the quotidian world and the technology of its presentation in a way that will make their stories most powerfully satisfy an audience. Sometimes a virtual reproduction of the real world's sight or sound or movement or dimension serves that goal. But, just as frequently, it does not.

Interactive presentations, just as other media, gain their appeal as much by the ways in which they depart from reality as by the ways in which they mimic it. Bazin's insights need to be understood by those people who see interactive and virtual reality technologies as the next heirs to storytelling. The technophile who believes that full-motion video and the holodeck are natural progressions of an aesthetic principle that demands the reproduction of reality misunderstands what it is that makes make-believe different from reality.

A technology that perfectly mimics reality cannot be satisfying as a storytelling form. A user in some future holodeck will likely hear a soundtrack. And if she calls up Waterloo, she will not need to worry, really, about bayonets or grapeshot. Though her virtual battlefield may even provide the stimulating aroma of gunpowder and sweat-drenched horses, the less pleasant odors of war, you can bet, will be discreetly masked.

The differences between the story world and the real world are crucial to the participating experience of all media. Radio, novels, plays, and films, all failing in some respect of mimesis, require their audiences to use imagination. Future storytelling technologies will require the same. Absent the necessity to engage imaginatively—to suspend disbelief, immerse in the text, connect the dots—is it possible for us to have an experience of the story at all? What, then, is the difference between being a spectator and a participant? If the text does not demand something from us imaginatively, what kind of authentic interaction is possible?

We could spend more time seeing what interactive texts borrow from other sources and could spend even more time, probably, discussing what makes these presentations of stories feel different for their viewers than the experience humans have with novels, poetry, or cinema. But it's more important to end by reminding ourselves what all these storytelling technologies have in common.

We've spent some time looking at the particulars of interactive scripts. What kind of language shows instead of tells? What is the dramatic point of view? What needs to happen when we establish a scene? These are a few, only a few, of the specifics that interactive writers need to master. We've also spent time taking what might be called a macro-look at stories. We've analyzed the underlying navigational structure of the interactive application. But we specifically abandoned structuralist paradigms when we began looking at ways to distinguish good stories from bad ones. That distinction led us to consider the ways in which make-believe characters come to life.

We took a look at the thread that weaves through the development of interesting characters. We traced the relationship between context, conflict, and choice. We developed patterns to explain the thread that must always exist between a narrative's inner story and its outer story. All this work can help you. It's honest. It will give you a decent start. But it's not enough, by itself, to guarantee you'll originate a good story. No analysis, in fact, is sufficient by itself to produce a "satisfying" story.

Where do you go for the rest?

You have to go to yourself, first. Write *from* your experience as much as you can, but be wary of writing *about* your experience. Second, you need to read. It's interesting how books still fuel the narrative fires. Why is it that filmmakers, in particular, people who laud the moving image above all else return so often to the printed page for their stories? Why does that happen over and over again? And why is it happening, even now, for cyber-presented products?

I think, ultimately, literature will always fuel new media, either directly or indirectly, simply because the imagination is engaged through language. Language provides the structure from which we make meaning. Language allows us, maybe even forces us, to invent stories for the people we see at bus stops, to see bat wings in ink blots, to make faces in the clouds. Without language, we cannot have imagination. Would you broaden your imagination? Heighten it? Fill it with new and exciting possibilities? It's useful and maybe even important to see movies, television, and interactively based stories, but these are passively received things, still as a stone compared to what happens when the human mind engages the printed page.

Read, then. Read often and well.

And maybe, occasionally, just to keep yourself honest, you ought to tell somebody a bedtime story.

12

Conversations with Kaplan, Stephenson, and Roach

I think the novelist is going to become an important part of the world of interactive writing. Novelists write worlds. And some of the best movies originated from novels.

HOWARD BURKONS

Michael Kaplan

Michael Kaplan has been working as a writer/designer in the multimedia community for over five years. As a contributor to *Meet Media Band* (Phillips Interactive), he created the structure and interlocking scenarios for *Undo Me*, an interactive music video that was awarded Grand Prize at the QuickTime Film Festival in 1994. He was the primary writer on *Pony Express Rider* for McGraw-Hill Home Interactive, which was awarded both the Family Channel Seal of Approval and the National Parenting Center Seal of Approval. Working with John Sanborn and Jim Simmons, Kaplan developed an unprecedented form of interactive movie—one that seamlessly links audience choice to the unfolding drama. The result is *Psychic Detective*, a film that is "thirty minutes long, five hours wide," and described by *Wired* magazine as "a glorious mindf**k." In 1995, Michael Kaplan and new media auteur John Sanborn formed LaFong: a creative partnership that is committed to writing, directing, and producing the next level of content for new technologies. Recent products include *Paul Is*

Dead, an original rock-and-roll murder mystery produced by Microsoft and MGM Interactive, premiering online in April, 1998; *Strife*, a 3-D adventure game (Velocity); *Blue Funk*, a deconstructed online sitcom currently in development at MGM Interactive; and *Dysson*, an immersive e-mail fiction/hoax that was described by *Time* magazine as "a new interactive art form." A sampling of these projects can be seen at *www.lafong.com* and *www.dysson.org*.

Q: Where is the interactive industry today?
A: We've gone past the gold-rush feeling and we are waiting for the next breath to be drawn. That next step will probably involve role-playing, artificial intelligence, and smart bots. I'm not talking about virtual reality. I'm talking about the online version of what shows up in *The Diamond Age* by Neal Stephenson. Ractors and all of that.

I think it's going to be tricky to find experiences that people will want to pay for. The general impression of the Internet is that everything is free. It's anarchy.

One thing is for certain. There are less commercial opportunities right now to do interactive stories. That may be because we are very much in an experimental stage as an industry. People are still trying to figure out what kind of stories need to be interactive. But another factor is economics. The CD-ROM industry is very much like the record industry. It's about unit sales. And, ultimately, a successful product becomes one that people want to play over and over.

With an interactive story like *Psychic Detective*, you'll probably play it a dozen times. Each play-through is about thirty minutes long. Is that the value we are looking for with CD-ROM? Does that make the product currently on the market illegitimate? No. But it may mean that interactive movies are not suitable for CD-ROM.

One of the more legitimate forms of interactive narrative I found was Interfilm. That whole process of an interactive theater experience was completely undermined by the fact that the company made two or three really bad interactive movies. But the interactive "mob mentality" that Interfilm promoted—where everybody in the theater was voting to see which plot variation was going to win out and how it played out—could have been a lot of fun. One of the first interactive movies Interfilm released was called *Mr. Payback*. It played out very slowly—like your grandfather's idea of story branching. Should I go left? Should I go right? Should I fall on the banana?

Interfilm's business model—where people paid $4 to interact with the movie, say, two times—was smart.

Q: *What role is the writer playing in the development process of an interactive application?*
A: Unfortunately, most of the time the writer is brought in after the fact to create a mythology that ties things together. Or to create some reward sequences and splash screens. With online, it's the revenge of the English major. The Web needs people who can write complete sentences. The problem is, you may end up writing the Web site for Farmers Insurance.

Q: *Since interactive narratives involve some degree of user choice (multiple endings, variations of scenes, entertaining click-ons, etc.), how does the writer maintain an honest story line?*
A: You've put your finger on the real challenge with interactive writing, which is to make the player feel like every choice they make is critical, and that they have a lot of power, but never make it feel as if the story is meaningless and that players are simply editing an MTV video.

It is my belief that there's got to be a solid through-line, but the spine of an interactive story ends up looking like a skeleton for Siamese sextuplets. I got into some of this in *Psychic Detective*. If the user did not make choices, the linear movie kept playing. And, choices came up, then went away. That felt very legitimate to me in terms of how interactive drama might play out. It also provided a certain sleight of hand, because if people are concentrating on what's becoming available (and quickly unavailable), they're distracted from thinking, How come I can't go over here? How come I can't do this?

Interactive writers are always looking for ways to let players impact a story all the way to the end—taking them on a truly different, parallel route—but also finding points where you can reign in all the elements to a common location. I broke *Psychic Detective* into chapters. At the end of each chapter, you're going to come back to the same general place. Let's say the main character is going to be in jail. No matter what path you took to get to the end of that chapter (you might see a different scene as a prelude to the jail scene, for example), you have got to go to jail. If I don't steer you to a common point of reference, I'm going to loose my mind trying to write the interactive story. I call this technique bottlenecking. Once the player is in jail, I can spin them off into many different directions again.

Coming off of *Psychic Detective*, my mind was exploding with great possibilities. John Sanborn and I had begun to map out an interactive story that would start off at a different place each time, depending on how you played it previously. These things are structurally possible if somebody is willing to bank-roll the concept.

Neal Stephenson

Bestselling science-fiction novelist Neal Stephenson is the author of *The Big U, Zodiac: The Eco-thriller, Snow Crash,* and *The Diamond Age.*

Q: Is it really possible to marry narrative and interactivity?
A: I think we are almost hardwired to want our narratives told to us. If users can change the outcome, it's not really a narrative. From the beginning, when we were cavemen sitting around the fire telling each other stories, stories had a beginning, middle, and ending. The ability to tell those stories and understand them was crucial to survival. If one caveman can tell you a story about how he tangled with a bunch of hyenas and survived, and if you listened to that story and understood it, you would have the benefit of his experience and the ability to live another day.

Narratives that you fiddle with—interact with—just don't work in my opinion.

Tony Sheeder (my creative partner I've worked with on several projects) and I created an interactive title called *Daymare.* Tony's original idea didn't start out as a narrative. It was more of an environment that would change its shape as you interacted with it. Over time, as we developed the project, more and more narrative elements were added. The closer we came to making *Daymare* a narrative, the more problematic it got. In the end, it became difficult to surmount some of the obstacles that we created for ourselves.

Q: Such as?
A: There is a particular point of view about how to create interactive products which comes out of the video game industry which says that you need to keep the "click rate" up. Users need to be clicking the mouse every few seconds or else they will drop out of their interactive mode and slip into a passive state. If that should happen and the user is suddenly called to interact, users find it kind of startling and annoying. If you go with that philosophy, it forces you to come up with a pretext for some kind of interaction every few seconds. That philosophy is not compatible with coherent writing.

Every time you have a mouse click, the user has to affect the program. Clicking implies some sort of decision or branching point in the story. Either that or it is an obstacle of some kind. There are two basic approaches people take to tackle this click rate problem. One is the so-called tree of death, where the story line keeps forking every twelve seconds (or whatever the click rate interval is) until it ends in a zillion possible outcomes—most of which are bad. The other is where the narrative stays fairly linear but in order to give you something to click on, you get these puzzles or obstacles that are slapped down in the middle of the story. The user is forced to solve the puzzle before they can go on.

The problem with the tree of death is that the writer ends up creating a one-thousand–page script that costs a billion dollars to produce. The problem with the puzzle approach is that most people hate puzzles.

On *Daymare*, we spent a great deal of time grappling with these issues. I think we created a lot of material that had merit. But in the end, we ran into the tree of death problem, along with everything else.

Q: *Tell me about the final written document.*
A: The problems with writing an interactive script, as you can well imagine, are piled up on top of the normal problems of writing a feature film script.

The material was written around a dozen or so memories that the main character is trying to reconstruct. These memories are linked together, not as hyperlinks, but as associations. I might look out of a restaurant window, see a swimming pool, and remember stopping at a motel on the interstate when I was a kid. My mind creates links between the things I see around me and memories that I have.

To track all this, I originally created a two-column script format in Microsoft Word using Word Basic—utilizing a number of built-in features of Word such as the ability to create bookmarks, etc. The page layout was in the landscape mode (paper laying horizontally). One column was as wide as a normal sheet of typing paper, containing normal script formatting within its boundaries. The column adjacent to it was a couple of inches wide containing notes about how everything linked together. These notes were active links that transported you to another location in the script when clicked (see fig. 12.1).

Later in the development process, Tony was hired to write more material. The page format was changed to portrait mode (vertical page) and the document evolved into its existing form.

```
SIN CITY


Chapter 7, Scene 3



INT. FOYER, ST. MARK'S HOTEL

AT THE BUILDING'S DIRECTORY: Johnny examines the list of tenants. He
spots the name: CLAUDINE CHRISTIAN. And below the name: ROOM 303.

Johnny enters the hotel. The old place is long past its prime, but what
an ornate red velvet heyday it once had. A huge chandelier hangs over-
head.

An OUT OF ORDER sign hangs from the elevator door. Johnny pokes his head
into the elevator. Peers into the shaft.

                        VOICE (O.S.)
                Hey!

Johnny pulls out too fast. SMASHES his head against the elevator door.

A WHEEZY LAUGH accompanies a tiny bald head and a pair of hairy arms
down the corridor. The whole package belongs to LENNY BERTOLUCCI, 50,
cigar stub between his teeth.

                     LENNY
                OUT OF ORDER, kid. You want I
                should write it in Swahili?

Lenny LAUGHS to himself. It turns into a thick COUGH and WHEEZE.

                     JOHNNY
                Where's the staircase?
```

CALLMODEBEGIN
THIS INTERACTIVE
ENVIRONMENT IS
TRIGGERED BY A
HYPER-MEMORY.

001.500.030
>303MEMORIZED

001.500.040
>JOHNNYLOOKSHAFT

001.500.050
ANTAGONIST
>LENNYSNOOPS

001.500.060
ENDSTMARKSSCENE

Fig. 12.1. Sample page from *Sin City,* written by Jon Samsel and Robert McDonnell. Copyright 1998. Based on the script format for *Daymare* as described by Neal Stephenson.

***Q**: Will* Daymare *ever be produced in any form?*
A: We used a portion of the script—which focused on one of the character's memories—to produce a prototype. Beyond that, I think it's unlikely that anything will ever come of it.

***Q**: In today's frenetic world, is the technology tail wagging the story dog?*
A: In some ways, that is true. Nobody admires CD-ROMs as a technology. Everybody wishes they were faster and could store more information. In some ways, that's an annoyance. In some ways, it spurs greater creativity. Writers really have to use their heads to conform to the limitations of the technology. For a creative person, technological limitations are not necessarily that bad because in all media there are constraints. The measure of a good artist is how well they deal with the constraints that are handed to them.

Having said that, in some ways, technological limitations are clearly annoying. When it became clear that *Daymare* would have to be placed on more than one CD-ROM, that presented a major obstacle to us. We did not want to limit ourselves to a linear narrative. We wanted it possible for the user to experience the program in any order. But when you've got a series of discs you are working with, it forces you to organize your material in a fixed order. The material located on one disc can't be immediately accessed when you are using another disc. To do so, you must stop everything, eject the first disc, and insert the next disc. This technology constraint directly interfered with what we wanted to do.

Sometimes artists can deal with limitations. Sometimes it changes the nature of what you are doing. An example is comic books. Characters in comic books wear masks and skintight clothing because it is easier for the artists to draw. That's one way creative people got around a problem.

At a certain point, the costs involved with drawing starts to affect the art itself. The story lines of comic books tend to be real pulpy and involve big, intense, obvious emotions because those expressions are easier to draw.

Q: It's been said that when we talk about plot, we are not talking about merely the action of a story, we are referring to the meaningful manipulation of character as well. Do you believe complex characters can be developed for interactive applications?
A: It comes down to the question of can you create a computer program that can simulate the human mind. The only way to deal with the problem that you just described would be to write software—code—that could convincingly exhibit human behavior. Among people who are knowledgeable about computers, there are two basic opinions about this. One opinion is that our brains are just big digital computers and if you wrote a big enough computer program, you could create conscious human beings in a computer. But we are nowhere near being able to do that. The other opinion is that it is impossible to create human consciousness in a piece of digital hardware. No matter which opinion you take, we cannot currently write computer software that can mimic human behavior. For that reason, I expect that the problem you describe will continue to exist until applications can be networked so that actual human beings can play roles in these systems.

To succeed at this, we would need better input devices—sensory input such as video and audio—plus some way to include human players in the loop. It's easy to imagine a great big building in the Philippines or Sri Lanka filled with thousands of cubicles—with actors sitting at computer terminals earning a nickel a day—making human decisions for networked games.

Q: *Are there any consumer products on the market today that use interactivity in an intelligent way?*
A: I admire *Myst* and *Riven*—largely because the creators were clever enough to not even try to put humans in it. They just knew that the minute they added humans to the environment, it would be lame. Both titles are splendid—they are gorgeous, evocative.

Players embark on a mission of discovering a narrative that happened in the past. The story—what the family members did to each other long ago—cannot be altered by the players. The player uncovers the story one bit at a time as they play the game. This is a very new way of experiencing a static narrative. It is also a clever way of getting around the limitations of today's technology.

Greg Roach

Greg Roach is the CEO and artistic director of HyperBole Studios. Considered a multimedia pioneer, Greg wrote and designed *The Madness of Roland*, the world's first original interactive multimedia novel. As a filmmaker, Greg created the world's first narrative interactive film, *The Wrong Side of Town*, the Best of Show winner at the first QuickTime Film Festival. He also created Virtual-Cinema®, which is both a technology and a design philosophy for creating interactive video-based properties. This technology served as the foundation for HyperBole's three latest interactive CD-ROMs: *Quantum Gate, The Vortex*, and *The X-Files*.

Q: *What is VirtualCinema?*
A: VirtualCinema is an interactive engine, interface, and structural approach to interactive story games. My company, HyperBole, won the contract from Fox Interactive to produce *The X-Files* in part because of the strength of our dramatic awareness and a powerful prototype we produced using Virtual-Cinema. VirtualCinema measures the responses and activities of the player and applies them back to the story line. This continually evolving software gives the user a seamless viewing experience because it was developed out of our creative need to tell better interactive stories.

It's the techniques and tools for combining cinematic storytelling with the interactivity of games.

Part of the VirtualCinema architecture is an object-oriented database, which stores all the logic associated with a title. It contains a set of rules that determine how media elements are put together—so that a degree of continuity can be synthesized on the fly—accounting for player choice, interactivity, and the accumulated impact of the player's decisions.

Other key factors include our production design and a production methodology that determines how we approach filming the material, how it then gets integrated inside the playback environment, etc.

There are also certain geometric assumptions built into VirtualCinema that relate to how an interactive narrative can be structured. We've tried to create a new grammar for cinematic interactivity by synthesizing all the best elements of what has come before us. On a technical level, VirtualCinema is built in C++ and allows users to interact directly with video streams. We can track moving objects through video streams and know when certain actions in the video are taking place (characters speaking, walking, etc.)

VirtualCinema uses concepts called "über variables" and "über psychology," which constantly track and monitor what the player is doing and then fold that psychological profile back into the title. There is a sort of psychological loop between the player and the program that influences, tracks, and implements the aesthetics of the piece, from how characters behave to how the narrative unfolds.

For example, if a player chooses action A, then a corresponding psychological variable gets increased x number of points. When this particular variable hits a certain level, then a corollary event will happen.

Q: *Tell me about* The X-Files.
A: We've brought the world of the show to life on player's computers—allowing them to be an active participant in the drama, solving problems as an FBI agent would.

The X-Files has six hours of video, which translates into at least forty hours of gameplay. That video is divided up into highly granular little pieces of cinematic action—from five to fifteen seconds long.

The "seven second rule" is one of the design principles built into *The X-Files* experience (and VirtualCinema)—something I learned from Ken Williams over at Sierra Online—which says that you should never take control away from the player for more than ten seconds. Our foremost goal was to keep the player in control and connected at all times. Because what happens is that there is a dichotomy of experience between watching and doing. We wanted a complete integration between those two modes so that the process of doing automatically generated something to watch, but immediately following this, the user resumes control. More than that, the cinematic sequences which play in response to player choice are themselves interactive—you can interact with anyone (or thing) constantly.

There are several action sequences in the title—like those found in popular twitch games—segments where quick reflexes and quick thinking are required. As a matter of fact, the final act of the piece is all in real time. Ultimately, what we were shooting for was a balance—a balance of story, gameplay, character interaction, physical manipulation of the environment, intellectual pursuits, emotional pursuits, and the like.

Our goal with *The X-Files* was to create something that has the same degree of suspense that you might find in a traditional film—only more so because the experience is wrapped around you. A lot of games have puzzles that are just sort of tacked or stuck into the middle of the story. Very often, the user wonders, What does this puzzle have to do with anything? I feel very strongly that all the obstacles to your progress, all of the problems that you are presented with to solve, need to arise organically out of character and situation. In *The X-Files*, all of the natural impediments to your forward progress are as organic to the story as we could possibly make them.

Q: *Describe the structure of* The X-Files.
A: *The X-Files* is a single story which allows for an high degree of player freedom or nonlinearity within the structure of the narrative. As the user navigates the game, what you think is the explanation for a situation will inevitably change as you complete one of the acts of the story and enter another.

You could reverse-engineer *The X-Files* and call it a three-act structure. As a matter of fact, I could easily boil the story down into a story synopsis that would suffice for a standard feature film.

A number of different design structures are built into *The X-Files*. Part of what we always search for in a design is balance and a good variety of activities—from character interaction to the intellectual challenge of trying to solve a crime.

Q: *Tell me about the interactive writing process*
A: I start at the 20,000-foot level and work schematically. I believe that the underpinning of successful interactive design is a geometric understanding of the spatial possibilities of what the media represents. I like to start with a map. There is a conceptual space presented by an interactive experience. Once you map out your story, you can then go in and write in an almost linear fash-

ion. But all of those pieces and their relationships must be predefined by the writer.

In *Myst*, the story is predetermined. It is just a matter of what order are you going to stumble across the elements in that world. Once you have your map and its geometric form laid out corresponding to the pieces of your story and its acts, you then have a template by which you are going to sit down and do the job of writing.

With *The X-Files*, we received a story treatment from Chris Carter and Frank Spotnitz at 1013 Productions. The type of linear treatment you'd see in any feature film. It was three to four pages in length and detailed the flow of the story. There was an iterative process where the two sides—HyperBole and 1013—went back and forth making changes. We were identifying the things that needed to change in the story in order to fit properly inside of the interactive medium. Some of those elements were character related and some of the changes were related to plot concerns. Very often, in a traditional linear media, it is acceptable for a character to act as a courier for information . . . your phone will ring and somebody says, "Hey, this has just happened." In the interactive world, you want to avoid that deus ex machina experience. You want to allow the player to discover material proactively, through their own efforts.

Once we went through that iterative process, we had a story treatment that both sides felt was appropriate—true to *The X-Files*, a good story, and something that worked for us in terms of interactive design.

We next sat down and translated that story into our interactive map. Our VirtualCinema authoring environment was still under construction at this point so I created a scriptwriting tool inside of Filemaker Pro and HyperCard. Rather than using a traditional word-processing program to write with, I used a database program. With the map and treatment completed, I sat down and wrote the script, while, at the same time, hammering out the details of the interactive design inside of this database tool. The combined map, treatment, script, and interactive design specifications made up the final design document—one thousand pages of material. Remember that with over six hours of video, *The X-Files* is bigger than six episodes of the television show. In traditional cinematic terms, *The X-Files* is the size of a miniseries.

That document also contains a lot of detail that doesn't necessarily translate into screen time, but needs to be there in order to make the world come to life. It contains everything from dialogue to physical action to things that are contained in the environment. It's a document that works for the entire production crew—actors, designers, programmers—everybody.

As the interactive writer, I was also in charge of monitoring key psychological aspects of the piece. For *The X-Files*, we were keeping track of loss, paranoia, and the X-Track (your belief in paranormal phenomena). Certain sets of choices factored into the status of these variables. These variables, again, determine what the experience ultimately becomes. Sometimes that will demonstrate itself in what characters say. In the script, there might be a dialogue line for a character. Immediately following it will be a note that says, "Unless paranoia is high" (in which case, the character will say something else). On the set, we might have the actor deliver the same line two different ways—one with an ambiguous tone and one that's menacing. Which one is revealed to the player is determined by the status of these variables.

III

Hybrids
and
Hypertext

13

Away from Narrative: Hypertexts, Open Texts, and James Joyce

As audience, we've been conditioned—we've been told stories for so long. Film has been the best way to tell a visual story. It's beautiful. It sounds great, you have great actors, and it's a wonderfully rich experience. But now there are different ways of telling or showing a story. Now, for the first time, we're really thinking about audience participation. How is the audience going to interpret this vision and make it their own vision? We've never had to think that way before.

JARYL LYN LANE

So far, we have been concerned with a certain species of interactive work, that is, a work that incorporates a linear narrative and is for the most part narratively presented. *Wing Commander III, The Pocahontas Animated Storybook, The X-Files: Unrestricted Access, Phantasmagoria,* and *Johnny Mnemonic* are representative of this type. Interactive writers interested in these kinds of texts need to apply the past chapters with some rigor.

When we talk about linear narratives, we are talking about systems that are to some extent closed. Endings are resolved, all parts relate. The further you move away from narrative, the more open the systems become and the less tied they are to narrative. These tangentially dramatic presentations demand user participation in ways that Syd Field and three-act structures are, pardon the pun, virtually irrelevant. Games like *Quake, Tomb Raider, Doom,* and *Diablo: Hellfire,* for instance, do not depend on a narrative spine for their appeal. They are, instead, extremely addictive twitch games. Greg Roach says this kind of participation isn't interactive at all.

Other projects such as *Blade Runner, HyperCafe, Myst, Seventh Guest, Post-cards from the Radio, Victory Garden,* and *Psychic Detective,* have a narrative of sorts, but their story lines are not always resolved with any real closure. Their sense of pace and rhythm are not enforced at all in the way demanded by linear narrative experiences. These texts, in fact, are not intended to be experienced as pure narrative. They are examples of digital experiences, which do not, at their heart, depend on narrative appeal. They are designed precisely for people who enjoy puzzles, games, exploratory environments, and simulacre of all sorts. These kinds of cyberproducts don't usually follow three-act structures and the attempts to see them as some kind of "new narrative" are misguided, or sometimes plain silly.

A game doesn't have to resolve a complex set of interrelated human decisions that hinge on a serious moral choice. Let's suppose you enter a virtual interactive experience that specializes in police simulations. You click on "hostage crisis." You're in an inner-city convenience store. You become a virtual cop going into a hostage situation. The bad guy holds a gun to a hostage's head. Does the cop shoot or not? Do you shoot or not? In the real world, this is a deadly serious situation. In the fictive—i.e., narrative—world, the situation *ought* to be serious. We ought in fiction to vicariously experience the cop's decision making. We ought to feel the anxiety that the officer will undoubtedly endure when debating whether he or she should shoot the bad guy, or talk the bad guy down. Shoot or talk. In the real world, and the narrative world, a hostage's life hangs in the balance.

But the world of fiction takes us farther. Unlike the real world, our responsibility in story land broadens to include the inner lives of the hostage and of the bad guy as well as the cop. Is the bad guy bad? What brings him to this time and place? Does he know his victim? Is there a moral context we need to know to evaluate the scene? Has the hostage, for instance, committed some grievous crime against his assailant which mitigates in some way the bad guy's holding him hostage? Or is the bad guy simply a random killer? What brought these two characters together? What unifies their past with this present? What motivates their separate actions and the actions of the police officer in this single, dramatic moment? And what happens afterward? A story must give us a sense, however emasculated, of ever after. These are only some of the things that fiction obligates one to do. It is an ageless contract between a writer and the audience. A timeless trust.

An interactive game is bound by no such obligation. In a game, the only thing that matters is how many points you get. You beat the bad guy to the draw, you get one hundred points and, oh yes, the hostage survives. You don't beat the bad guy to the draw, you lose a hundred points and, gee whiz, you also lose the hostage. If you try talking the bad guy down and it doesn't work, the game most likely will penalize you two hundred points. Why? Because the point of a game is to make you respond, not deliberate. An interactive writer's job, for these texts, is simply to stimulate, to create situations that demand ten or twelve or twenty clicks a minute.

Puzzles and cryptograms dole out rewards for more analytical behavior. Neal Stephenson says people hate solving puzzles, but the fact is that the hottest selling interactive products by a good stretch are *Myst* and its follow-on, *Riven*, which, on the surface, seem to be nothing but elaborate puzzles. Besides games and puzzles and live-action role-playing games, the spawn of *Dungeons and Dragons,* you have MUDs and interactive Web sites where people ostensibly gather to tell stories. But these quilted group transactions, often compared to soap operas, seldom reach soap-opera quality.

"What we are working with now are incanabular forms of interactive communication," claims John F. Barber, an instructor in writing theory, computers, and composition in the Department of Language and Communication at Northwestern State University. "The kinds of things we are doing now are not what we will be doing next year. And certainly not what we will be doing in the next five or ten years when other iterations of electronic-based writing, communication, art, and interaction break through. We are developing a series of place markers now for what will have been."

Hypertext

There is an enormous volume of presentation on the Web that, like games and puzzles, breaks with standard narrative conventions, but that, at its best, stretches the bounds of literature. Hypertexts are sites that involve their users in long, complex chains of fact, incident, and presentation, interwoven by association, logic, or randomly to create warrens of interrelated if open-ended text. These texts frequently abjure the kind of closure demanded of even modernist narrative, opting instead for a collage of association that many critics insist on describing as a "readerly" text.

A word regarding "readerly" and "writerly" texts. We shouldn't have to invent vocabulary to state the obvious fact that each time we see a film, read a book, or participate in an interactive environment our experience from one time to the next changes. And no one, so far as I know, has ever insisted that two persons viewing, reading, or interacting have the same experience of a given film, book, or interactive text. But modern literary theorists, wanting to empower critics and, ostensibly, readers, use the term "readerly" to suggest that a reader cocreates, with an author, a book. A viewer cocreates, with the director, cinematographer, makeup person?! the film. In his essay "A New Art Form: Hypertext Fiction," Howard Becker cites an interactive appropriation of this readerly/writerly vocabulary: "if we remember that one of the cooperating parties in the production of any work of art is the audience, we can think of a work as coming into existence anew every time someone looks at it, reads it, or hears it."

This isn't a new or original assertion. But the suggestion that the audience is involved in production, if by production we mean origination or authorship or creation of any text, is a false card. A viewer at a movie, a reader of a book, or a user interacting within a hypertext, whose environment, presentation, and logic are predetermined by a programmer/designer/writer, are not originating the text that they experience. They cannot, in any procedurally determined system, change a byte's worth of information. They don't create, or produce, anything.

That's not to say that audiences of all kinds don't bring something essential to any text. A musician or diva is going to have a different experience of an opera than that had by someone completely untutored in music or opera. Furthermore, the authors fully grant that, other things being equal, the musician's experience of an opera, or the diva's, is an experience not only different, but better informed and qualitatively superior to our own. But we don't give the musician or the diva credit for writing the score for the cello, composing the opera, or originating the libretto. This readerly, writerly "thing" seems somehow tied up much more in popular sentiment, or politics, than in an honest look at what happens when we read a book, watch a film, or interact with a hypertext.

Participating in a world does not make us an author of that world. I don't think I can improve on Janet Murray's summary of this concern in *Hamlet on the Holodeck,* so let me offer this passage taken from her chapter on agency:

> One of the key questions that the practice of narrative agency evokes is, To what degree are we authors of the work we are experiencing? Some have argued (with either elation or horror) that an interactor in a digital story—not just the improvising MUDer, but even the navigating reader of a postmodern hypertext—is the author of the story. This is a misleading assertion. There is

a distinction between playing a creative role within an authored environment and having authorship of the environment itself.

. . . Authorship in electronic media is procedural. Procedural authorship means writing rules by which texts appear as well as writing the texts themselves. It means writing the rules for the interactor's involvement, that is, the conditions under which things will happen in response to the participant's actions.

. . . Contemporary critics are attributing authorship to interactors because they do not understand the procedural basis of electronic composition. The interactor is not the author of the digital narrative, although the interactor can experience one of the most exciting aspects of artistic creation—the thrill of exerting power over enticing and plastic materials. This is not authorship but agency."

Murrays' remarks ought to influence literary and film theory as well as interactive critics. Hypertexts, to return home, can make their participants powerful agents within a marvelous environ. But they aren't *producing* the text. Clicks on a mouse can give only the illusion, however powerful, of creation. The illusion of choice. The front porch, by contrast, or the bedside story offers a true potential for production since the audience in those cases *can* actually assume authorial power, creating material not determined by the initial yarn-spinners and in many cases not intended by them.

Some Web sites provide forums for a kind of cooperative attempt at storytelling. Those forms engage their users explicitly as authors. Hypertexts, on the other hand, are procedurally defined and finite arenas, offering predetermined interactions for a potential user. A hypertext doesn't make its users authors, but it does make them agents.

What's it like to be inside a hypertext? The experience can be disconcerting or tiresome for someone seeking the closure normally expected of linear narratives. Most hypertexts are clearly not puzzles, nor are they games, though puzzle and gaming elements may be present. Hypertext, at its best, demands a different kind of involvement from its users/agents than do puzzles, games, or linear narratives.

Noted hypertext author and instructor Stuart Moulthrop, is quoted on his Web site as saying, "The postmodern critics are right: hyperfiction (as I do it anyway) is a word-game more than a world-game."

In her online essay "Dinosaur or Postmodern Mutant? Narrative in the

Age of Information," N. Katherine Hayles explores two works of hypertext fiction in great detail—Shelley Jackson's *Patchwork Girl* and Marjorie Luesebrink's *Califia*. She finds that, "In these fictions, narrative functions less as a text to be read than a topology to be explored; less a pre-set linear sequence than a network of possibilities; less as an object to be consumed than an interactive engagement in which reader and author collaborate in bringing the narrative into being."

Roots

Antecedents to modern hypertext are clearly evident in experimental literary works by author/artists such as Jorge Luis Borges and Raymond Queneau.

Argentine writer Jorge Luis Borges (1899–1986), wrote stories that can be read as potent metaphors for hypertext and the World Wide Web, where knowledge is archived without beginning, without end, and beyond the concept of linear time. One of Borges's most famous works is *The Garden of the Forking Paths*, a story of a deception of history perpetrated by the British government to cover up an incident involving a breach of national security. One of the book's characters, a chinese assassin, discovers that his ancestor's novel is more than it appears to be—functioning on two levels—both as a story and a puzzle. Borges's work is significant because it forces readers to look beyond the obvious and to question all possible outcomes of a story.

Innovators such as Raymond Queneau (1903–1976), a French author who produced some of the most important prose and poetry of the mid-twentieth century, dabbled in early hypermedia stories. In 1969, Queneau created *A Story As You Like It*, a machine-generated experiment in creating hypertext verse and prose (see figs. 13.1 and 13.2).

While it is notable that the writing quality in Queneau's experiment was mediocre at best (hey, it was generated by a machine!), it was a striking example of the conceptual advances in multilinear thinking.

What, Then, Is Modern Hypertext Fiction?

Hypertext refers to two or more nodes of information that contain embedded, easily navigable links to each other. Hypertext and hypermedia are the building blocks of the World Wide Web, informational kiosks, and popular multimedia CD-ROMs. Hypertext fiction is a complex narrative whose links communicate meaning as the reader traverses his or her own unique path

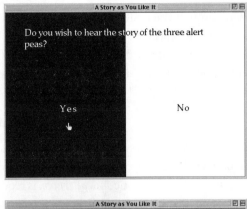

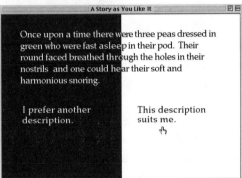

Figs. 13.1 and 13.2: Screen shots from a freeware HyperCard version of *A Story As You Like It*, by Raymond Queneau.

through the story. Or, as author Michael Heim puts it, "Hypertext is non-sequential writing with free user movement."

Michael Joyce builds on Heim's definition, stating, "Hypertext fiction tends to be closer to our normal experiences—the narratives that make up our lives. Closure is a matter of rhythms and of transient episodes . . . where we find the story of our lives and the story of the things that are important to us in successions and recurrences."

Hypertext is experienced over the Internet on Web sites or via mediums such as CD-ROMs and floppy disks. These hypertext fiction programs frequently combine language and dramatic presentation to produce the cyberheirs of James Joyce, or Dos Passos, or Beckett. Some are very much like conventional novels while others are experimental expressions of poetry and wordplay.

Stuart Moulthrop's *Victory Garden* has been praised by well-established critics as has Michael Joyce's *afternoon, a story* and Shelley Jackson's *Patchwork Girl*. What do these works have in common? How does the reader actually interact with the work? How does the user create a unique navigational pathway through the material? How do multiple pathways influence the reader's eventual interpretation of the text?

Let's examine two works of hypertext fiction—*afternoon, a story* and *Postcards from the Radio*—and see what all the fuss is about.

afternoon, a story

Michael Joyce's *afternoon, a story* is perhaps the most celebrated hypertext fiction written to date. Eastgate Systems proudly describes the work as follows: "A classic of electronic fiction, *afternoon* is required reading. Complex and richly imagined, this is the story of Peter, a technical writer who (in one reading) begins his afternoon with a terrible suspicion that the wrecked car he saw hours earlier might have belonged to his former wife. *afternoon* is a rich and lyrical exploration of the tangled strands of knowing and memory, the interconnections that bind and unravel the intersecting lives of its postmodern characters."

The story was created by Michael Joyce, a prize-winning novelist and a professor of English at Vassar College. Joyce's works include the hypertext fiction novel *Twilight, A Symphony;* a novel, *The War Outside Ireland;* and a work of nonfiction, *Of Two Minds: Hypertext Pedagogy and Poetics.*

According to the author, *afternoon* is made up of 539 nodes and 951 links. Each node contains only a small portion of the overall story. Readers start from a common "title page" of the story, yet, from that page on, the reader navigates the piece to his or her own drum (see fig. 13.3).

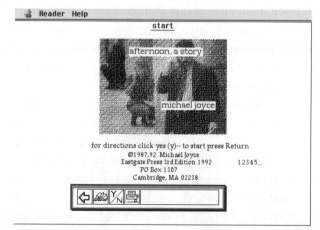

Fig. 13.3. The "title page" of Michael Joyce's *afternoon, a story*. Published by Eastgate Systems, Inc., 1987. Created with Storyspace. Reprinted by permission of the publisher.

Readers can navigate *afternoon, a story* by interacting with a menu bar (located at the bottom of each page). The user may also advance the story linearly by hitting the return key (although in "linear mode" the user will only be able to access 40 of the 539 nodes). The arrow button (⟵) functions like the "back" button utilized by the popular Web navigation interfaces such as Netscape Navigator and Microsoft Internet Explorer. It allows the reader to re-trace his or her steps back through the story (if the person so chooses). The browse icon (the little book located to the right the arrow button) allows the reader to quickly browse links between screens. The yes/no key permits the reader to respond to questions posed by the text. Readers who click the print icon can print the text of a screen. Readers can also type some words—and occasional one-word questions—in the text box to the right of the menu keys.

On the "first page" in *afternoon,* titled "begin," the reader is prompted by the text to continue (see fig. 13.4).

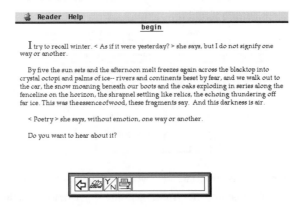

Fig. 13.4. Screen shot of the first page of Michael Joyce's *afternoon, a story*. Published by Eastgate Systems, Inc., 1987. Created with Storyspace. Reprinted by permission of the publisher.

If the reader hits return, a new page, titled "I want to say," materializes onscreen, which says, "I want to say I may have seen my son die this morning." (See fig. 13.5)

If the reader instead clicks "yes" in response to the question, "Do you want to hear about it?" the reader is transported to a completely different "next page," which, in this case, happens to be titled "yes" (see fig. 13.6).

As you can see, there are a number of possible navigational pathways or "readings" through *afternoon.* That's both the strength and weakness of hypertext fiction. Hypertext is cool because it empowers readers to dictate how

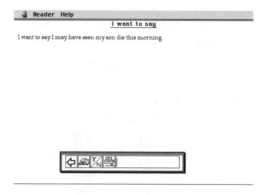

Fig. 13.5. Screen shot of "I want to say," from Michael Joyce's *afternoon, a story*. Published by Eastgate Systems, Inc., 1987. Created with Storyspace. Reprinted by permission of the publisher.

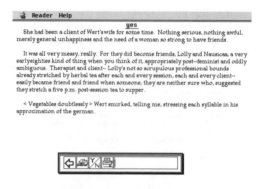

Fig. 13.6. Screen shot of "yes," from Michael Joyce's *afternoon, a story*. Published by Eastgate Systems, Inc., 1987. Created with Storyspace. Reprinted by permission of the publisher.

the material is presented to them—whether they make deliberate choices or simply follow their natural impulses to explore. The seemingly random unfolding of interrelated story elements appeals to many readers, in much the same way as following hypertext links from one Web site to another. You don't quite know what material is coming next and you almost certainly will never experience the same "story" twice. Some readers believe that multiple navigational pathways are the greatest weakness of hypertext. The labyrinthine structures of hypertext fiction, they argue, make it difficult for the reader to enjoy the work as prose. How does one make sense of the author's story when the work is 539 "pages" long and 3,678 "pages" wide? Does the work even have a true beginning, middle, and end?

Joyce himself answers this query by identifying *afternoon* as a work in progress, saying, "Closure is, as in any fiction, a suspect quality. Although here it is made manifest. When the story no longer progresses, or when it cycles, or when you tire of the paths, the experience of reading it ends."

Postcards from the Radio

Postcards from the Radio is John F. Barber's intriguing work of experimental Web hypertext. Barber, a "hybrid" instructor, author, and futurist, has published numerous professional papers discussing the use of technology in teaching and teacher training. He currently teaches undergraduate and graduate courses in advanced composition, composition theory, creative writing, technical writing, and computers and composition in the Department of Language and Communication at Northwestern State University.

Postcards prompts users to choose from a variety of hyperlinked phrases that first appear in neat, ordered rows on the home page. Barber himself describes *Postcards* in the work's introduction: "This collection of random thoughts, observations, and fantasies is being written while traveling in search of something I'm not sure of. Many things described in these postcards actually are happening in different ways, but they make more sense to me like this. After all, it doesn't matter what you are doing or where you are bound, but how you go about it." (see fig. 13.7).

Fig. 13.7. Home page from John F. Barber's *Postcards from the Radio*. Courtesy of Webgeist (*www.webgeist.com*). Copyright April 1997. Reprinted by permission.

After reading through a myriad of twenty-nine unique phrases, the user has the option of choosing any one of the underlined hypertext links. For example, if the user were to choose the phrase, "The Collision of Realities," he or she would be transported to the node displayed in fig. 13.8.

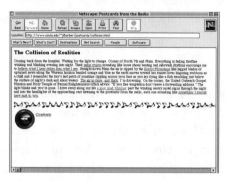

Fig. 13.8. "Collision of Realities" node from John F. Barber's *Postcards from the Radio***. Courtesy of Webgeist (***www.webgeist.com***). Copyright April 1997. Reprinted by permission.**

The Collision of Realities

Coming back from the hospital. Waiting for the light to change. Corner of North 7th and Main. Everything is fading fireflies winking and blinking evening into night. <u>Tired radio voices</u> sounding like loose shoes beating sad sidewalk rhythms encourage me <u>to believe what I hear rather than what I see</u>. Straight down Main the air is ripped by <u>the Rocky Mountains</u> like jagged blades of upturned saws along the Western horizon banded orange and blue as the earth moves toward her sunset lover lingering stubborn as a child and I remember the day's last patch of sunshine rippling across your face as you lay dying like a fish trembling just below the surface of night's dark and silent waters. <u>The air is close, and thick</u>. I'm drowning. On the corner, the United Outreach Gospel Mission and Holy Temple of Eternal Enlightenment offers advice: "If you flee temptation don't leave a forwarding address." The light blinks and you're gone. I drive away along my life <u>a long road winding</u> past the winking sentry motel signs through the night and into the headlights of the approaching cars listening to the postcards from the radio, each one sounding like <u>something I should have said to you</u>.

The user can then choose one of six underlined hypertexts, which link to related nodes of information. For example, if the user next decided to click on the hypertext phrase "Rocky Mountains," he or she would be transported to:

Sad, Lonesome, and Cold

East Rosebud Lake nestles against the Beartooth Mountains. High rock cliffs on either side, snow covered at the top, provide lookouts for Rocky Mountain Sheep. The trail for Phantom Lake, Lake At Falls, and Froze To Death Lake leaves from here, a pathway for the wind blowing sad, lonesome, and cold from my heart.

After pondering the significance of the author's mountain memories, the user might next decide to click on the hypertext phrase, "lonesome." In doing so, the person would be transported to the following node:

Veg-e-Matic Love

Sliced and diced like ripe vegetable dreams by cold tongued Ginzu blades (not available in stores anywhere) blended and pureed beyond recognition my heart is stored neatly in airtight jars on cool back shelves of the wheezing refrigerator its iron lung rapidly failing signaled by the high-pitched microwave beeping and the dishwasher sloshing away the polish of uncompleted dreams.

Get it?

Barber drawns a parallel between hypertext fiction and the way the human brain thinks. For him, and other advocates of hypertext, the relationship between text and reader is paramount. Barber explains:

"Hypertext fiction allows the reader to become an interactor. By making conscious selections of which links to follow, the reader determines a pathway through the material. We're doing hypertextual and associative thinking within the framework of our personal worldviews all the time. As we learn more, we can establish more links to other worldviews—we expand our intelligence. In this sense, what we are doing with hypertext fiction is new in that it facilitates our exploration of new and different or alternative worldviews, intelligences. That's the way the human brain works."

Eastgate, Storyspace, and the Self-Reflexive Text

What interests me about hypertext is its root in modernist literature. Even before the end of World War I, authors were beginning to move away from the narrative expectations that had become, to their taste, too rigid in novels or plays of the period. After the war, with the rise of the surrealists and dadaists, literature, in a sense, began to emulate the plastic arts. Where painters began to abandon representationalism on canvas, authors sought to subvert narrative structure on the page.

It's no accident that readers/users of hypertext fiction often compare their experience to reading works like *Finnegans Wake, Ulysses, Waiting for Godot, The Labyrinth,* or *U.S.A.* Hypertexts are firmly rooted in the conventions of modernity, self-consciously aiming for a self-reflexive text, calling attention to the way in which the story is rendered as well as to the incident of story itself, loosely associating impressions and language and graphics in an unresolved, open-ended papyrus that strives, in a sense, to appear authorless.

The modernist movement in literature wanted to see how far from "narrative" literature could move. In the plastic arts, painters abjured the idea of representation altogether, creating the modern abstractions that alternately delight, irritate, or confound its viewers and critics.

The best hypertext, as with the best modern art, is not a text without rules. It is, above all, not an expression absent of human context or concern. The problem for cyberfans seeking quality hypertexts is that most people who enter this arena are not Stuart Moulthrop or Michael Joyce.

"A lot of people can sit down and write an interesting sentence or an interesting paragraph," offers interactive evangelist Greg Roach. "Fewer people can combine those into a cogent, compelling short story. And fewer still can combine those into a decent novel. So to say, 'I can write a bunch of interesting paragraphs on note cards and throw them into a wind tunnel and let you pick them up at random, and you'll have something that is compelling and sensible,' I think is kind of stretching it."

The great democratization offered by the Web doesn't come without some downside. There are no editing houses or publishers or critics to pass judgment on what enters the Internet and what doesn't. Fans of cyperspace cheer this as a new freedom, a release from shackles. I fully agree that there is no need for any restriction at all on the Net's literary expressions. But just because something is *on* the Internet doesn't mean its any good. Persons who aspire to see hypertexts become the next evolution in human expression, as it definitely can be, need to be more rigorous in their critiques of the texts produced.

Already we are seeing the categorization and capitalization of certain works of hypertext fiction over others with the rise of electronic publishing houses such as Eastgate Systems, Inc. (*www.eastgate.com*). In their own way, these publishers legitimize an author's work by granting them worthy of being published—albeit in electronic form rather than the traditional perfect bound paper format. As Eastgate's own Web site proudly proclaims, "At Eastgate, we create new hypertext technologies and publish serious hypertext, fiction and non-fiction."

Eastgate Systems has published many of the most highly regarded works of hypertext fiction, including the multilevel tragedy of Edward Falco's *A Dream with Demons*, the incisive poetry of Stephanie Strickland's *True North*, the lyrical intelligence of Michael Joyce's *Twilight, A Symphony*, the historical prose of Deena Larsen's *Marble Springs*, and the frenetic plot and incident of Stuart Moulthrop's *Victory Garden*.

Eastgate is also the publisher of a unique hypertext authoring software known as Storyspace (originally developed by Jay Bolter, John Smith, and Michael Joyce). The software tool was designed for both writers and readers of hypertext who need to collect, organize, and express the structure of their ideas both textually and graphically (see fig. 13.9).

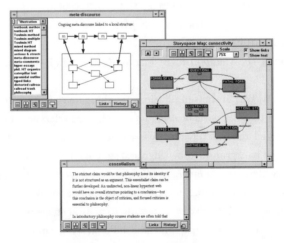

Fig. 13.9. Three views of structure for David Kolb's *Socrates in the Labyrinth*. A Storyspace map view (top) and writing space (to its left), a connectivity map (right), another writing space (bottom). Map views allow writers to see and manipulate the structures and interconnections of their work.

The basic component of Storyspace is the writing space (or node). Writers can compose text and images and quickly link them to other related writing spaces. Storyspace also lets you create hypertext works for the World Wide Web. At the click of a button, Storyspace can translate your hypertext—with its content, structure, and links—into an HTML file ready for posting on the Internet.

Popular Web hypertexts created using Storyspace include Jane Loader's *Flygirls,* Mark Amerika's *Grammatron,* Arnold Dreyblatt's *Memory Arena,* and Adrianne Wortzel's *Ah, Need.*

Narrativeless Narratives

The move away from narrative requires greater rigor of its writers, not less. Samuel Beckett took these experiments to the extreme, creating in his plays a minimalism that tries (how successfully?) to present literature/drama with no narrative restraint at all.

Critics quickly discovered, at least in James Joyce's case, that his apparent streams of consciousness were mated to a rigorous, complex, and classic substructure. With the decoding of these texts came the notion that readers were as responsible as the text's writers for the creation of whatever experience resulted in the reading of these kinds of stories. Sound like a user's role in cyberspace? It ought to.

In his book *The Metaphysics of Virtual Reality,* Michael Heim writes:

> *Finnegans Wake* spins nets of allusions touching myriad other books and often alludes to other parts of itself. Its complex self-references and allusions have daunted and frustrated many a reader: few books outside the Bible call for so much background knowledge and so much outside commentary. The secondary literature on *Finnegans Wake* is enormous, with glossaries of puns and neologisms and etymologies of the many foreign and concocted words. More important, this book embodies the structural shape of hypertext. It is the ne plus ultra of nonlinear and associational style, a mess of hidden links and a tangle of recurring motifs. Joyce worked on *Finnegans Wake* for over seventeen years, in a nonlinear fashion not unlike the way a person typically uses a word processor. The book was not created with a beginning, then a middle, and finally a conclusion. Rather, Joyce produced sections as the muses moved him. Sometimes he wrote only a single large word across the page in crayon (he was nearly blind at the time). Yet everything in *Finnegans Wake* dovetails like a wave of fractal structures . . . the hermeneutic structure of the novel matches hypertext.

Literary critics love the idea of viewing literature as a readerly text—gives 'em more status. So you frequently see literary critics speaking of critical exegesis as literature since, after all, the activity of decoding, say, *Ulysses*, is not unlike the writing of it. Using this logic, Moulthrop has no more claim to be the author of his text than the users who participate in *Victory Garden*.

In hypertexts, as in modernist literature, there is a challenge to deconstruct the systems of structure that unite the apparently disparate ranges of language, image, and so on. A user/reader is challenged to decode layers of signs and signifiers to experience, finally, the foundational themes and structures that connects the work and, ostensibly, gives it significance (if not meaning). *Ulysses* and *afternoon, a story*, become, in this view, a species of cryptogram. They become puzzles created jointly between writer and reader, the sense of authorship now shared because, unlike your crossword puzzle, the enigmas posed by Michael Joyce or Stuart Moulthrop do not have an empirically verifiable result. The endgame will differ from one reading/participation to the next. Every resulting experience will be unique.

Well-known visual poet Eduardo Kac, has devoted nearly his entire adult life to experimenting with visual language and verbal images. In his essay "Holopoetry and Fractal Holopoetry: Digital Holography as an Art Medium," Kac explains: "Language plays a fundamental role in the constitution of our experiential world. To question the structure of language is to investigate how realities are constructed. . . . The temporal and rhythmic organization of my texts play an important role in creating this tension between visual language and verbal images. Most of my pieces deal with time as nonlinear (i.e., discontinuous) and reversible (i.e., flowing in both directions), in such a way that the viewer/reader can move up or down, back and forth, from left to right, at any speed, and still be able to establish associations between words present in the ephemeral perceptual field."

To demonstrate Kac's methodology, here is a humble attempt at creating a visual poem that mimics the visual look and feel of Kac's poetic style (see fig. 13.10).

What the interactive writer should appreciate from this discussion is that hypertext, though related to systems of structure and complexity that may be nominally narrative in origin, aims to produce an experience that is not tied to a sense of closure or story. A linear narrative keeps human values at the center of its attention. In linear narrative every line and element is designed to involve the reader in a world that is complex, but not stochastic. It frequently resolves its plot line(s) ambiguously, but does not abandon the responsibility

Fig. 13.10. *Waiting for a Tram,* **by Jon Samsel. Copyright 1988.**

to provide some sense of closure and catharsis. And, of course, linear narratives create a sense of pace and rhythm. Things happen at predictable times in this kind of presentation.

Hypertext author Michael Joyce goes so far as to claim that "hypertext fiction replaces the Aristotelian curve (of beginning, middle, and an end) with a series of successive, transitory closures . . . transitory coherences in which you come to satisfy your understanding until the next time around. You build from that. Each of them enriches the previous. The core of hypertext fiction is not to get to some secret ending. It's more about successive understandings of kaleidoscopic perceptions that I think characterizes any art and makes our lives worthwhile."

Let's say you want to go past three acts and mainstream narrative in much the way Michael Joyce suggests. You want to break out. You're not interested in straight narrative at all. Shouldn't you just start out writing hypertext?

It's a bit like answering someone who's never held a paintbrush asking you whether he or she should skip the still lifes and nudes and go straight into abstract expressionism since that's really what he or she would rather do. I could dodge this question, but I won't. I'd say no to that beginning artist who hates drawing class just as I'd answer no to the neophyte writer who wants to jump-start his craft in hypertext. Don't try abstract art before you can draw a pear in a bowl. Don't "do" hypertext until you've made a serious effort to become competent at the business of "simply" telling a story.

Picasso, we should recall, did not prepare for his art by picking up bicycle handles or distorting nudes into cubes. He mastered the old forms before he began changing them. Writers of hypertext, if they want to be taken seriously, should at least be familiar with their literary ancestry. Too many writers manqué want to take shortcuts in their art. They use the excuse of their "new" technology to excuse shabby work. Don't be one of these people. If you can't write a good short story, novel, or play, it's not likely that you can develop six or eight or ten hours of extended and interrelated text that deserves to be taken seriously. Do your homework; know your literary and dramatic heritage and become competent in its forms, first. Then, by all means, stretch your wings in hyperspace.

Toni Morrison, after all, is every bit as interesting in her use of language, allusion, design, and complexity of signifiers as James Joyce. The difference is, with Morrison you get a rattling good story to boot.

A Conversation with Michael Joyce

Michael Joyce is a prize-winning novelist and a professor of English at Vassar College. Joyce's works include the hypertext fiction novel *Twilight, A Symphony*, and the much celebrated *afternoon, a story*. Joyce has been active in the interactive and collaborative arts communities for many years.

Q: How do you define hypertext fiction?
A: From the beginning, I referred to hypertext fictions as multiple fictions. Not because I wanted to steer attention away from the technology or the modality of the telling, but because my own experience reading and teaching these fictions is that they are, in some sense, almost lifelike structures.

I say this because a good deal of my recent writing life has been devoted to steering people away from the notion that these things are branching fictions and to try to elucidate what, in fact, they are if they are not branches.

For me, the term "multiple fiction" gathers much more the sense of what these things have (which my students tend to call an "oddly lifelike quality"). Carolyn Guyer, the hypertext writer, says "the thing about hyperfictions is that, for art, they tend to be extremely lifelike."

Hypertext fiction tends to be closer to our normal experiences—the narratives that make up our lives. Closure is a matter of rhythms and of transient episodes . . . where we find the story of our lives and the story of the things that are important to us in successions and recurrences. The term "multiple fictions" or "multiple stories" seems to capture that for me.[Laughs] Of course, after using it for a decade and not seeing it catch on, I leap at any opportunity to mention it.

Q: *What are the common misconceptions about hypertext fiction?*
A: Sometimes when I give a reading someone will say, "Isn't this every writer's dream? You can throw in all your backstory—you don't have to cut anything. It's so undisciplined." Usually, those comments are from people who haven't read really good hypertext fiction. Many writers fail to realize that there is a great deal of composition in this format.

Another misconception is thinking of hypertext as branching. Hypertext is not about a story and its variations, but, rather, the inner possibilities of the story. A better term is multiplicity. We don't go about our lives like branches. We choose our lives instead by inclination, by urges, by happenstance, or seductions.

A third misconception is to think that links are notes or annotations. As soon as the reader clicks a hyperlink, one must ask, How much more does the reader understand about the way this story is unfolding? It shouldn't be simply that you are getting another episode; it should be that you are coming to understand the way the characters think or see their lives. Too often, you see a poorly crafted narrative Web site where you see the word "sex" and you know that if you follow that link, you will go to a sex scene. If you click on "soccer," you will get a sporting contest. Language and storytelling rarely work that way. The things that are sexy to us sometimes are soccer matches—sex can sometimes seem like a contest. You want to evoke for your reader a sense of discovering story. The link doesn't just get you to another part of the story, the link is part of the story.

Q: *How does* Twilight, A Symphony *differ from* afternoon, a story?
A: I am willing to claim that some things I did in creating *afternoon, a story* were original. In fact, I've been deemed the originator of some art form, or at least, a first something. But when you are a first, you come to a certain humility. You become aware that what you set in motion is not under your control. If somebody deems your creation a literary art form, they will create works which test your understanding of what it was you thought you were doing.

In *Twilight*, there were a lot of obvious changes. Unlike *afternoon*, I included graphics, sounds, and QuickTime movies in *Twilight*. I tried to be very careful not to just seed things throughout the work because it was possible. I tried to define the relationships between the sounds, images, and the text. There were also hypertextual changes. In *afternoon,* there aren't any long screens. Part of that was due to the fact that Storyspace, the hypertext system Jay Bolter and I created, was designed for the Macintosh classic and its little ice block–size screen. We only had so much textual space to work with. Partly though, it was due to the fact that we wanted to move the story along in bite-sized, pulsing rhythms. When I came to write *Twilight,* I bridled under my own discipline and went back to very long scrolling windows in some cases. I love the sense of the text sort of taking you beyond the point were you can hold onto it.

Another change is the overview or libretto. For over a decade now, I've been interested in whether there is such a thing as true interactivity. Because true interactivity, to me, means that the story would change as a result of my reading it. I don't know of any stories or systems as yet that are truly interactive according to my definition. It strikes me that a fundamental aspect to creating true interactivity is that the reader in some sense, has to share a conceptual map with you. To share an idea of what the scope of the work is so that she can, at various turns, test her sense of how this landscape is evolving against what she perceives to be your sense of it.

In *Twilight,* it starts with a screen I like to think of as a libretto, something that says, Here's what was going on before you got here. However, it is written quite consciously in the prose of something like the *Texaco Saturday Opera.* At a time when Texaco used to sponsor radio operas, they would have these librettos where there was this odd third person telling of the story to come. It sets in motion a set of expectations and rhythms and thematics that are not met by the opera.

Where *afternoon* gave you few cues of its wholeness (and the user had to discover the big picture through its linking), in *Twilight,* there is an overview of sorts. An overview, which is, in itself, part of the work. It's not really front matter. It's not direction. It turns out to be an active part of the story too. The question I pose in *Twilight* is, Whose is this voice here?

Q: *Tell me about your most recent project,* Twelve Blue.
A: *Twelve Blue* is the first project I've written directly for the Web. It's my most recent work. It was copublished online by Eastgate Systems and Postmodern Culture.

In *Twelve Blue,* as in all of my interactive fictions, voices come and go. It's a pronominal sense of English—the fact that language allows you to have one character merge into another. Not in a morphing way, but in a way that, viewing the same screen or similar screens in different sequences, it can seem to be one or another of the characters.

For example, one scene in *Twelve Blue* finds two drowning men. One is a very bad man and one is a good and very innocent man. At different times, they share the same language on the same screens. The technique allows my themes and variations to become almost musical. When readers [come] upon these voices, they see the text differently.

Twelve Blue (excerpt) "a white witness"

He settled like the tide, then sank eventually, floating aimlessly and softly, not at all like a log but languishing and plump, a white witness to the darkness.

After the first spike of pain and the panic there was a settling sense of inevitability, the body pitted against itself, both longing for breath and at the same time snuffing it with each gulping inhalation of the frigid, pungent water. The first swallow tore against his lungs but successive ones softened them and made him heavy. Soon he was beyond panic.

There was a pinging echo as if someone hammered against a nearly empty air tank with a wrench.

A sense of someone swimming nearby in dark water.

A woman came to visit him bearing a garland of dried vines strung with flowers of various shades of blue and a few stray blossoms of pink and yellow. She sang a strange song of a Portuguese sailor and a witch. Above him water lilies floated like green clouds. They were tethered to the muck on swaying cords of soft green. Another girl signed his name over the water, singing as she formed the letters.

Q: Is multiple fiction a new art form?

A: There is an absolute newness to it, but before I even talk about that, it seems important to point out that newnesses don't spring out of nothing. Newnesses are, in fact, a result of successive attempts and experiments. It seems obvious that throughout the twentieth century, there has been an attempt on the part of various writers to open up the ability of the story to talk to itself, to talk to its readers, to contain multitudes. For instance, James Joyce, Gertrude Stein, Virginia Woolf. The computer has not created these media as much as enabled them. There has been this longing for multiplicity and complexity throughout the twentieth century.

That said, the absolute newness that I think exists here is that—here let me digress a minute. . . . There is an odd backlash going on now in the mainline culture where, with the advent of the Web, hypertextuality is establishing itself as a cultural reality. I find colleagues and literary critics saying, "Well look, the book did all this. The book can do all this. The book sustains multiple stories and can reflect consciousness and do all the things that you want to claim as unique to hypertext." What the book doesn't do—and that is the newness here—is change every time you read it. I mean literally change the presentation of the text in a way that a very complex disk-based hypertext fiction does. Even Web fictions, which have less complexity yet have the advantage of being increasingly universally available; any reader on two successive occasions reading the "same hypertext" will discover that the work presents itself differently. So that when you come to discuss your experience of reading a hypertext work such as *afternoon, a story* or the Web fiction *Twelve Blue,* with someone who has read it, one of the things you inevitably have to do is discuss with one another what your experience with the text was. What is it that you saw? What is it that you read?

Now I realize that if you put a few students together and ask them to read and discuss *Madame Bovery,* each of them will have had a different interpretation of the text too. If you ask them to explain their thoughts, they will point to different pages in a way that someone could argue that the reading changes depending on the reader. But, you wouldn't say to the group of readers, "Did you read page fifty-seven after reading page fifty-six?" In hypertext, you find yourself in that position. Did you see this screen? Did this happen? In my reading, this scene followed this, which made me think she was afraid. Someone else might say, "No, in my reading, the second scene came first and I found that she was much more confident."

These conversations sound vaguely gamelike when you first hear them, but they are actually very old literary questions—how we see character and how we see event. They are, in fact, the satisfactions of the form. What is it that sustains the form? What sustains them is the psychological reliability of knowing that as we view the events of our lives from multiple perspectives, they seem to show up differently.

Many Luddites and others in the academic community argue that our ever-increasing reliance on visual communication will kill the word. I don't think that's going to happen. The word now takes on a very interesting power. Words can do some things that images can't. Words in conjunction with images can do some things that neither can do alone.

Hypertext, like life, is subjunctive—as in, "it could have been otherwise." Had I only made this turn, my life would have been different. Our lives take on a certain sadness and a certain glory because when you choose one path, that means you haven't chosen another hundred.

Q: That reminds me of the famous stanza from Robert Frost's poem "The Road Not Taken":

> I shall be telling this with a sigh
> Somewhere ages and ages hence:
> Two roads diverged in a wood, and I—
> I took the one less traveled by,
> And that has made all the difference.

A: That is true. There could be someone down the other path who could be saying those same or similar words. That's what makes great stories. It's what keeps an audience coming back.

14

The Web and Popular Entertainment

Within the next few years, online interactive entertainment will make it big. When you mix a story with interaction, it creates the thrill of sports because no one knows what's going to happen. It's like improv with a worldwide audience.

SCOTT ZAKARIN

Bill Gates has never been accused of missing an opportunity to make a buck. So a lot of people got excited when Gates launched his new online "network" Microsoft Network (MSN), dedicated to harnessing the Internet's awesome potential for delivering products to bring entertainment in a myriad of interactive forms to a computer screen near you. The network was designed to carry loads of original programming. Didn't work out. MSN the network is already a distant memory in the nanosecond attention span of the digital world. Only the online service remains. Gates has folded his tent and gone home. A lot of investors who have tried to profit from Web-based entertainment were not suprised that the effort failed, though most everyone was unnerved at how quickly Gates decided to jump ship on the effort.

What are we to conclude from MSN's failure? Well, we shouldn't conclude from any single debacle that Web-based entertainment is dead. Not by a long shot. It's hard to imagine that somebody, someday isn't going to make a lot of money delivering entertainment products over the Web. After all, compared to the hundreds of channels, films, or tapes provided by competing systems, the Internet's capacity to provide variety is nearly endless. And by giving customers the capacity to interact with new products, the Internet would seem to have a clear advantage over older technologies.

But there are some problems. With time and money, the technical ones can be overcome. But the challenge to those who seek to bring new, interactive products over the Web may be more intransigent. Let's look at one or two technical concerns. Online technology does provide greater user control and access than any other previous entertainment/information medium, but the Internet's platform is not yet developed sufficiently to accommodate the demands of many products that consumers want online. An aircraft combat simulation over the Web, for example, can look like two perambulators negotiating corners in a park.

Bandwidth bottlenecks the Web. The bandwidth necessary to interact with a sci-fi serial featuring decent motion and sound and involving role-playing and combat simulation with multiple players in real time is huge. The rate of play for most gaming/role-playing/simulation products on the Web is slow, even at present rates of penetration. Play will move even more lethargically as new immigrants arrive on the Web's enticing virtual shores.

But technical problems related to capacity and speed we expect (perhaps optimistically) to be solved. Al Gore recently christened a program for academic institutions, nicknamed Abilene, which is dedicated to data compression and bandwidth technologies aimed at jacking up the flow rate of Web-borne information to 9.6 billion bytes per second. That rate would allow you to download all thirty volumes of the *Encyclopaedia Britannica* in one second! The notion is, of course, that if universities can develop this system and work out the bugs, then Abilene might become a future platform for all Web-based traffic.

That doesn't mean that the average household would benefit from the new technology. Present home-delivery technologies are completely inadequate for accommodating the Abilene pipeline. But setting aside the related problems that would have to be solved before an Abilene-like system could be accessed by folks in inner cities, suburbs, or farms, let's assume for purposes of this chapter that huge bandwidths will, at some point, be widely and cheaply available. If that's true, you certainly shouldn't have trouble finding a market.

According to Odyssey, Inc., the Web presently penetrates only about 23 percent of U.S. households. A 40 or 50 percent penetration seems likely in the not-distant future. Those consumers will be interested in new forms of entertainment, provided the product offered is convenient, reliable, and relatively inexpensive. Note that I say relatively inexpensive. We should remember that no one thought consumers would pay at all for television when it was available for "free" over the airwaves. But it only took multichannel TV twelve years (beginning in 1968) to achieve meaningful household penetrations of 30–45 percent nationwide. Market studies of radio's development, and also network television, demonstrate a similar evolution.

So let's suppose that the Net becomes the newest delivery boy on the block with tons of people eager to buy. Then we turn from technical issues to concerns related to product. If you're going to sell entertainment over the Net's platform, you'll need to develop products for which people will pay. As a distribution and delivery medium, the Internet has to compete for audience income and loyalty with every other broadcast medium: television, movies, games, videos, books, comics, CD-ROMs, and DVDs. Which brings us back to Bill Gates and MSN.

In spite of the Internet's potential, Web-based entertainment simply isn't taking off the way its prophets predicted. Simply put, audiences are small, product is fleeting, and profits are hard to come by. Even the major film studios— early on the most optimistic players in the Web-based entertainment game—are now reluctant to invest much in online properties without a clear line-of-sight business model or path to profitability.

But there's a joke about Hollywood. The joke is that a genius in Hollywood is the second guy to recognize a trend. It's obvious that this new frontier is a frontier. There are hazards around every corner. There are bound to be a lot of casualties along the virtual trail. But for those who persevere, a gusher, gold mine, or cattle drive has got to be out there somewhere.

So, if you're an interactive writer, what's the best way to homestead on this strange, new land? I'm going to suggest a very pragmatic approach. Start by learning what's already out there. Past chapters have outlined in some detail information related to interactive design, storytelling, and gaming. What we're going to do now is cite products where these lessons are applied. You're about to read excerpts from Web-savvy writers who are experiencing success in all areas of interactive writing and programming. These writers will describe samples of Web-based entertainment that they feel are worthwhile.

Learn from them.

But before discussing products on which writers work, I want to mention some places where Web-based entertainers are employed—places where *you* can work. We'll discuss some suggestions for story- and game-based Web entertainment that have legs. I'll be suggesting that you take a look at these producers and products. Bring your own original ideas into play, certainly, but test those ideas against what survives on the Web.

Let's suppose you like the idea of getting paid while you write entertainment product. Who'll hire you? To answer that question, we'll sample some producers, people you might write for. I'm talking about online networks, the ABC, NBC, and CBS of the Web.

Television networks hire more writers year in and out than all other dramatic media combined. Paul Palumbo is a man familiar with the virtual networks. Palumbo is a writer himself. His career has spanned the gamut from working as an analyst for Paul Kagan Associates to writing for Apple Computer, Inc., *Multimedia Wire,* and *Electronic Gaming News.* We interviewed Paul and he gave us this rundown of networks that are presently active in bringing product to the Internet.

Besides the big four networks—ABC, NBC, CBS, and Fox—there are numerous other online players, including:

- *AOL Studios* America Online (*www.aol.com*) is composed of three companies: AOL Networks (distribution and content), ANS Communications (technology, backbone facilities), and AOL Studios (composed of ImagiNation Network, Digital Cities, and Greenhouse Networks). Thrive (a joint venture of Time Warner and AOL) is a "channel" producing health, romance, or erotic content. The Hub is a Generation X–themed channel.

- *CityWeb (a.k.a. Warner Bros. Online)* CityWeb (*www.warnerbros.com*) is designed to be the first community-based, affiliate-centric online network of broadcast-TV stations. Warner Bros. Online's strategy is to partner with a leading news and information TV station in each market on an exclusive basis, and to syndicate content across those sites reaching in excess of 70 percent of the country. Warner Bros. Online is the production entity that feeds programming to CityWeb, and also self-distributes on the Web. Warner Bros. plans to utilize a television syndication model for CityWeb programming, producing content that appeals to the general broadcast-television audience.

- *Disney Online* Disney Online (*www.disney.com*) is creating an extensive channelized network of kids content based on franchise properties in the tradition of "living books." Disney.com is more promotional in nature, and acts as an aggregation point of related Web sites that make up a network of all things Disney (films, TV programs, and other media).

- *HBO.com* HBO.com (*www.hbo.com*) is an online entertainment network that naturally cobrands with HBO's premium cable network. HBO.com combines interactive promotions and extensions of HBO's television programming with original content made exclusively for the Web.
- *The Station@Sony.com* The Station@Sony.com (*www.sony.com*) is an online entertainment service that provides users a range of entertainment options from games to chat-based programming. Current entertainment partners include Columbia/TriStar Interactive, Sony Interactive Studios (producer of Playstation games), Sony Music, SonyWonder (kids entertainment), and Sony Signatures (product merchandising).
- *Universal Studios Online* Universal Studios Online (*www.universalstudios. com*) is a division of Universal Studio's New Media Group and is primarily in the business of taking existing company franchises and moving them in a new creative direction online. Universal Studios Online can draw on 3,500 different properties, thousands of music albums, its theme parks, and Location Based Entertainment (LBE) sites for content.
- *Warner Bros. Online* Warner Bros. Online (*www.warnerbros.com*) is a mass entertainment multiplex offering a range of content from feature films, television, music, animation, and original programming. The site contains promotional information about Warner Bros. properties as well as original elements that extend the franchise in an interactive way.
- *Women's Wire* Women's Wire (*www.womenswire.com*) is an Internet infotainment network deployed in electronic magazine (e-zine) format. The network specializes in programming for women. It has channels for news, style, work, body, buzz, cash, shop, and Beatrice's Web Guide. Current entertainment content partners include *Women's Sports and Fitness* magazine, Yahoo!, Columbia TriStar (movie copromotions and contests), CompuServe, match.com (dating service, cross-promotion, and traffic links), iChat, and Macromedia.

Okay, let's move from employers to product. Earlier chapters discussed the myriad shapes in which interactive material can be realized. Web entertainment borrows from all those paradigms. Let's start with Web-accessed entertainment that is story centered. To get a take on the quality of that interactive product, we contacted Harry Youtt. Youtt is the writer of the breakthrough pilot-season Web site for David E. Kelley's ABC television series *The Practice* (*www2.thepractice.com*). Youtt teaches conventional and hypertext courses in the UCLA Writers' Program and designed and taught that university's first online course.

"My assignments," says Youtt, "have included everything from a major entertainment Web site to design of law-firm Web sites, and consulting in development of a Web site to launch a newly branded automobile."

A successful and avowed enthusiast for Web-based entertainment and for interactive writing, Youtt explains: "Writing in conventional media is like serving a formal, several course meal, where the diners sit down and are served in the order the preparer decides, with portions the preparer doles out. There is an art to serving a formal meal, but the art of serving a buffet is entirely different. The presentation becomes important, but immediately the participants begin to enter into the process, choosing the order and combination of tastes, and the amount of each. They are free to return to the table whenever they wish and to focus only on what they have enjoyed. An entirely different sensation."

Youtt offers the interactive title *Stone Soup* as a product worthy of emulation. *Stone Soup* is designed for children. It begins when a couple of hungry soldiers come into a selfish town and announce in the town square that they are going to prepare the most scrumptious soup imaginable, using only water and three large stones. The townsfolk gather about, their curiosity piqued. With a fire built and a cauldron bubbling, one soldier announces that of course the soup would taste even better with an onion or two.

"Oh, I have some!" a townie offers and hurries off to get onions. In they go.

How about some carrots? Potatoes? Spot of beef? You get the idea. The soup is made, interactively, with the contributions of the user/townspeople and the virtual community they comprise.

Stone Soup sets a standard that Youtt does not often see met. When asked which Web sites he likes best, he replies, "Unfortunately there are not many. . . . Most television-show sites have become cookie-cutter billboards. Motion-picture Web sites have become showplaces of action graphics and self-important ad-agency design that may win prizes but will not truly engage the site visitor." Youtt sees this kind of tag-on product as a waste of time. He wants Web entertainment to aspire to something like *Stone Soup*, to "amplify the horizons presented by the core entertainment vehicle."

I was interested to note that "the core entertainment vehicle" that Youtt mentions is generally a noninteractive, archaic product to which interactive and digital product is attached. Youtt's television-related site offers a familiar example; an established noninteractive, videotaped platform, *The Practice*, makes Youtt's interactive product possible and viable. *Titanic*, to offer a current example, drags a raft of related Web sites in its celluloid wake. This sort of thing is common. Even radio spawns Web sites. And this is a good thing for interactive writers because without an impetus from older media, a great many interactive opportunities would not exist.

This has all happened before. It's common to see product developed for one mode of distribution sponsoring that produced in another. We take for granted television networks' reruns of Hollywood movies. Those reruns generate revenue for television-originated programming, including the dreaded movie of the week. Cable-bound companies like HBO and Showtime do something very similar, using profits from Hollywood-generated films to fund cable-originated movies and programming.

The same kind of mix-and-match is bound to happen on the Web. It's interesting to me that most things I read assume the Web will always offer product in which the audience participates. I'd be very surprised if Internet technology does not one day offer noninteractive entertainment to be downloaded right alongside product that is user-participatory. In that scenario, a film or TV episode would be packaged with interactive games, sims, MUDs, and hypertexts of great variety. I can also see producers on the Web creating original programming that is noninteractive, straightforward, linear stories and episodes which will themselves be linked to interactive sidebars, thus offering the user opportunities to participate interactively or to become immersed in an uninterrupted narrative.

You can bet that the marketplace will force some kind of symbiosis between interactive and noninteractive producers. Just as revenues derived from reruns of celluloid product contribute to TV sitcoms and movie of the week, I can see product generated by the movie industry and television redistributed over the Net to create profits that Web producers will use to subsidize their own interactive and noninteractive projects.

What about the independent guy? Where is the cyber equivalent of the independent filmmaker? Right now independents in the virtual world have a hard time keeping a profitable audience. But as the Web becomes more entertainment friendly, that should improve. There will continue to be obstacles, of course. Stand-alone interactive products will probably always have a harder time finding solid niches in consumer psyches than products associated with some sort of core vehicle. And stand-alone interactive products are always going to represent a big risk for investors. After all, even when a product is acknowledged as good, it doesn't always succeed.

"There are some really creative people out there who are doing some incredibly fun and innovative stuff for the Web," asserts Deborah Todd. "Those are the ones who get me excited about online entertainment. Is there much opportunity? Sure, if you make it for yourself. In terms of writing for other sites, I think writers really have to search for those opportunities with the good sites, otherwise, well, who wants to write brochureware?

"I still believe that technology has some catching up to do, and I've seen some things coming that are very cool. Perhaps by taking new technology and creating around that, and also pushing the edges, we'll see some more things approaching the *wow* factor."

Take the case of *The Spot*. *The Spot* was arguably the most famous episodic Web site ever created. With its appealing cast of twentysomethings (all dimwitted and self-absorbed), *The Spot* generated an interactive, lightweight drama focusing on issues of sex and scandal. In its heyday, the program garnered more than 100,000 page hits and 560,000 server requests per day. As a Spotmate, users explored the daily diary entries of the show's characters soaking up gossip about friends, family, and their innermost fantasies. Voyeurism was predictably one of the product's main draws. This tendency in users was exploited cleverly. For instance, a request for bikini shots of lead character Michele Foster might lead to a connected episode finding Michele pondering life's challenges while lounging beachside in that same suit. Additionally, users could activate QuickTime movies, download photos, and send e-mail to favorite characters.

As with other popular cybersoaps like *East Village* or *Fernwood*, *The Spot* was popular largely becaused it delivered entertainment at a variety of levels. Narrative experience and interactive arenas were combined to create a virtual community of Spotmates. This was a good show. It received good notices and good critical reviews. But it didn't make money.

There are other online shows struggling to carve out a niche, build an audience, and generate revenue just like *The Spot* attempted to do many months back, extending in different ways concepts exploited by traditional television to the digital world. This list isn't extensive, but if you're wondering what kind of work you might find as a story-centered interactive writer, these titles represent a smattering of possibilities:

Neurostatica

Neurostatica (*brain.themarket.com*) is a multicharacter story set in a time-based environment. The story is twenty minutes long and features ten characters and forty locations. Every thirty seconds, the story progresses. The user is able to follow individual characters or go on his or her own journey. Since time always moves forward, being in one location means missing what is happening elsewhere. This is very similar to the *Tamara* model.

The user is rewarded for repeated viewings of *Neurostatica*, and, in fact, the only way to get to the über ending is to actually piece together "hints" from each of the ten interconnected story lines. Aside from multiple characters, the user discovers valuable plot points by interacting with the environments.

One of the most interesting things about the project is that the twenty-minute length provides two important elements to the experience: first, it ensures the dramatic semblance of the three-act structure, in that each of the story lines plays out over twenty minutes, and second, it fulfills the same type of "contract" that a sitcom makes with a viewer, in that it agrees to deliver a complete experience in a mutually agreed-upon time frame.

Online experiences that have no shape—that provide users with no sense of where they are in a story—will never work, so *Neurostatica* is valuable from the standpoint that it explores how to capture the bounded experience principles we get from TV. The project was created, directed, written, and designed by Douglas Gayeton; produced by Glenn Kaino; drawn by Steve Vance.

Plug In

Plug In (AOL keyword: plug in) is the premier teen site for original content on AOL, created in the low-income community of East Palo Alto in 1996 as an experiment to see what would happen if kids without previous access to computers and the Internet could be trained to not only master the technology, but use it to present ideas about themselves, their community, and the world around them. In eighteen months, the site has become a popular destination where teens get together to riff on the ideas that matter most to them.

It functions somewhat like a teen version of *Politically Incorrect*. Each week, the cast of twelve thirteen- to eighteen-year-olds choose a single theme and attack it in everything from interactive essays ("Rave and Rant") to chat rooms to highly provocative message boards.

Present plans now call to turn Plug In into a franchisable model that can be extended to other low-income communities. Creator and executive producer: Douglas Gayeton; creative director: Sheva Gross.

Waking Hours

Waking Hours is a project currently under development with AOL Australia. The show examines twenty-four hours in the interactive lives of twenty-four kids, with interactive Web pages designed and created by the teens themselves. Much like *Neurostatica*, it is both a highly structured, yet completely open architected experience. Creators and executive producers: Douglas Gayeton and Boxtop/IXL; creative director: Sheva Gross; producer and interface designer: Glenn Kaino.

Blue Funk

Blue Funk (*www.lafong.com*) is an interactive sitcom currently in development at MGM Interactive. It was developed both as an online program and as a traditional television show. Six HTML pages push the narrative forward; the remaining thirty-six are fantasies, wild metaphors, midstory digressions, cartoons, and comic songs that all spring organically from the linear movement of the user. Created by Michael Kaplan and John Sanborn.

Vanishing Point

Perhaps the largest online narrative ever attempted, *Vanishing Point* was funded by MSN and produced by Sunshine Digital. It is an inhabitable, fully navigable online world that documents over seventy-five years in the history of the "Circuit," the most mysterious drop-out culture in twentieth-century America.

To tell the interconnected story of over a hundred Circuit travelers, the project uses real audio (250 interviews, tapes, songs, etc.), graphics (paintings, drawings, woodcuts, etchings, murals, graphic novels, etc.) and writing (letters, diaries, journals, transcripts). In all, over five thousand pieces of content.

The only way for the user to experience the complete story is to travel around the online version of the Circuit and seek out individual pieces of content. Since all content is treated as a rare object, online travelers must actually barter with fellow travelers in order to assemble narrative. In other words, *Vanishing Point* is an online world where the stories are the currency. Creative director and interactive designer: Douglas Gayeton.

Notice that these products are all in some way narratively centered. This kind of programming is very ambitious, in many ways the most challenging kind of product to develop, and also the riskiest to finance. What other kind of product attracts interactive writers? Let's extend our sample from online stories to online games.

Our first guide in this new arena is Jeff Sullivan, president and a senior writer/designer at Digital Arcana, Inc. His background includes artificial intelligence research, screenwriting, game and computer journalism, and a lot of gaming. His interactive credits include *Spycraft: The Great Game, Planetfall II: The Other Side of Floyd, The Outer Limits Online,* and *Space: 1998 Online.* He's also presently developing products for both major studios and game publishers.

Sullivan's *Outer Limits* clearly fits the paradigm of an interactive product piggybacking on a previously existing, nondigital, and noninteractive product. Following are portions of an interview in which Sullivan described his thoughts on online gaming.

Q: What are your favorite multiplayer online games and what makes them so special?
A: Acrophobia, because it's easy to learn and gets you in there rubbing virtual elbows with others very quickly.

Quake/Quake II, because it only promises a "quick fix" for adrenaline junkies, and largely delivers what it promises.

NetStorm, because it's a beautiful and fun online game to play (although it's not especially an online-only game).

Q: I assume that The Outer Limits Online *was based on previously created material . . .*
A: Yes, it was based on an episode of the series called *Resurrection* by Chris Brancato. We started with the episode as our launching point, advanced the story a generation into the future, and then evolved things from there to create an interesting and balanced conflict between two basic "sides" in a war for survival.

Q: Can you compare the written documents you created for The Outer Limits Online *with those for* Spycraft?
A: The documents were about as different as night and day. For *Spycraft,* we knew the exact branches that the story could take, and laid them all out in exhaustive detail: each branch, option, object, character, and interaction was defined in advance.

For *The Outer Limits Online,* we can't possibly know exactly what the players will be doing, so instead of designing the game's story line, we had to design a collection of systems that players could use (e.g., the combat system, the exploration system, a game-world expansion system, an NPC [nonplayer character] interaction system) and then just set it all loose in the pot to see if it made soup.

Q: *How would you describe the underlying structure for* The Outer Limits Online? *Is the is "look and feel" of an online game generally different from a* CD-ROM *game?*
A: The underlying structure of *The Outer Limits Online* is a multiplayer role-playing game. As such, it has a large game world, a variety of NPCs [nonplayer characters], and a loose collection of story lines driven by NPCs and player characters.

There are CD-ROM games (and by this, I assume you mean single-player games, since *The Outer Limits Online* is going to ship on a CD-ROM, as many online games do) that have this same framework, and there are CD-ROM games that are entirely different. I don't think that any hard-and-fast rules can be drawn between stand-alone and online games, except that multiplayer is much more prevalent in online games, since, by definition, you've already got the network connection required.

Jeff Sullivan sees multiplayer games as being the backbone of Web-based entertainment. Marc Saltzman would undoubtedly agree. Saltzman wrote an article for the Cable News Network (February 11, 1998) in which he reminds us that when you think of Web-based gaming, you absolutely *must* think in terms of global interaction. A boy in Boston might engage a grandfather in Pakistan. The Web crosses all borders, generations, and tastes; its growth has spawned a huge digital playground, connecting players with a PC and modem to playmates from all corners of the globe. And gamers today enjoy a multitude of choices tailored to any taste: "head-to-head action blastfests, strategic resource management, tactical troop formation, fast-paced sports games, fictitious worlds filled with magic and mayhem, battles in space or over war-torn skies"—not to mention chess, solitaire, and *Scrabble®*.

Saltzman's article goes on to describes a variety of gaming products used on the Web today, such as *Quake, You Don't Know Jack,* and *Ultima Online.* These are excellent examples; the kind of product that new or veteran writer/designers can use as models to emulate.

Let's take a quick look at some popular online games.

- *You Don't Know Jack* is the quiz show where high culture and pop culture collide.With wall-to-wall studio sound effects and original music, *You Don't Know Jack* and its sarcastic host will whisk you from the green room to prime time at a pace so fast it'll chap your lips. Get the question right and score some cash; get it wrong and pay the price.
- *Quake* From a first-person point of view, *Quake* players explore a wild collection of gothic/industrial mazes, consisting of hallways, moats, ramps,

catwalks, elevators, and secret rooms—and kill everything in sight.

- *Ultima Online* is a magical world of spells and monsters, quests and heroes. It's a living, growing world where thousands of players from around the globe discover fantasy and adventure twenty-four hours a day, every day of the year. Chat with other players in real time. Dialogue appears directly onscreen above the speaking character, not in a separate chat window. With its own virtual economy and ecology, *Ultima Online* is unmatched in realism.

- *Hellbender* is a multiplayer online game for up to eight players. You enter the twenty-ninth century and the Bions—violent cyborgs—are on the attack. The Coalition of Independent Planets needs your help! You and your Hellbender™ attack craft must deliver the final blow to the Bions.

- *Lords of the Realm II* is a multiplayer experience that immerses you in the harsh world of thirteenth-century England: where life is held cheap and conflict is epic. In this world, reality is harsh, peace rare, and combat brutal! Rise to become king—brutally defeat your enemies, conquer neighboring realms, and build your empire on their remains.

- *Trophy Bass II* In this multiplayer fishing simulation, you challenge your fishing buddies online in a frantic race to find the best spot, the best lure, and land the best fish before time runs out. Play on any of ten lakes, each featuring photographical and topographical maps, accurate depth readings, structure, lily pads, stumps, snags . . . the works. Get over one hundred tips from top bass pros in smooth, full-motion video.

Marc Saltzman's prognosis for gaming on the Web is very optimistic: "as modem speeds climb, with ISDN, cable, and ADSL becoming the new speed standards in the short years ahead, it looks like this next generation of 'multiplayer gaming' will continue to soar well into the next century."

That's probably a good note on which to end this discussion. What you've seen in this chapter are models for you to emulate. Whether you find yourself moved to online programming, story-centered material, hypertext, or games, these titles comprise a reading list you ought to sample. Past chapters have detailed principles related to the design and aesthetics of interactive texts. With these titles, you can see how those abstract principles get applied.

But you have to start. You have to get your feet wet. Get on the Net. Log onto an entertainment network. There's a place for you in there somewhere—it's time to find out where.

15

Paul Is Dead: The MGM Online Series

A detective novel is a story about a story. The detective novel is a story about somebody working backwards with pieces of evidence to recreate another story, which is the murder or the mystery or whatever. In interactivity, it's a story about a story also. The user enters a new experience and has to piece together all the given objects, the clues and all of the information which is embedded in that story. It is your mission to reconstruct a plot which is a reasonable facsimile of the über, or higher arcing story that you've entered.

DOUGLAS GAYETON

aul Is Dead is an episodic murder mystery designed to be experienced over the World Wide Web. It was created by Michael Kaplan and John Sanborn; written by Michael Kaplan, Todd Krieger, and John Sanborn; directed by John Sanborn; produced by Leda Maliga and Scott Schaffer (MSN); and executive produced by Ken Locker (MGM) and Bob Bejan (MSN). The series is scheduled to debut on MGM's Web site in 1998 (*www.mgm.com*).

In this original series, players use their cursors to roll over elements on the screens to reveal links and clues, so you can help the series's lead character (and reluctant detective) Elly Clyde solve the mystery. Did rock legend Paul Lomo drown? Or was he murdered?

The series was produced as a thirteen-week series, not unlike a standard television series. However, *Paul Is Dead* is *not* television. It's more like a deconstructed narrative that invites the audience to actively navigate the experience. Using Macromedia Flash animations, crisp graphics, witty dialogue, hidden clues, red herrings, and alternative Web sites built into the series, *Paul*

Is Dead is the realization of next generation, Web-based entertainment. Players can in no way affect the outcome of the story, but they are able to forge their own paths through each week's episode, and, in the process, help Elly Clyde solve a dastardly crime.

Creating the Series

We sat down with Michael Kaplan, cocreator of *Paul is Dead*, to learn more about this breakthrough interactive series.

Q: How did you first go about creating Paul Is Dead?
A: I didn't want to get into a situation with *Paul Is Dead* where we would let people dictate the outcome of the story. After MGM optioned the project, John Sanborn and I were contracted by Microsoft Network to follow a television production model with thirteen weeks of programming that was refreshed five days a week. I'll be damned if I was going to start spinning out parallel scenarios that had cookie programs charting where each user is in the story. That would have been much too difficult. More to the point, I don't think anyone would have cared. You can't make the assumption that with online anybody will start the story over to see what kind of variations they get. I think people are wondering, How much longer do I want to be here? or How soon can I get out of here?

With *Paul Is Dead*, you've got the main character moving forward in real time, interviewing people and trying to piece together the clues in a murder mystery. As the story unfolds, it opens up a cultural paper trail: the albums, the songs, the e-mail messages, the Web sites, and the newspaper clippings. At the same time, there are mock Web sites, alternative worlds on the Web, that tangentially intersect with the story. The whole project had a great multimedia feel to it.

Paul Is Dead invites the user to go in as deep as they want to. If all you want to do is experience a new episode, you can call up the episode and watch the linear, animated story unfold on your screen. If from there you choose to travel deeper into the program and interact with some of the archived material, or visit the alternate Web sites, you can do that too.

Paul Is Dead is an attempt to play with the medium. We used many of the communication tools people are becoming familiar with as part of the story. What frustrates me about many online stories is that they feel constrained by the metaphor. For example, if people are reading a story online, 90 percent of the time they are reading from a character's journal. That's what *The Spot* did. And every cybersoap that came after that mimicked their presentation style. Developers then began to realize that Web stories could be like books. Our feeling was, online stories can be a lot like the Internet.

Analyzing the Series

The story unfolds every day through new scenes of streaming audio and still pictures. These scenes will play by themselves, giving you new story information, clues, and backstory. At the end of each week, a cliff-hanger will make you think over the weekend about what happened and what to do next. Attached to each scene are links to related screens, which contain more clues and information, and related alternate Web sites, run by characters within the story (see fig. 15.1).

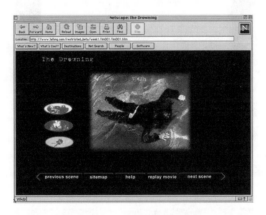

Fig. 15.1. Screen shot from the opening scene of *Paul Is Dead,* created by John Sanborn and Michael Kaplan. TM and Copyright by MGM. Reprinted by permission.

Navigation Bar

You can access all *Paul Is Dead* material from the navigation bar at the bottom of each scene. Using the navigation bar, you can get to the next scene, return to the previous scene, or link to related screens or related alternate Web sites (see fig. 15.2).

Getting Involved

From the start, use your mouse and cursor to roll over elements on the screen. This will reveal links and clues, some of which are hidden. As you move deeper

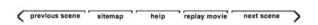

Fig. 15.2. Navigation bar (navbar) from *Paul Is Dead,* written and designed by John Sanborn and Michael Kaplan. TM and Copyright by MGM. Reprinted by permission.

into the story, you will be visited by characters who will want to chat with you via pop-up screens. Don't be afraid to chat—you may learn valuable information, clues, and secrets from them. And you'll want to visit the bulletin boards and chat areas of the alternate Web sites to hunt for clues, and discuss the intrigue that will grow deeper every week (see figs. 15.3 and 15.4).

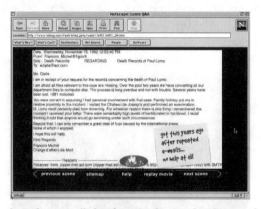

Fig. 15.3. Screen shot of an e-mail clue from *Paul Is Dead,* written and designed by John Sanborn and Michael Kaplan. TM and Copyright by MGM. Reprinted by permission.

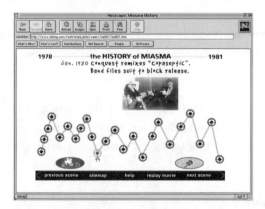

Fig. 15.4. The history of Miasma—an interactive time line, from *Paul Is Dead,* created by John Sanborn and Michael Kaplan. TM and Copyright by MGM. Reprinted by permission.

Related Materials

Like any good detective story, you never know what bit of information is a clue you need to pay attention to . . . and what's just a red herring (see fig. 15.5).

Fig. 15.5. Screen shot of hidden audio clues from *Paul Is Dead,* created by John Sanborn and Michael Kaplan. TM and Copyright by MGM. Reprinted by permission.

Paul Is Dead contains links to numerous alternate Web sites, which will pop up as new browser windows when clicked on by the user. To return to the main story, users simply close the separate browser window (see fig. 15.6).

Fig. 15.6. Screen shot of an alternative Web site from *Paul Is Dead,* created by John Sanborn and Michael Kaplan. TM and Copyright by MGM. Reprinted by permission.

Site Map

A site map is also available so that you can go anywhere within the boundaries of the story you've seen so far. As the days go by, this will be very important as you will need to review material, listen again to songs, and match one

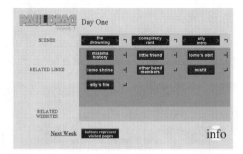

Fig. 15.7. Day One site map from *Paul Is Dead,* created by John Sanborn and Michael Kaplan. TM and Copyright by MGM. Reprinted by permission.

person's version of the story against another's. Who's lying? And why? (see fig. 15.7).

The Flowcharts

The two-part flowchart that follows was created by the writers using StoryVision, an interactive writing and flowchart tool for Macs and PCs (see figs. 15.8 and 15.9).

As StoryVision cocreator, John Vourlis explains, "StoryVision provides writers with the tools and space to create a diagram or flowchart of an interactive product, which is the first thing you really need to do when you write for interactive. Writer's need to be able to create some kind of graphical outline of the story to complement the text. StoryVision allows writers to connect that flowchart directly to the text—and attach text files to each node of the flowchart."

The Script

The screenplay for *Paul Is Dead* is organized into weekly episodes, thirteen episodes in all. Each episode is further subdivided into daily segments, and each day is even further subdivided by "theme" or "location"—each of which reveals bite-sized nuggets of rich, interactive content to the user.

The page format is similar in look and feel to a conventional Hollywood feature film screenplay. However, it's more modularly organized than a standard linear screenplay. It really has to be. This is an interactive experience! And although the story has been precreated by the writers and cannot be altered by the user, no two users will experience the flow of tangible interactive events in exactly the same sequence. In other words, the story events are organized

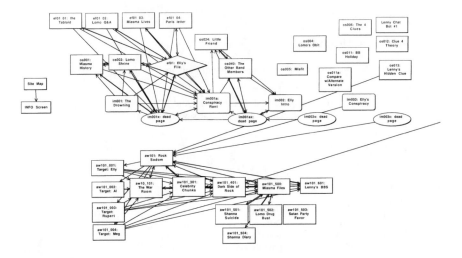

Fig. 15.8. Day One site map from *Paul Is Dead,* created by John Sanborn and Michael Kaplan. TM and Copyright by MGM. Reprinted by permission.

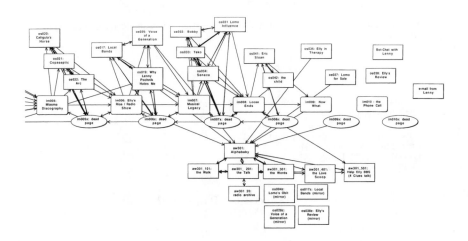

Fig. 15.9. Day One site map from *Paul Is Dead,* created by John Sanborn and Michael Kaplan. TM and Copyright by MGM. Reprinted by permission.

MONDAY

im001: The Drowning

Burst of rock music as we see the close-up shot of Paul, underwater, bubbles a-bubbling...

ELLY (V.O.)
Yes sir. One genuine dead rock star. And MY all-time personal fave. Can you guess who it is?

Giant question mark.

ELLY (V.O.)
Its not Jimi, not Janis, not even that other Paul...

ELLY (V.O.)
Nooooo.... You gotta go way back, early 80's. They were ahead of their time then... but they're red hot right now. A crazy band called: Miasma.

Icon for Miasma History (os001) appears, along with images of the band in their glory, focus on Paul...

ELLY (V.O.)
October 21st, 1981. Their lead singer, Paul Lomo, drowns mysteriously hours after the final mixes on what is now considered a rock and roll masterpiece.

Icon for Paul Lomo shrine (os002) appears. Image of "The Arc" on screen.

We see the murder sequence played out, hands being stepped on and Paul being kicked in the head.

ELLY (V.O.)
People say it was an accident. They whisper that he jumped. But I know...he was *pushed*.

He floats face down in the water. This dissolves into...
The tabloid headline.

Linked to: im001a: Conspiracy Rant
Linked to: os001: Miasma History
Linked to: os002: Lomo Shrine
Linked to: ef01: Elly's File

PID Week 1 - Revised Beta Draft -10/8/97 - Page 5
MONDAY

Fig. 15.10. Sample page from the interactive screenplay *Paul Is Dead*, created by John Sanborn and Michael Kaplan. TM and Copyright by MGM. Reprinted by permission.

modularly, into themes and locations, because of the nonlinearity of the content.

The screenplay for *Paul Is Dead,* episode one, Monday, starts off with the following phrase:

```
im001: The Drowning
```

For those of you with a background in feature film screenplay formats, this phrase is essentially the script's "slugline." Kaplan, Krieger, and Sanborn label this phrase a bit differently, with "im001" being the name that identifies each fragment of the piece and "The Drowning" being the title of a segment. The title alerts us that we've moved onto the next "beat" almost like a chapter heading and when users look at the time line, they can see the division of information. The abbreviation "im" refers to "interactive movie," and the content of that movie is "The Drowning" (see fig. 15.10).

The names and titles were developed early on in the design process of the series, as the writing team created structure before dialogue. As John Sanborn explains, "We actually lay out screens of information (what is an *im, os,* or *aw*) as the first collaborative writing step."

- "OS" means off story—tangential pieces that almost allow you to annotate the story as you go
- "AW" means alternate web site
- "EF" means Elly's file
- "QA" means question-and-answer segments
- "SR" means story repository—used with the conquest records vault

After the structure, names, and titles are agreed upon, the writers next go on to write the visuals—the text and images that appear onscreen—followed by Elly Clyde's voice-over narration. The entire first page of text that Kaplan, Krieger, and Sanborn have fashioned for *Paul Is Dead* essentially describes the streaming Flash animation sequence that launches the series—a thirty-second montage of text, images, sound, and music.

Flash animation is an ideal choice for Web entertainment such as *Paul Is Dead* for several reasons:

- The movie files are small ("The Drowning" is only 153K!), which makes them ideal for delivery over the Web.
- They are downloaded into your browser's cache in real time, which means that you can view the animations as they are downloading, rather than downloading the file and viewing it later.

- They pack a creative punch (they are more like television than magazines).
- They are interactive, therefore the user can do things with them that they can't do with the media used on the vast majority of Web sites on the Internet.
- They allow the writer to show rather than simply tell a story. Most other Web sites are too text-heavy. Users don't like to read a lot of screen copy. They would rather see and do things.

Sanborn, Krieger, and Kaplan refer to this animated sequence as an interactive movie. As "The Drowning" movie ends, the screen becomes a static page—like any other standard Web page you might find on the Net (see fig. 15.1). The writers have labeled this type of static Web page a "dead page."

The dead page for "The Drowning" contains three "roll over" icons to the left of the screen: "Miasma History," "Elly's File," and "Lomo Shrine." There is also a navigation bar at the bottom of the screen made up of five links: previous scene, site map, help, replay movie, and next scene. When a user's cursor rolls over any of these eight hot links, a hyperlink is activated.

For example, if a user where to roll over the Lomo Shrine icon, it would highlight to reveal the words "Lomo Shrine," identifying itself visually as a link. Clicking on the icon would transport the user to a new node—the Lomo Shrine page (see fig. 15.11).

Five new icons appear on the Lomo Shrine page that the user has never seen before: "Poet," "Rock Star," "Bad Boy," "Drug Addict," and "Dead Man."

Fig. 15.11. Screen shot of the Lomo Shrine page from *Paul Is Dead*, created by John Sanborn and Michael Kaplan. TM and Copyright by MGM. Reprinted by permission.

os002: Lomo Shrine

| The Five Acts of the Life of Paul Lomo

POET: At Bard College, Paul Lomo enters a "poetry slam" and blows everyone away with his beat-era influenced verse and leather pants. The girls swoon, the boys glare and Paul learns to play the guitar.

ROCK AND ROLL STAR: Fame comes hard and fast to Lomo. And he loved it at first. The women, the money, the power. But he ended up hating it all. Except the women.

ANGRY YOUNG MAN: When Conquest Records remixed "Copasceptic" and released a butchered version, Lomo went nuts. How could the record company so misunderstand his vision? And how could the public BUY such trash? Paul drives a truck into the lobby of the Frank Gehry designed building. "Good architecture" he muttered.

DRUG ADDICT: It started with booze and ended with what would now be called heroin chic. Paul claimed to have kicked his habit with Shanna a month before their deaths, but if there was one thing that Paul Lomo knew, it was his image.

DEAD MAN: Buried in Golden Gate Headlands Cemetery (where Jerry Garcia and Stanley Jenkins were laid to rest), Lomo's grave becomes a shrine for fans of several generations, who leave tokens on his tombstone. Lomo would have HATED the woods.

Linked to: im001a: Conspiracy Rant
Linked to: os001: Miasma History
Linked to: im001x: dead page
Linked to: ef01: Elly's File

PID Week 1 - Revised Beta Draft -10/8/97 - Page 9
MONDAY

Fig. 15.12. Sample page from the interactive screenplay *Paul Is Dead,* created by John Sanborn and Michael Kaplan. TM and Copyright by MGM. Reprinted by permission.

As the user rolls over these icons with his or her cursor, text descriptions of each icon appear onscreen.

Fig. 15.12 is taken from the page in the *Paul Is Dead* screenplay that corresponds to the Lomo Shrine screen shot shown in fig. 15.11.

Notice the name and title at the top of the page:

```
os002: Lomo Shrine
```

What does this phrase signify? Well, "os002" is the name and *os* stands for off story—a sequence that is "off" the main track of the story line, and is an aside to the *im* or interactive movie. Get it?

Let's look at two more pages from the *Paul Is Dead* screenplay that correspond to Elly's File (see figs. 15.13 and 15.14).

Paul Is Dead cocreator Michael Kaplan recaps the behind-the-scenes business history of this highly innovative interactive series:

> When MGM initially sold *Paul Is Dead* to the Microsoft Network (MSN), John Sanborn and I were contracted to write, design, and produce the series. We felt like we were getting a chance to build a Cadillac. We were well paid for our work and Microsoft was not terribly worried about the business model. I don't think we will see the likes of that again. In fact, Microsoft later closed down MSN as a production/distribution entity and signed over the series to MGM. They took a tax write-off on the project. MGM is now responsible for generating advertising and marketing support for the series. They plan to launch the series in 1998. MGM is in a win-win situation because they didn't have to fund the production of the series. It's the *Masterpiece Theater* business model. Too bad all interactive projects aren't funded this way!

ef01: Elly's File

A cork board with various clippings and pictures and post-its forming a clutter that will grow larger and larger with each passing week.

Every item that appears on the board is hot. On the bottom of the screen is the following text:

These are odds and ends I've been collecting about this case over the years. Maybe I'm building a theory. Maybe I don't know how to throw anything away.

Linked to: im001x: dead page
Linked to: im001a: Conspiracy Rant
Linked to: os002: Lomo Shrine
Linked to: os001: Miasma History
Linked to: ef01_01: the Tabloid
Linked to: ef01_02: Lomo Q&A
Linked to: ef01_03: Miasma Lives
Linked to: ef01_04: Paris letter

PID Week 1 - Revised Beta Draft -10/8/97 - Page 10

MONDAY

Fig. 15.13. Sample page from the interactive screenplay *Paul Is Dead,* created by John Sanborn and Michael Kaplan. TM and Copyright by MGM. Reprinted by permission.

ef01_01: the Tabloid

LOMO IS NO MO!!

Bordeaux, August 7

"Live fast, die young, and bury a good-looking corpse."

Paul Lomo-- lead singer, sex idol, bacchanalian beast--and as of late Sunday evening...drowning victim. Wild stories of all night drug parties, communal orgies and sacrificial burnings had been circulating on both sides of the Atlantic as the final tracks were being laid down for what was to be the definitive MIASMA release. Holed up in their Southern France stronghold, Chateau De Jossigny, the band had been in a headlong effort to finish what had been a difficult string of sessions.

As band member Bobby Jared put it just two weeks ago in this very paper, "We need a little r 'n' r, right? Just too much crap flying 'round up in Paris, had to go get ourselves some quiet..." Well the silence is now resounding as their number one draw and front man is now six feet under with no forwarding address.

No details have yet come forward from the authorities, though Francois Michel from the local Department du Mort had these words to share, "We have learned from close associates of Mr. Paul Lomo that very early this morning his body was discovered face down in the Olympic sized pool behind the Chateau de Jossigny. While the matter is currently how do you say *"en train de recherché"* , under investigation, it is the departments belief that Mr. Lomo's drowning was an accident--no evidence of foul play has been unearthed." The police however have not said whether they will perform an autopsy and for that matter, did not indicate in any way that they had viewed the deceased.

(A post-it or hilight marker shows the following comment from Elly: WHY NOT? IS THERE A COVER-UP? IS THERE A BODY!!??)

Still one can't help but wonder what strange happenings might have been occurring in the French countryside. Lomo's passing follows closely on the heels of another fatal accident ending in tragedy, the death dive of 19 year old Shanna Mason, groupie, girlfriend and plaything du moment, who expired just one month prior. Since exploding on the scene with "Caligula's Horse", MIASMA has been consistently in the headlines, if not for their music than for their outlandish off-stage antics.

A button on the bottom of the screen says: More Files

Linked to: im001a: Conspiracy Rant
Linked to: ef01: Elly's File
Linked to: im001x: dead page

Fig. 15.14. Sample page from the interactive screenplay *Paul Is Dead,* created by John Sanborn and Michael Kaplan. TM and Copyright by MGM. Reprinted by permission.

16

The Reconstructed Text

Interactivity is something that draws you in and makes you a participant. Like *Myst*. The visuals make it really intriguing. You're sucked into
the environment and made to explore it. I know people who are totally
hooked on *Myst*. People who actually did not go to their jobs for days.
There's something very compelling about discovering the story.

CAROLYN MILLER

In his book *Deconstruction: Theory and Practice*, Christopher Norris rightly warns that "deconstruction" should not be viewed as a system, method, or settled body of ideas. Instead, the deconstructivists, working out of a profound skepticism for the possibility of discovering truth or meaning in language, act as critical watchdogs, preventing those pragmatic, "Anglo-American" academics from absorbing and homogenizing new, fresh, radical theories into existing moderate and tame ones. Done well, the deconstructivist is still bound to use reason and logic and textual analysis to say something about a story, film, or text that provides worthwhile insight and understanding.

But because deconstruction's method explicitly denies any assumed correspondence between mind and meaning, because it is hostile to the idea of "meaning" at all, and because it rigorously attacks critics who respect these notions (which includes practically anyone who wrote before the sixties), deconstructive projects can be completely irresponsible, or simply nihilistic, claiming exemption from any "older" critique and feeling no responsibility to relate specific textual concerns to an existential, human condition.

In practice, writers don't deconstruct texts, they analyze them. A critic's analysis will certainly reflect the person's notion of ontology, his or her personal life, ideology, culture, and so on. But we don't really need the new word "deconstruction" to describe this practical, day-to-day activity. The word "analyze" should suffice. Critics and theories analyze texts and themselves—endlessly. So what I'm about to do is offer a short analysis of an interactive text.

I am not picking a fight with the postmoderns and deconstructionists when I use the word "reconstruction." I'm just using the word in its ordinary definition! That is, I am seeking nothing other than to describe its completely mundane implications.

If I construct a house of cards on my kitchen table, then knock it down, and then decide I want to build the house anew, I must *reconstruct* it. But how? There are fifty-two cards. Were I a better mathematician, or poker player, I suppose I could say that with these cards we have fifty-two to the *n*th power of possibilities for a new house. But I don't want the *n*th power house. I want *my* house. So how do I reconstruct my house, my first house, with all the cards arranged in exactly the same way? Moreover, how do I recover that first thrill when, having placed the final card, I realize, "This is it! This is my house!" How do I put all that back together?

The real answer is—I can't. Even if by some miracle I succeed in resurrecting my house, the experience that came when I looked at that house on my table and said, "Wow! This is it! This is the one I want!" can never be the same because I can never fully recover that first, seminal, naïve activity nor recover that first spontaneous flush of pleasure that came when I created my card-thin castle.

But I can try.

I can, to use Owen Barfield's words, "save the appearances." I can recover some vestige, if only a penumbra, of the experience I had when first I realized I had created my perfect house of cards. The recovery of original meaning, anathema to any deconstructivist, continues to drive, entertain, and instruct human beings. It is definitely a powerful element which attracts users to the most popular, by far, interactive text.

Myst and its follow-on *Riven* find their genesis in Rand and Robyn Miller who, with a handful of loyal cohorts, began work in the rural outskirts of Spokane, Washington. One of the first decisions the makers of *Myst* made was that their text would develop from a classic linear story, a story with a beginning, a middle, and an end, which would underlay and be completely consistent with their interactive environment, but which would also be, for the most part, invisible.

The sand these authors threw into the digital game was that they didn't *tell* anybody, certainly not the user, that there was a story at all. They didn't even tell the user that he or she was supposed to be looking for a story, or that a story lay somehow at the end of the cybertunnel.

The first thing you see when you pop the *Myst* CD into you computer is a book. Clicking the book casts you inside the pages—into a fantastic, meticulously graphed environment. What do you do next? You look around.

There is nothing to *tell* you what to do, nor even if there *is* anything to do. All you know is that there are a hell of a lot of cards scattered on this table and you have no idea whether a house ever existed at all, nor that your real purpose for being here is to find that house, card by card, and reconstruct it entirely.

Myst can be a frustrating experience. Many, many people never get past the first challenges or puzzles that would allow them to discover Atrus's narrative—the house of cards, so to speak—that lies deeply beneath. Lots of people simply give up. Other people are content to simply stay in the environment, letting the game/story/puzzle/cryptogram lead them endlessly through a world that, as played, increasingly begins to betray the existence of order and purpose beneath.

Older media construct stories for us to hear. *Myst* constructs a story for you to discover. But you never get all the cards at once. You have to first of all figure out that you're supposed to be looking for something! And then, not yet knowing what it is, you inhabit this exotic, fantastically arrayed world, looking for clues.

But unlike most hypertexts, the clues in *Myst* and *Riven* lead to closure. Once that cat is out of the bag, the trick is then to see if the world extends from that closed point to someplace else. It does, of course. The story's conceit that marvelously written books give their authors access to other times and worlds leads to complications, power struggles, heroes and villains, and on to other stories, as well integrated as Tolkien, where one episode, leading to the next, arrives to meet or trigger an even larger story.

Get back *NYPD Blue.* Go home soap opera. *Myst*'s narrative is super-serial, episodic by ages and eras. Its scattered clues, coffers, icons, mirrors, weapons, and paraphernalia at least as associationally complex as any hypertext's, but at this text's deep center, there beats a heart of order.

A narrative and linear order, in fact, was from *Myst*'s genesis its creators' credo. Quoting Rand Miller, "When you're working on children's software, you can draw the door first without knowing what goes behind it. But with *Myst*, there was an enormous amount of planning to ensure that everything was tight and consistent."

At this point I'd like to give you an idea what the reconstruction of *Myst*'s world feels like from a *user's* point of view. The following excerpts do not come from the makers of *Myst*. There is no official sanction of the remarks you're about to read. What we've done is simply download an enthusiastic user's remarks, which give his impressions of the world of *Myst*.

We're only going to produce an excerpt of this experience, just enough, I hope, so that you can see how this text takes you from a mere experience of environment to the *hint* that some kind of story waits to be reconstructed beneath. Encounter *Myst* in a user's words:

The Myst Journals

1. Arrival

I felt a cold chill run through my body. Not terribly cold, but cold enough to bother me. The only other feeling was a dull ache in my head. I usually only feel like this when I sleep in an uncomfortable position. . . .

Sleep?

I lifted my head up, only to bring about a jarring sensation similar to a hangover. I looked around my surroundings. I had fallen asleep . . . on a shipping dock.

I attempted to slowly lift my body up from the ground, fighting muscle fatigue and the ringing inside my ears. I could hear seagulls in the distance and the ocean gently breaking on the dock I had rested on.

Where am I? How the heck did I get here?

There was only one ship at the dock, and I doubt that I could've arrived here on it. It had sunken to the point where only the lookout mast was sticking above the surface of the water. It looked as if water had slowly crept through the bottom of the hull, bringing the mighty vessel to its knees.

I managed to get myself in an upright position and gave my surroundings a quick once over. At the other end of the dock was a staircase spiraling up the base of a hill, leading up to a giant monument of some sort. By the base of the stairway was a podium with a large electrical switch on it, like you'd see in an old industrial fuse box.

To my left was a long retaining wall, with a walkway going alongside the top. On the other side of the walkway was a large building which resembled something out of ancient Greek architecture.

I'd better find out where I am.

I did a quick inventory of myself, making sure I wasn't the victim of a mugging from the night before. Satisfied that everything was in order, I decided to go about and find someone.

I walked up the stairs until I came to the very top, where the strange monument sat. I now noticed that it resembled a large gear wheel, half buried into the ground, and another gear laying on its side. Next to it was a podium similar to the one at the base of the stairs.

From here, I could see a great deal around me. I could see the first building, with another one along side it. The second building seemed to burrow deep into a mountain where a strange looking tower stood. I could also see the sunken ship, and what appeared to be a small forest surrounding one particularly massive tree that blocked the rest of my view. Wherever I was, I certainly didn't remember coming to this place.

I continued looking around, and I suddenly realized that I was on an island. In almost all directions, all I could see was ocean, and from my high vantage point I was getting a good strong whiff of the sea air blowing in from the south side of the island (assuming that the far side of the island was south). How the bloody hell did I get here?

I walked halfway down the steps and then along the concrete retaining wall. At the other end was another set of steps leading around to the front of the first building. From there, I followed a path that was made out of wooden beams laid down across the ground. I was about to enter the first building when I noticed a note on the ground. It looked yellowed and crumpled, but I was still able to read what it said. . . .

Catherine,

I've left you a message of utmost importance in our fore-chamber beside the dock. Enter the number of marker switches on this island into the imager to retrieve the message.

Yours,

Atrus

Who's Catherine? Who's Atrus? I put the note in my coat pocket and decided to try looking inside the two buildings.

The Myst Journals: The Arrival, by Chris Josephes. Copyright 1997. Reprinted by permission.

What greatly interests me about this user's remarks is the obvious fact that, at the outset, he has no idea what, where, or how this environment is to be engaged. Even the makers of *Myst* and *Riven* can only say, "look around." Notice the user's reactions to the environment are at first only practical, "Where am I? How the heck did I get here?" And later on, "I'd better find out where I am."

The dominant ego in these opening passages is the user himself. Note how often the word "I" occurs in these remarks. There is clearly a separation between text and user, here. A deliberate and careful boundary. But at specific junctures that changes. And it changes when the user encounters someone in the story besides himself. Then the user's identity vanishes. He's concerned now to know the other. "Who's Catherine? Who's Atrus?"

Our user has just dealt himself two very important cards. A story's plot can be seen as character in action. Atrus's note to Catherine is our user's first indication that this world is not simply an exotic place of plastic. He doesn't know, yet, that there is a story to reconstruct. But by knowing that Atrus's message is of the "utmost importance," he is motivated to keep looking, and if he keeps at it long enough, he'll find out. He'll discover the Miller brothers' story. He'll rebuild the house of cards. He will have saved the appearances of that first, seminal act.

Myst's story is buried in cyberspace. Most cybercritics looking at arenas like *Myst* or *Riven* see a clear divorce of digital storytelling from any other form, particularly stories in print. It's interesting to me that the creators of *Myst* and *Riven*, far from exhibiting that kind of hostility, create stories in print and in cyberspace that are intended for *the same audience.* There was no great leap of faith, here. The Miller brothers simply found *Myst's* users so enthusiastic over the narrative underpinnings of the CD world they created that they found it necessary, and profitable, to satisfy their audience's yearning for story by publishing ordinary, hard-paged books whose narratives precede, parallel, and anticipate the CD's cyberstory.

The first book in this series, *The Book of Atrus*, informs readers how Atrus, son of Gehn, learns the art of writing books that link to other ages. Backstory is supplied in this book, worlds that precede *Myst* are explored, and the book's story concludes at the point where the game starts. Similarly, *The Book of Ti'ana* and *The Book of D'ni* take characters on a complex, classic narrative that ties in, point for point, with the stories hidden in *Myst's* and *Riven's* cybergrammed procedures.

Indeed, once you pop your *Myst* CD into your computer, the first thing you see is a book. Books, and writing, are at the heart of this arena's concern, the art of writing, in fact, is posited as magic, an art that allows its author to travel between ages and worlds. That's a dangerous power to have, of course. And real jeopardy ensues for the characters who delve into *Myst's* dark secrets.

It's very chic for postmoderns to pen stories that, if weak on story, claim the serious purpose of self-examination as some kind of critical artifact. *Myst* manages to be self-reflexive *and* to tell a story. Its thematic concerns, we need to interject, are not those of Tolstoy or Toni Morrison. *Myst* doesn't pretend to interpret the human condition. Its story, for all the apparent parallels with Tolkien (the quest, good overcoming evil, the elements of magic and encryption), are only superficial. And that's fine! There's nothing wrong with creating a wonderful world of fantasy and escape.

The point ought to be made, however, that there's nothing to keep some cyberwriter from creating a world which, assembled and self-reflexive as *Myst's*, buries another kind of story that aims for a serious exploration and interpretation of the human condition. Would users want to spend the time to reconstruct such a story? I don't know. Users visit hypertexts that are no less complex and usually not as interesting as either *Myst* or *Riven*. What interactive writers ought to see in these very popular texts is a model for developing serious cyberliterature.

Clearly, a reconstructed text offers possibilities for serious writers as well as for those interested in science fiction or fantasy. *Myst* and *Riven* show the interactive writer that complex and associational stories do not have to dump linear narratives to be interesting or profound. In addition, these works show us that digitized stories can work in partnership with stories on the printed page to enhance a reader/user's immersion and pleasure.

But the Millers' creation also shows that plotting a story for worlds like those of *Myst* and *Riven* takes lots and lots of work. To use the excuse that one's text is "beyond narrative" is too often an excuse for either sloth or incompetence. You can create worlds that lead in all directions. If you want a *really* good story, find an honest way to tie those worlds together. The tighter you make your digital world and the stronger you make its stories and characters, the better your finished product will be.

IV.

Informational
Multimedia

17 Informational Multimedia, Education, and Training

We've been teaching writing for over 150 years. We started by looking at writing as a product. Then we changed our minds over a period of many years to think of it as a process. Now we have further defined our thinking to look at it as a collaborative, socially constructed process. Now there are some people among the writing faculty that are beginning to look at writing as a socially constructed environment in which collaborative writing can be facilitated easier and in many different ways using computer technology.

JOHN F. BARBER

We've spent a great deal of time discussing the practice and theory of bending digital technology to storytelling and gaming applications. But you don't have to work on Wall Street to see that some of the busiest interactive writers are those developing digitally based multimedia products that are intended to teach or train individuals or groups for just about anything you can imagine.

Training is expensive and businesses seeking to cut costs in this crucial area are turning to interactive designs for support. Manufacturers, professionals, and, increasingly, academic institutions have a huge need for digitally designed products that covers everything from Socrates to silicon chips. Multimedia products don't have to be digitally conceived, of course. Robert Heinich says that the generic term "multimedia" refers to "any combination of two or more media formats that are integrated to form an informative or instructional program."

The chief characteristic of multimedia products is that they engage more than one sense to stimulate learning. This idea isn't new. Comenius was an early pedagogue who, in the 1600s, applied theory to practice by developing a textbook for children that used both pictorial and verbal presentations as a teaching method.

What *is* new is the power of participation that the computer adds to other multimedia products—the ability to have a student, or professional, or dockworker interact with the material being presented onscreen. For all the reasons discussed in earlier sections, computers have huge advantages in this regard. They are able to supply vast quantities of information within a stimulating aural, graphic, and spatial environment while allowing the user to determine the pace or path of instruction.

Interactive writers can take advantage of learning theory as they design products for industry or academia. We now know that learning is a process best accomplished when *all* our senses are engaged. Sophomores retain more of a lecture's detail if the professor's remarks are accompanied by visual punctuation and repetition. Children with a hands-on experience of a science lab retain more information than do children who only hear the lab described or read about the lab in print. Frank Capra applied these lessons, I don't know how unwittingly, in the Why We Fight series in which he enlisted dramatic devices, visuals, and sound to indoctrinate GIs during World War II.

Multimedia is big business. The application of digital technology to education, information retrieval, and training is, in fact, so vast that it deserves a book unto itself. About all we can do here is offer the writer a few broad areas to consider.

Corporate Uses of Informational Multimedia

Want to write for the deep pockets? You could easily wind up writing an interactive text for Motorola or Wal-Mart that is designed to teach or train employees on topics as broad as you can imagine. Corporations take digitized training for granted. You can see proof of this in the generation of acronyms that refer to the subject. A company brochure, for instance, may boast of its CBT (computer-based training) on-site, or a university may tout its ILM (interactive learning modules) as a way to develop multimedia software for educational applications.

The demand from manufacturers and companies for educational and training software is huge. The instruction or training can come in any format, local or long distance, via hypertext, Web sites, or in CD-ROM. What kind of application can you expect to write or design? Anything. A schematic interface for an aircraft's maintenance schedule, for instance, allows technicians to point to a problem area and obtain specifications, detailed instructions for routine maintenance, and suggestions for troubleshooting problems that might arise. You might produce a text for managing offshore assets that would allow Wall Street executives to attend a seminar on the subject from their offices.

In today's corporate environment, informational multimedia and new technology are being used in a myriad of business activities, including the following:

- Product demonstrations
- Research and development
- Customer support
- Electronic presentations
- Competitor assessment
- Management indoctrination
- Corporate communications
- Small group interactive video conferences
- Employee training

In an attempt to cut costs and streamline the power and reach of its marketing, customer support, training, and sales efforts, many companies are turning to CBT and Web-based training (WBT) methods in greater numbers than ever before.

Laurie Windham, president and CEO of Cognitiative, Inc., a San Francisco–based technology consulting firm, observes, "The Internet has increasingly becoming a strategic vehicle for both business-to-business and business-to-customer communications. We help our clients—some of the largest brand names in the computer industry—develop Web strategies and content, as well as the testing of new concepts and site usability."

Informational interactive applications are designed to:

- Provide individualized, self-paced instruction
- Support *or* replace traditional offline media (training manuals, textbooks, customer support guides, employee manuals)
- Reduce costs
- Strengthen relationships between businesses and their employees/customers

No matter how it is being used or what it is being used for, businesses need to ask themselves, Does multimedia serve our purposes and meet our needs? and How should we work with content specialists, such as writers, to create informational multimedia programs that will achieve our objectives? To assess whether the multimedia solutions are really right for business usage, it is important to consider the following questions:

- Is there a need for your employees or customers to work in a self-paced environment?
- Are you tackling simulated occupation environments (such as flying an airplane or disarming a land mine)?
- Do you need to provide a consistent level of instruction/information?
- Are quantitative testing or assessment measurements necessary?
- Are you addressing a group of people with special needs (handicapped employees or a dangerous production process)?
- Do you need to reduce learning time, build customer loyalty, empower employees, or increase motivation?
- Must you maintain your competitive edge in the market, build your brand, or increase market awareness in bold new ways?
- Does the material being taught contain elements of mixed media?
- Does some of your material involve repetitive instruction of analogous material?
- Are time or safety issues involved that make computer-based instruction more feasible?

The Writer's Role in the Business Training Environment

It is the writer's task to assist a company's interactive content planning team in creating both functional and dynamic applications that combine page layout, multimedia content, interactivity, network tools, commerce, and human interface design. Writers must play a deeper role than simply copyfitting for the screen. They need to assist the production team in building a multimedia application that delivers the goods.

The following diagram outlines the development process for a typical multimedia training title. In this case, the title is *TutoHelp,* a step-by-step tutorial for novices learning how to use AutoCAD (a complex design software used by architects and engineers). *TutoHelp* is published by Objective Reality, Inc., in Irvine, California (see fig. 17.1).

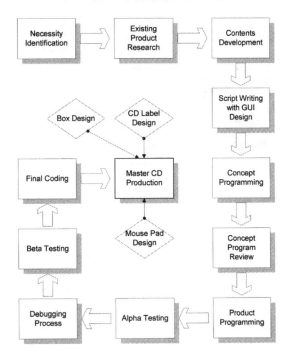

Fig. 17.1. Development Process Flowchart. Courtesy of Kenneth Lee and Objective Reality, Inc. Reprinted by permission.

Needs Identification

Next comes the company's need for creating the project. Why is this project being produced? What are the learning objectives? What is the best way to organize this content? How can the learning modules be created so that they most effectively convey the concepts and objective of the application?

Research Phase

Most companies will hire a content expert to work with a writer so that the writer better understands the scope of the material to be explored. Additionally, outside consultants are often called in to offer businesses help in developing and maintaining what Cognitiative calls "beginning-to-end focus," where facilitators conduct specialized research such as focus groups, one-on-one interviews, customer segmentation, and dyads to better understand the needs of the user.

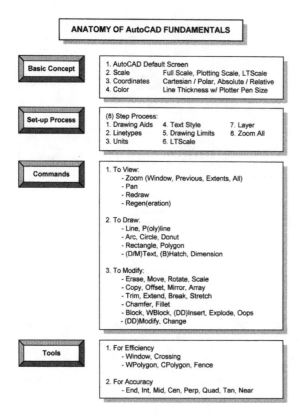

Fig. 17.2. Anatomy of AutoCAD Fundamentals. Courtesy of Kenneth Lee and Objective Reality, Inc. Reprinted by permission.

Kenneth Lee was the lead writer on the CD-ROM tutorial *TutoHelp*. He needed to write an interactive document that walked users through the fundamentals of the AutoCAD software program. Lee was his own content expert—he teaches AutoCAD at the University of California, Irvine, and is a principle at Objective Reality, the publisher of *TutoHelp*. Lee listed all of the steps involved in building an AutoCAD design before he even thought about writing a script or designing an interface for his title (see fig. 17.2).

Look, Feel, and Structure

Next comes the look and feel of the learning modules. What onscreen images will be used? What color schemes work best with the content? What is the underlying design structure for this application? If you recall, we discussed design structures in detail in chapter 2. Writers should feel free to mix and match different design structures to come up with a matrix of interlocking access

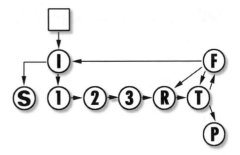

Fig. 17.3. Training structure model

paths that best works for their applications. One design structure we have not discussed, however, is training structure. In a training module, for example, an interactive writer might want to sketch a map that outlines the content to be taught and the learning objectives to be achieved. A basic training lesson might look something like this (see fig. 17.3).

A basic training structure, like the one shown above, is ideal for simple WBT projects or simple CBT applications. Module *I* stands for "introduction." This is where the course content is discussed, objectives are reviewed, and expectations are explained to the user. If the user needs more information, such as a list of course prerequisites, she hyperlinks to module *S*, the sidebar. If the user is able to satisfy the course prerequisites and finds everything he or she needs, the person leaves the sidebar and returns to the introduction.

Continuing on to module one, also known as lesson one, the user learns about the first concept. After interacting with all available content in lesson one, the user moves on to lesson two, then lesson three. After completing lessons one through three, the user hyperlinks to the recap module (*R*), where he or she can review summaries of all the course material presented up to that point.

A test module (*T*) follows the recap. If the user passes the test, he or she can move on to other lessons. If the person fails the test (*F*), he or she is sent back to either the recap module or the introduction module (depending on how the training application is programmed).

Content Template

After all the content structures are mapped out, the interactive writer should complete a content template for each screen of the lesson that will be displayed to the user. The content template is something like a storyboard except that the focus is on the media and the interactivity rather than a "story told in pictures" (see fig. 17.4).

INTERACTIVE CONTENT TEMPLATE

Module Title: _____   Module Code: _____

CONTENT CHECKLIST

Images: _____
_____
_____

Audio: _____
_____
_____

Video: _____
_____
_____

Other: _____
_____
_____

OPENING SCREEN ACTION UPON USER ENTRANCE

INTERACTIVITIES

Fig. 17.4. Interactive content template

Scriptwriting

The scriptwriting phase is the final stage of the interactive writing process. In chapter 3, we described several different types of interactive documents that can be created for interactive applications—concept documents, design documents, and interactive screenplays being the most prevalent.

A narrative interactive screenplay, you may recall, is a story written in a series of scenes dramatized through actions and dialogue, which contain characters, locations, and scene descriptions, and are arranged in a particular format. Informational interactive screenplays are messages/objectives written in a series of modules dramatized through lesson plans and activities, which contain characters, text, video, graphics, and sound—arranged in a particular format. Note that there is no standard format for what an interactive screenplay should look like. Writers are currently adapting formats they may have used for other types of projects—formats with which they are comfortable. Some writers choose to modify Hollywood screenplay formats, while others modify the traditional two-column radio format.

Here are two different page formats used for informational multimedia

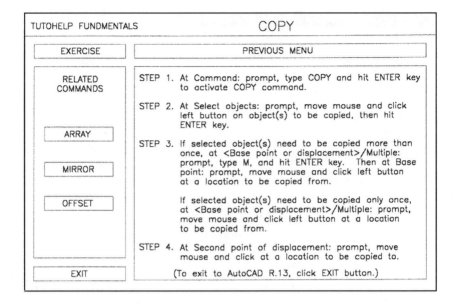

Fig. 17.5. Copy page or "script page" from *TutoHelp*. Courtesy of Kenneth Lee and Objective Reality, Inc. Reprinted by permission.

projects. The first is Kenneth Lee's writing format used to create the interactive AutoCAD tutorial *TutoHelp*. The script's page format is similar in look and feel to the actual screen interface used in the final product (see fig. 17.5).

A second screenplay example is the two-column page format commonly used to create radio advertising spots and traditional videotape training titles. The visuals and onscreen instructions and/or interactivities are placed in the left column and audio and dialogue are placed in the right column (see fig. 17.6).

Interactivity in the Classroom

How is informational multimedia being used at the university level? Schools of higher learning are quickly finding how beneficial, and profitable, "distant learning" can be. Many universities already allow their students to receive credit for courses downloaded distantly from the Web. And already we're seeing the embryos of universities without classrooms, growing axons of Web-based curricula where distant students receive credit for everything from applied calculus to Celtic history in a virtual university.

TWO-COLUMN SCREENPLAY FORMAT

Module Title: **BE A SURVIVOR**   Module Code: **K3-109**

INSTRUCTIONS	AUDIO
We SEE the Lange Productions Logo dissolve to screen, then fade to black.	10 second splash music.
The names of the program's four sponsors then appear on-screen:	
BRISTOL-MYERS SQUIBB ONCOLOGY SALICK HEALTH CAR INC. ZENECA PHARMACEUTICALS	
Followed by the title screen:	
BE A SURVIVOR: YOUR INTERACTIVE GUIDE TO BREAST CANCER TREATMENT	
The title screen dissolves into a reception counter at a doctor's office. We are greeted by a pleasant office manager named JILL.	JILL HELLO. WELCOME TO OUR BREAST CANCER RESOURCE CENTER.
	IF YOU WANT INSTRUCTIONS FOR USING THIS PROGRAM, USE THE MOUSE AND CLICK THE POINTER IN THE WINDOW AREA.
	TO START USING THE PROGRAM IMMEDIATELY, CLICK ON THE DOORS.
If the user CLICKS on the WINDOW AREA, they are hyperlinked to the Resource Center, where they are greeted by a friendly FEMALE DOCTOR. She is the resource center guide.	FEMALE DOCTOR HELLO. I'M GLAD YOU CAME. I'LL BE YOUR GUIDE AND HELPER WHILE YOU'RE HERE. TO MAKE ME STOP TALKING AND DISAPPEAR SO YOUR CAN GET ON WITH THE PROGRAM, CLICK ON ME. I'LL COME BACK IF YOU CLICK ON THE CHAIR.
The following images are roll-overs which are highlighted as a user rolls her cursor over the object.	YOU CAN SELECT ANY TOPIC YOU WANT BY CLICKING ON THE RIGHT OBJECT: ON THE STATUE TO LEARN ABOUT BREAST ANATOMY AND BREAST CANCER; ON THE MICROSCOPE FOR INFORMATION ON DIAGNOSIS AND STAGING; IN THE TREATMENT AREA, YOU CAN SELECT...
STATUE MICROSCOPE WINDOW TELEPHONE BOOKSHELF	

Fig. 17.6. Two-column script format based on the educational CD-ROM *Be a Survivor: Your Interactive Guide to Breast Cancer Treatment*, produced by Lange Productions.

How about secondary and elementary education? Do we see digitized, multimedia texts in these classrooms? Yes, we do. In some cases, it's done well. In other cases, it is not. This raises an important issue. The application of computer-generated multimedia technology to the education of children is turning out to be a much more complicated problem than computer mavens initially perceived. The difficulty isn't so much one of technology, but rather that teachers can't agree on how to teach.

Businesses aren't afflicted with this dilemma. Companies like Oracle, Apple Computer, Sybase, and Sun Microsystems develop product for their clients that is stimulating, certainly, but which is also very task- and content-oriented. This is precisely the kind of product that many educational theorists deride.

I'm going to spend a little time discussing this problem; the debate that is ongoing about how we aim to use computers to teach our children is too important a subject to gloss over. The computer is not a magic bullet for teaching children. People who think that computer-driven technologies make rote memory unnecessary, or that computers make a mastery of basic skills anachronistic, are simply mistaken.

Fig. 17.7. Screen shot from the educational CD-ROM *Be a Survivor: Your Interactive Guide to Breast Cancer Treatment,* **produced by Lange Productions.**

Interactive writers need to understand that much of what drives the development of multimedia for educational applications derives from education theory. Most contemporary pedagogues have made their fortunes rejecting "traditional" approaches to learning. The early behaviorist learning theory pioneered by people like Thorndike and Skinner from the early 1900s to the late 1960s is largely criticized by contemporary theorists for producing rote knowledge without analytic skills. But do the new theories lead to greater skills in critical thinking or analysis?

It isn't something that is easy to ascertain. Standardized test scores that evaluate math and language skills for students exposed to the "new" theories indicate that these young people aren't doing better than students traditionally schooled. Modern theories of education, particularly the constructivist and cognitive approaches, dominate current pedagogical theory. But their claims for superiority over traditional methods are too often assertions that haven't received empirical support. Additionally, it seems that proponents who urge the abandonment of traditional methods are often guilty of loading the rhetorical dice.

In his paper "Teaching, Learning, and Reform in the Twenty-First Century Classroom Tech Forum: Year 2000–2003," Mark E. Gabehart, director of technology, curriculum, and training for Cypress-Fairbanks ISD, compares a traditional with a constructivist educational environment (see fig. 17.8).

TRADITIONAL

- Curriculum is presented part to whole, with emphasis on basic skills
- Strict adherence to fixed curriculum is highly valued
- Curricular activities rely heavily on textbooks and workbooks
- Students are viewed as "blank slates" onto which information is etched by the teacher
- Teachers generally behave in a didactic manner, disseminating information to students
- Teachers seek the correct answer to validate student learning
- Assessment of student learning is viewed as separate from teaching and occurs almost entirely through testing
- Students primarily work alone

CONSTRUCTIVIST

- Curriculum is presented whole to part with emphasis on big concepts
- Pursuits of students' questions is highly valued
- Curricular activities rely heavily on primary sources of data and manipulative materials
- Assessment of student learning is interwoven with teaching and occurs through teacher observations of students at work and through student exhibitions and portfolios
- Students primarily work in groups
- Students are viewed as thinkers with emerging theories about the world
- Teachers generally behave in an interactive manner, mediating the environment for students
- Teachers seek the students' points of view in order to understand students' present conceptions for use in subsequent lessons

Fig. 17.8. Excerpted from "Teaching, Learning, and Reform in the Twenty-First Century Classroom Tech Forum: Year 2000–2003" by Mark E. Gabehart, directory of technology, curriculum, and training for Cypress-Fairbanks ISD, Region 20, Education Service Center, April 21, 1997.

As you can see, the constructivist classroom is characterized as highly valuing "pursuits of students' questions," whereas the traditional environment is said to value "strict adherence to fixed curriculum."

Come on. Isn't it possible for a teacher adhering to a fixed curriculum to *also* value students' questions? And won't these questions lead back to the subject being discussed or to some related aspect of the fixed curriculum? Isn't there a balance to be struck between a train-schedule approach to curriculum development and total chaos?

Let's try another comparison. Traditional educators, Gabehart tells us, view students "as 'blank slates' onto which information is etched by the teacher," whereas constructivists view students "as thinkers with emerging theories about the world."

This comes close to nonsense. A student can't theorize about anything without basic building blocks of knowledge. On the other hand, any teacher who views his or her students as slate isn't going to be effective under *any* pedagogy. The comparison continues, traditional teachers being characterized as "didactic" while constructivist teachers are "interactive . . . mediating the environment for students." Enough already. Traditional teachers who are effective interact with, stimulate, and respect their students just as much as any newcomer fresh from the School of Constructivist Education. And believe me, any new teacher will find that mediating the environment for her students sometimes requires a firm, and very didactic, No!

The constructivist classroom, we are told is "nontraditional" and "student-centered." Students "work collaboratively on problem-based, project-based curricula." In other words, students will receive a general topic, then be placed in small groups and tasked with defining specific problems related to that topic. The group will then work to research facts related to their problem, will engage imaginatively to reach conclusions or "perceptions," and will produce something well written that demonstrates skills related to critical thinking and reflection.

Once again, it ought to be recognized that an exercise along the lines outlined above can be observed in schools that would regard themselves as traditionally oriented. The group project wasn't the invention of constructivists. But most of us who have actually been in a group of four or five teenagers know that in any such group, one or two students will inevitably write the report, build the model, or slice the frog, while the rest hang on. That's not the way it's supposed to work! cries the constructivist. But that's the way it *is*, and when it comes to educating our children, a theory that takes reality heavily into account is of the utmost importance.

That doesn't mean that we're stuck with Skinner and the sixties. There is no doubt that process-oriented education can greatly benefit students. It would be wrong to infer, simply on the basis of present test results, that new approaches to teaching can't be worthwhile. But I do see a problem when any method—traditional, constructive, cognitive or otherwise—is touted as superior to older pedagogies or is implemented in isolation of other methods. It seems to me that traditional and constructivist approaches, as a specific example, complement each other and ought to both find a place in the classroom. A child needs phonetics when he or she begins learning to read. A child needs to master phonemes to spell and to encounter new words. That's a traditional approach. But a child also needs a broader experience of learning, a reading experience that emphasizes purpose and context as a way to teach the child skills that are more analytic and abstract.

Interactive writers and educators ought to work together to create products that strike a balance between process and content, a balance between rote memory and analysis, between group and individual efforts. And then the keepers of our children have to be honest with whatever results are observed. They should be charged to voraciously incorporate what works—and to throw out what doesn't. Some of the spin-offs of the newer approaches to pedagogy have become tagged with terms like "whole math" or "whole language." In general, schools wedded exclusively to these approaches to math and language learning have not done well. California has seen a precipitous decline in the ability of its school children's rote and analytic skills since the whole-math model was adopted. The news came on the front page of the *Los Angeles Times* that the Golden State, for years a leader in math achievement scores, had fallen to thirty-eighth nationwide, competing for dead last with traditionally poor-performing states like Mississippi and Louisiana.

Many factors, of course, have contributed to California's decline, but state educators are beginning, if belatedly, to consider that the whole-math model may be a significant part of the problem. What's true for math seems also true for reading and language skills. States experimenting with whole-language approaches to reading and writing have gone back to their districts urging a traditional, phonetic curriculum as the basis for reading, and, consequently, traditional instruction in grammar is on the rise.

What does this mean for the interactive writer? I'd say it means that if you're going to write product for educational applications, you need to understand the tug-of-war between the traditional and the new. You need to understand the basic tenets of current pedagogical theory. Nothing can be more important than the tools we use in the twenty-first century to teach our children. The best curriculum, it seems to me, would be one which takes the best of the old and the new. Constructivist and cognitive approaches to learning have produced worthwhile insights, but they should not be applied in the classroom to the exclusion of traditional approaches. Why not use both tools? Students need interactive product that drills basic skills and they need software that provides more open-ended, process-oriented challenges which demand analysis and critical thinking. It's not an either-or thing; it's a "both/and" proposition. Educators should (as they claim constantly to do) practice inclusion.

A balance of traditionally and cognitively based software is what the twenty-first century student will need. Basic skills not applied to problem solving are indeed inert. But a student lacking basic skills in arithmetic and reading, or geometry and grammar, won't be able to tackle problems requiring higher-level cognition. Interactive writers can contribute greatly in this regard by designing texts that provide both content and process, texts that, in their coded procedures, integrate Piaget with Skinner.

18

Global Window Japan:
A Content-Rich Web Site

Edutainment is neither fish nor fowl. It's neither educational nor entertaining. Greatness comes from integrity. What weakens the story is when
you try to be all things to all people. That's what you get when a marketing wizard tells you that there's a market for something that's educational and entertaining.

ROBERT TERCEK

lobal Window: Japan (*www.anderson.ucla.edu/research/japan*) is one of
those breakthrough multimedia projects that is so overwhelmingly
useful and easy to use, one wonders why nobody has produced anything like it sooner. The site itself is a one-stop reference center for Westerners
who conduct business with the Japanese. Its fundamental purpose is to inform—and on that level, it garners high marks for its intent and execution.

Global Window: Japan was initiated at UCLA's Anderson Graduate School
of Management by Archie Kleingartner, professor of management and policy
studies, to address issues of global business effectiveness. The content of the
Japan Web site, developed in partnership with Japanese universities Meikai and
Asahi, targets what Professor Kleingartner has identified as a crucial but often overlooked issue: Roughly 25–30 percent of the perceived problems that
Westerners encounter in doing business with the Japanese can be attributed
to actual hurdles such as trade barriers. The remaining 70–75 percent result
from the inability or unwillingness of Westerners to learn the intricacies and

nuances of Japanese business culture. The *Global Window* site provides information on these cultural subtleties, in addition to factual data on Japanese business.

Synthesizing a vast body of information, the site is targeted to businesspeople with varying levels of interest and time. It provides convenient links to other comprehensive resources, as well as printable, take-along tips for business travelers. To help design, develop, and implement the site, the core *Global Window* content project team (Archie Kleingartner, creator and coexecutive producer; Susumu Miyata, coexecutive producer; Kate Winegark, project manager; Carolyn Miller, editor and writer) partnered with Internal and External Communication, a Marina del Rey–based developer of technology-delivered training and communications programs for multinational corporations.

Global Window: Japan was awarded the 1997 Gold Medal at the New York Film Festival, as well as the 1997 Gold International EMMA award. The EMMAs are Europe's premier independent multimedia awards (the site was entered in the competition's commercial online category).

The Role of the Writer

As noted above, Carolyn Miller was the lead writer for the *Global Window: Japan* project. Miller was kind enough to walk us through the writing process from her unique vantage point in the design team. Here is what she had to say:

Two Distinct Phases

I worked on this project in two distinct phases. During the research phase, my title was content editor. I oversaw and coordinated the work of our five researchers in the [United States], edited their documents, reviewed materials supplied by our team members in Japan, consolidated the notes made by our expert consultants, and played an active role in our weekly content meetings at UCLA. These meetings were attended by our researchers, faculty experts, and members of the production team, and were crucial in helping to steer the project on a straight course. During this phase we also hammered out some major design and content decisions.

The second phase was the production of the Web site. I never received an official title other than writer, though I was also a member of the design team. My chief role was to write about 98 percent of what appeared on the Web site. There was a staggering amount of material to write. I estimate it tallied up to at least five hundred "paper" pages, double-spaced. Part of my job was to indicate what words or phrases should be in hypertext and what they should be linked to; this meant I had to keep a complete inventory in my head of every piece of information, and consider how it related to every other piece of information. I ate, slept, and breathed this material for about five months.

Everything I wrote was reviewed by our group of experts in the [United States] and Japan; based on their notes, I wrote a second draft of each piece of material.

Goals, Objectives, and Target Audience

I came into the project after the research phase had already begun. At the time I arrived on the scene, some major decisions had already been made. For example, it had been determined very early on who the target audience would be: English-speaking business people, both in the [United States] and in other countries. (By the way, the fact that it was for an international market meant we had to be extremely careful to avoid exclusively American references). The goal of the project had also been crystallized: to offer a unique guide and resource for those visiting Japan on business. Furthermore, it had been determined that information would be offered on several levels, so that a person with very little time could gain a quick but useful overview, while someone with more time or a particular interest could delve deeply into a particular subject.

Though certain things had already been thought out, there was still a great deal of conceptual work to be done. For one thing, there was the huge job of organizing the material into different categories—a process that went on throughout the research phase. A more delicate issue we grappled with was how to present material that could, if mishandled, give offense to the Japanese, but if ignored would be a disservice to our users. There were a number of potentially volatile issues we had to handle with great care.

During the second phase, the development of the Web site, some of the most interesting work centered on design questions. We needed to determine the look of the main screens, the color palette, and a great number of navigation issues, and we also needed to determine how our limited budget for visuals and audio could best be utilized. We spent a great deal of time working on how to present the material in the most efficient, logical manner, from the point of view of the user. And as writer, I also had to wrestle with the style, tone, and organization of the major components.

The Challenges

Deciding what to put in and what to leave out was a huge problem. The researchers had produced a voluminous amount of material, much of it unique and fascinating. But I continually had to ask myself what would be useful from the point of view of a business person with limited time and specific needs. The touchstone was this: would a particular piece of information help our users have a successful outcome to their business trip in Japan? If the answer was yes, the information stayed in; if it was no, then it hit the cutting-room floor. Some of my favorite things didn't make it, and this was sometimes very painful, but I always had to think of our ultimate goal.

One of the biggest challenges in creating *Global Window: Japan* was sifting through all the material collected by the researchers and deciding what to use and what to leave out. Another big challenge was to take some extremely subtle Japanese concepts and present them in a way that would be understandable and meaningful to a Westerner. It was also very difficult to keep in mind that this material was not being given in a linear fashion; there was no beginning place and no ending place. A user could enter and leave at any point. Each piece thus had to stand on its own, but be linked to other relevant pieces via hypertext. You couldn't, as [the] writer, assume a user had already visited another part of the site and was familiar with related information or concepts. And in writing the articles (the sections which made up each topic), the challenge was to keep them short, sharply focused, and self-contained.

The biggest interface challenge, from my point of view as writer, was how to organize each topic with the three levels of difficulty we had determined (see below for description of how the topics were organized). The question was one addressed by everyone on the team, but it was the production company IEC that created the actual designs that we went with. I don't want to give the impression that I was in the decision-making position here.

It is important to note here that we were not trying to follow the paradigm of a book or executive report. It is true that some of the terminology we used, like "article" or "executive summary," comes from print media, but *Global Window: Japan* is very much reflective of the medium on which it is delivered, namely, the Internet. It is nonlinear; it is multileveled in terms of depth of information; it contains audio elements; it is written in short, self-contained articles; information is connected via hypertext; I could go on and on.

Design Structure

The information offered on the site is broken into nine large components, which we called "topics." They are more or less like chapters in a book, though they are not meant to be read in any particular order. The topics focus on such subjects as Japanese business practices, Japanese culture, and the Japanese economy. Each topic has three levels of information. The executive summary gives a quick, concise overview of the topic. The "take home pointers" are practical, important tips that are designed to be printed out by the site visitor and used as a kind of "cheat sheet" while on the business trip. The articles are self-contained pieces giving more detailed information, written in a readable magazine style. There are between five [and] eight of them in each topic. Each article is rich with hypertext links. There are other features as well. . . . including the glossary; the bibliography; audio elements; visuals like maps, photos, and diagrams.

A Sample Walkthru

To get a better feel for what makes this Web site work, let's follow one short pathway a user might choose to navigate their way through the *Global Window: Japan* Web site.

A user arrives at the main menu and examines the six navigation icons located in the left navbar, the nine content icons on the main frame (center), and five additional navigation icons located immediately below the content icons (below, center). The user must now make a choice—where to go next? To travel to an information-rich node, the user must choose one of the twenty hypermedia links that most interests him or her (see fig. 18.1).

The user finally decides on the topic "People and Culture." Clicking on the hypermedia icon transports the user to the "People and Culture" page (see fig. 18.2).

The user then browses the five information frames: navbar, topic, executive summary, take home pointers, and supporting articles.

"The idea behind the executive summary is that it provides a very quick overview of the material—usually only a couple of paragraphs of information," states project manager Kate Winegark. "The user can browse the topic, learn how it is important, and why. The take home pointers are meant for users who only have time to read the main bullet points about the topic. Coexecutive producer Archie Kleingartner said he envisions business travelers printing out the take home pointers, folding them, and placing them into

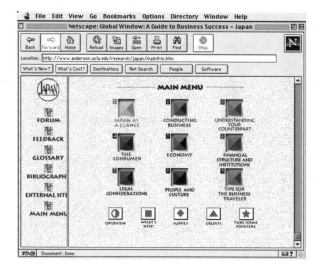

Fig. 18.1. Screen shot from *Global Window: Japan.* Copyright 1997, UCLA. Reprinted by permission.

Fig. 18.2. Screen shot from *Global Window: Japan.* Copyright 1997, UCLA. Reprinted by permission.

their pockets for quick reference later on. And, finally, the supporting articles are very text intensive. This is where the Web site's in-depth information can be found."

Let's say the user decides to return to the main menu. The person clicks on topic nine: "Tips For the Business Traveler." Intrigued by the numerous choices, he or she decides to learn about some of the common phrases in the Japanese language. By choosing the appropriate supporting article, an array of common English travel phrases appear onscreen, followed by their Japanese counterpart. The user can both see the phonetic spelling and listen to the audio pronunciation.

Choosing the phrase "Excuse me, what time is it?" activates an audio clip where a male voice recites, "Sumimasen ga, nanji desu ka."

19

PhotoPRINT CD: Interactive Sales and Training

The burden of interaction today has been placed totally on the shoulders of the human party. Something as banal as printing a computer file can be a debilitating exercise that resembles voodoo more than respectable human behavior. As a result, many adults are turned off and claim to be hopelessly computer illiterate. This will change.

NICHOLAS NEGROPONTE

P*hotoPRINT Training* is an interactive educational CD-ROM produced by the in-house production staff at Amiable Technologies, Inc. (*www. amiableworld.com*). Amiable is recognized as a world leader in the production of signmaking and digital color-printing software. Products include FlexiCAD, FlexiSIGN-PRO, and PhotoPRINT.

The PhotoPRINT product line is a comprehensive layout and print package software specifically designed to work with wide-format printers. The PhotoPRINT Training CD-ROM was designed for PhotoPRINT customers—mainly designers, production artists, signmakers, service bureau operators, and ad agency personnel—who don't have time to read user manuals. It teaches the user how to use the PhotoPRINT software, as well as how to print large-format color images. The CD is also a reference for many of the concepts required in daily production.

An Interview with Key Production Team Members

We sat down with key members of the Amiable Technologies in-house production staff—Brigette Callahan, writer/producer; An Nguyen, writer; and Tom Gundlock, lead graphic designer. We asked them about the unique creative challenges they encountered while writing, designing, and programming the *PhotoPRINT Training* CD. Here is what they had to say:

Q: What were your major creative challenges? writing challenges?

Brigette: Coming up with a simple yet exciting theme that was producible within the time frame was very challenging. Everybody had great ideas but we had to have forethought into production and our eventual capabilities before starting. This was especially difficult since we have never done a multimedia project like this before. Writing a training program was equally challenging because we had so many critics giving their input. It was difficult to please everyone. I eventually had to just dive into the project and make assumptions where I felt it was best in order to get the project off the ground. We initially evaluated using an outside source for writing our script. But we found that product knowledge was much more important than fancy marketing prose in creating this particular project.

An: Being constrained—we had to assume our end-users' educational backgrounds and our work had to stay within the boundaries of our company culture. As for writing, both Brigette and I come from a nonwriting background, so we had to quickly educate ourselves on writing training modules, copywriting techniques, and the like. Since two different writers worked on the project, tailoring the material to a consistent, fluid style was a challenge.

Tom: My biggest challenge was designing an engaging interface that was flexible enough to accommodate all of the subjects.

Q: Walk me through the major creative decisions.

Brigette: The initial concept of creating a training CD-ROM in interactive format as opposed to traditional printed manuals was proposed to the marketing and sales staff over a year before the project was started. They were very excited about the prospects. Once we were able to clear our slate of other projects, we started in late July of '97 talking about a theme and outline.

An: Next came the theme of an educational institute. We needed a theme that would encompass the tutorial aspects of the CD-ROM, as well as the creativity and design elements.

Brigette: The artwork began soon after the theme was decided. We never really had a written design proposal until the project was well into production. Both An and myself took a multimedia writing class to learn more about this new and exciting field. The resulting design proposal acted as a written description and goal for the project and was shared among the marketing and sales staff.

An: In hindsight, writing the design proposal put all our efforts (i.e., creative meetings, sketching, and programming) in perspective. We should have written the proposal first so that any problems encountered during production could have been anticipated.

Brigette: Since our client was in-house, we didn't really need a detailed design proposal to sell the idea. However, our project would have run a lot smoother if we did have it prior to our production.

Q: *What was your timetable to complete the job?*

Brigette: During the proposal process we started learning the different software needed to produce the CD-ROM. We created a three-minute demo that was shown to the sales staff to gain interest and enthusiasm. This happened in January of '97. We were also evaluating if this was a viable solution to communicate to our customers worldwide. Once the theme and outline were created, I estimated that it would take three months to produce the Mac version of the CD-ROM. We ended up taking four months for our initial release. I never considered it a rush job even though we were slightly late with the finished product. All our work is in a sort of rush-job mode with the various projects we produce, so this was just another job in that mode. The expectations of our employer was to have something that would emulate the quality of work that Amiable is famous for in their print designs as well as something of value that the competition didn't supply.

Q: How were you able to use multiple writers on the same production team?

An: We split the tasks between the two main writers. Because the CD-ROM branched into two separate types of writing styles—tutorials and marketing copy—it was easy to assign which part went to whom. Brigette took on the task of writing the scripts for each tutorial and I took the task of getting all the marketing copy done. When it came time to writing the tutorials for the Color Calibration and Contour Cut modules, I adapted Brigette's writing style in order to be consistent with the remainder of the tutorials.

Q: What kind of response are you getting from users of the final product?

An: Our dealers appreciate the effort Amiable makes in providing them with the best marketing collateral and training tools to help them sell. So, yes, they loved it. No one can compare to the tools we provide our dealers in this industry.

Brigette: Our dealers, resellers, and corporate partners all feel that this is an exciting product that has great potential. They are excited to see what the customer response will be as well as seeing what is coming next from Amiable. We did get some feedback about the specific tutorials being too fast and wanting to have more information on other aspects of PhotoPRINT. Overall, this project continued to keep Amiable on the map as a leader in the signmaking and color-printing industry and proves to our customers that we stay on the cutting edge (no pun intended) of our technology.

Q: Why do you think your project was successful?

Tom: In one aspect I think the project was successful because we were able to actually deliver a working product on time. We were all very new at multimedia going into the project and unsure about many aspects of it. We knew there would be a steep learning curve, and we all overcame many obstacles along the way. As a final product, I think the project satisfied the purpose it was intended for, and then some. Rather than being a straight training CD, it wound up being a sales/training CD. The training aspect of it could have been more interactive with quizzes and feedback, but with the timeline and ability at the time, I think the job was successful.

Brigette: Our project was successful because we were highly determined to make it successful. We had many hurdles and we learned a tremendous amount that should make our future projects run smoother. Our production team took time out to take some classes from a local college on multimedia writing and production and that helped catapult our idea to a finished project. We also did lots of research both within our industry and outside to see what is being done. We have a very talented team of artists and writers that was able to produce within the time frames allotted.

An: A major lesson learned is that you need to be prepared for all obstacles that may lay in your path—keep an open mind. And although we were actually producing while the writing team was being educated on all aspects of interactive writing, the learning doesn't end. With interactive media being so dynamic and constantly changing, what you learn today may not be necessarily applicable tomorrow. As long as you are able to put past experiences in perspective and apply it to future technologies, you'll be prepared.

Tom: Of course we learned quite a bit about the technical aspects of the process (software and hardware both). But I think the most crucial learning took place in the planning process. Having a solid foundation and overall plan before the project begins is the key. I think with a project this size, the order in which everything happens is crucial to the success of a piece.

Brigette: My advice to other writers and designers is to understand thoroughly what your client wants and do lots of research on similar projects. Cruise the Internet and attend industry-related trade shows to get ideas. Have many meetings with your client during the production phase to make them feel comfortable with the progress. Realize that most people are unaware of the time and cost it takes to produce multimedia. And, finally, it really helps to be organized and communicate with your team members clearly. Weekly meetings, storyboards, and discussion groups are what helped us. Good luck, have fun, and go for it!

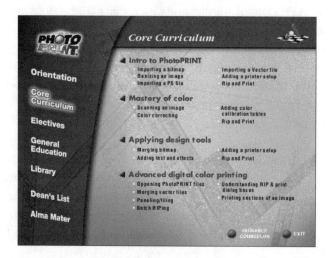

Fig. 19.1. Screen shot, *PhotoPRINT Training* **CD-ROM. Copyright 1998, Amiable Technologies, Inc. Reprinted by permission.**

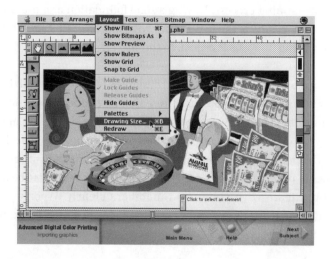

Fig. 19.2. Screen shot, *PhotoPRINT Training* **CD-ROM. Copyright 1998, Amiable Technologies, Inc. Reprinted by permission.**

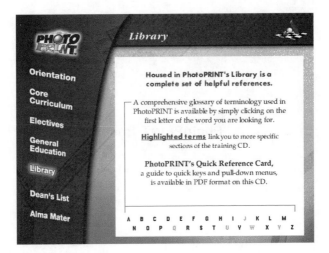

Fig. 19.3. Screen shot, *PhotoPRINT Training* **CD-ROM. Copyright 1998, Amiable Technologies, Inc. Reprinted by permission.**

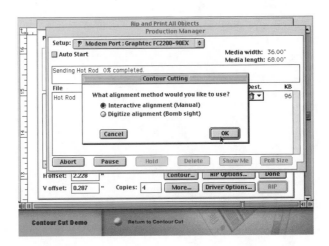

Fig. 19.4. Screen shot, *PhotoPRINT Training* **CD-ROM. Copyright 1998, Amiable Technologies, Inc. Reprinted by permission.**

PhotoPRINT Training
Version 1.0

Design Proposal

Written by
Brigette Callahan
(714) 248-8032

December 10, 1997

Fig. 19.5. Design proposal, *PhotoPRINT Training* **CD-ROM. Copyright 1998, Amiable Technologies, Inc. Reprinted by permission.**

PhotoPRINT Training CD   **Page 2**
Version 1

Summary

PhotoPRINT Training is an interactive educational CD-Rom based on the concepts and capabilities of PhotoPRINT software for large format color printing.

Premise

PhotoPRINT allows the user to create all kinds of signs and designs and print to large format inkjet and thermal printers. It also allows importation of graphics created in many of the popular design programs. By reviewing this CD-Rom the user will be able to learn the basics of PhotoPRINT and start printing large-format color images in as little as five minutes.This CD-Rom will also serve as an online ready reference for many of the concepts required in daily production. The target audience will be owners of PhotoPRINT software. They are designers, production artists, signmakers, service bureau operators, ad agency personnel, etc.

Story Summary & Purpose

Who has time to read a manual these days? When we buy a software package we want to be able to use it right out of the box. PhotoPRINT is simple to use. However, there are some concepts that people may not be aware of and this is where a training CD-Rom will help. Not only will it train and educate, it will provide general industry information and brief them on Amiable's whole family of products. They will learn about their current software purchase and the potential for upgrades. They will also learn how easy it is to get qualified technical support via our web site.

As usual, Amiable will be the first of its competitors to utilize this technology. The market has grown in the last two years to include upgraded computer equipment and CD-Rom technology. In the past, Amiable would use videos for training. This required the user to have a VCR next to his computer and view the movie while working in the software. This turned out to be an unsatisfactory solution to online training. With the popularity of CD-Rom drives it has become evident that the market is ready for a training CD. It's only natural that Amiable evolve to CD-Rom development.

Amiable evaluated the cost of distributing the original software on CD-Rom instead of diskettes three years ago. With its current international following, shipping on CDs is extremely cost-effective. Almost all of the customers have this technology so it will be easy for them to embrace the Training CD-Rom.

Copyright ©1997 Amiable Technologies, Inc.

Fig. 19.6. Design proposal, *PhotoPRINT Training* CD-ROM. Copyright 1998, Amiable Technologies, Inc. Reprinted by permission.

Interface Methodology & Technical Features

PhotoPRINT Training will be created using the latest technology for multimedia production. Immediately upon inserting the CD-Rom the program will start by searching the computer for the correct software for optimal play. If the computer is missing some software, a prompt will come up asking the user if he would like to load it. Then a short QuickTime movie will play as an introduction.

The main menu with be designed with a hip 90s look and a series of animated buttons to link the branching areas of the CD-Rom. Each navigational button will have a visual, as well as verbal, rollover and a different verbal cue when clicked.

The tutorial area will consist of a series of QuickTime movies created from moving screen shots. These movies will fill the screen to maximum width so the user can get a feel for the software interface. A voice over will describe what is being learned.

The Product showcase will include a series of text slides to describe each product with general features and upgradability. The interface will show all of the product boxes and, by clicking on each box, will access the text information. Music will be playing in the background.

The Library, or glossary, will have hot spots on various definitions so the user can access more information located in another area of the CD-Rom. For example, if the definition is color calibration, the word will be a different color, indicating to the user that this is a hot spot. Upon clicking on the word he can go to the section of a QuickTime movie for a more detailed description.

The main menu will have an animating corporate logo in one corner. Upon clicking on this logo the user can access the corporate and web site information.

The project will be created using Macromedia Director as the main programming language. Support software will be Adobe PhotoShop, Illustrator, Premiere, After Effects; Media Cleaner Pro; CameraMan and QuickEdit. The initial production will be on the Macintosh. Then, a Windows version will be created. The CD-Rom will be engineered to eventually run on both platforms. The initial release, however, will be for Macintosh only.

Future incarnations of the CD-Rom will be online connection directly to the software. When the user has a particular question about an area he can quickly click directly to that portion of the CD and get detailed information.

Copyright ©1997 Amiable Technologies, Inc.

Fig. 19.7. Design proposal, *PhotoPRINT Training* CD-ROM. Copyright 1998, Amiable Technologies, Inc. Reprinted by permission.

Navigation/Story Path Structure

The flow of the PhotoPRINT Training CD-Rom will be a basic branching structure with cul-de-sacs of information. At the end of each tutorial there will be a brief quiz to review. The test scores will not, however, limit the user from advancing. It will merely be utilized as a summary and basic feedback to the learner. There will be an option to skip the quiz.

The user can choose to take the linear direction in which he clicks on the main title and the program will automatically show all of the sections. Or he can select individual sections to watch.

Content Outline

Intro
The introduction will contain a 5 second animation of the Amiable 3D logo with accompanying music. The music will be up beat, modern, but not overwhelming. The logo bug will emerge from black and turn around 180° before ending up in full light. The logo text will zoom in from black to hit the beat of the music. The music will quickly fade.

The introduction will continue with a 30 second video featuring action shots of PhotoPRINT software. The video will be a quarter size of the original screen (320 x 240 pixels) and consist of quick moving images depicting signs and posters on display, as well as a sign shop utilizing PhotoPRINT on the computer and taking a print out of a printer. There will be other shots of different printers and various types of prints. Menus, legal graphics, promotions, point-of-purchase items will all be depicted. Again, music will accompany this video along with narration.

The music will continue to loop as the user is transitioned into the Main Menu.

Main Menu
The main menu, or table of contents, is the "lobby" for the whole CD-Rom. All of the action stems from this area. Since the project is a training CD-Rom the table of contents is described in terms of an academic theme. There are nine buttons total for this menu.

1) Orientation
Orientation contains three modules that are descriptive QuickTime movies.

Copyright ©1997 Amiable Technologies, Inc.

Fig. 19.8. Design proposal, *PhotoPRINT Training* **CD-ROM. Copyright 1998, Amiable Technologies, Inc. Reprinted by permission.**

Opening & creating a new drawing area - This movie will educate the user on the basic aspects of PhotoPRINT and its drawing size and area.

Working with PhotoPRINT palettes - There are many palettes in PhotoPRINT and this movie will describe, in detail, what each one does. They can be resized and reshaped and moved around to fit the users needs.

Printing comps to a desktop printer - Printing comps in PhotoPRINT is a different procedure than the more common Rip and Print. This movie will describe how to print comps for a client review. This involves a desktop laser or color printer.

2) Core Curriculum

The core curriculum contains the main aspects of this CD-rom. These are the training movies to learn all aspects of PhotoPRINT. Each of the four tutorials contain a specific function. The few items that aren't covered in this section will be covered in the "Electives" section. The tutorials will be created to work individually so that a full project is completed in each one. When the user clicks on the Core Curriculum button he will see a list of the four tutorials and the names of the individual movies. He can choose to click on a movie or click on a subhead to view all of the movies in that section. The button will lead him to the movie area where most of the screen is occupied by the QuickTime movie and the navigation buttons are a small strip at the bottom.

a) Intro to PhotoPRINT - Upon opening the software the user will immediately learn a simple skill and be printing in less than 5 minutes. The topics will include: Importing a Bitmap; Resizing the Bitmap; Importing a PostScript file; Importing a vector file; RIP and print.

b) Mastery of Color - This tutorial will discuss scanning and color correction. It will end with a basic Rip and Print featuring a different set of variables from the first tutorial. The topics will include: Scanning an Image; Color Correction of a bitmap; Adding a Color Calibration Table; RIP and Print.

c) Applying Design Tools - The design features of PhotoPRINT will be discussed in this tutorial. The pen tool, arched text, and photo masking will be explained. This is the most complicated of the four tutorials. The topics will include: Merging a Bitmap; Text and Shapes; Pen tool/Photo Mask; RIP and Print.

d) Advanced Color Printing - The last tutorial will cover those items that were not discussed earlier. It will also discuss the paneling feature and when the user would want to use it. Lastly, the project will be run through the batch rip and talk about it's features. The topics will include: Merging a postscript file; Paneling or tiling; Batch RIP and print.

Copyright ©1997 Amiable Technologies, Inc.

Fig. 19.9. Design proposal, *PhotoPRINT Training* CD-ROM. Copyright 1998, Amiable Technologies, Inc. Reprinted by permission.

3) Electives

The electives section will discuss features and give support documentation to help augment PhotoPRINT. These are the items that were not discussed in the "Core Curriculum" section. Clicking on this section will reveal the 5 sections. Clicking on one of these sections will lead the user to a descriptive text section. Photos and diagrams will be explained with arrows and text. There will be a music background but no voice over.

Color calibration- This section will give all the details of Color Calibration. The initial screen will be a descriptive paragraph of what it is. There will be six additional buttons as follows: Features, Benefits, Demo, A Necessity, Supported Devices, Back to Main Menu, and the benefits. A section will provide roll-over descriptions of each of the variable options.

Contour cutting - This will discuss an optional feature known as contour cutting. The initial paragraph will discuss the benefits of this feature along with the Benefits, Supported Devices, etc.

Diffusion methods - When the user is in the Rip and Print dialog box they are bombarded with many different choices. One of those is Diffusion Methods. This section will explain each method and when the user would want to use it.

Production Manager- This section will give comprehensive details of Production Manager and why the user would use it. The buttons are as follows: Dialog box, Preferences, Back to Main Menu. The Dialog box section will provide roll-over descriptions of each of the variable options. The preferences will will also have a roll-over interface to discuss each of the choices.

Adobe PostScript - With the new Adobe partnership PhotoPRINT has been redesigned to include Adobe's original PostScript 3 language. This section will describe the benefits of true postscript and the advantages.

4) General Education

General Education will contain information and descriptions to theories and practices that work with PhotoPRINT. These information items will be contained in a PDF file that the user can print themselves. Software for Adobe Acrobat Reader will be provided on the CD-Rom. The topics will include: Color discussion; Scanning/DPI; Creating PostScript file.

5) Library

The Library is also known as the index. There will be a separate interface with all the letters of the alphabet at the bottom. When the user rolls over a letter the letter is outlined. When the user clicks on the letter it changes color and goes to that section. If a letter contains lots

Copyright ©1997 Amiable Technologies, Inc.

Fig. 19.10. Design proposal, *PhotoPRINT Training* CD-ROM. Copyright 1998, Amiable Technologies, Inc. Reprinted by permission.

PhotoPRINT Training CD   Page 7
Version 1

of text the user will have the option to scroll through the text. There will be links for certain words. Links will either be to a particular text area or link to a particular part of a QuickTime movie that's in an earlier section of the CD-Rom.

6) Dean's List

The Dean's list will consist of the PhotoPRINT family of products; it will have an initial paragraph as follows, "In addition to PhotoPRINT, the PhotoPRINT Family includes digital color printing packages for every level of user, budget and business environment."

The products to be discussed in detail will be: PhotoPRINT Server; PhotoPRINT LE; PhotoPRINT Personal; PhotoCUT; PIA - Parallel Interface Adapter.

7) Alma Mater

The Alma Mater will contain all of Amiable's corporate information. Upon clicking on this button the user is whisked off to a new section containing a brief description of Amiable through its Mission Statement:

To create well-engineered, feature-rich software solutions which continuously satisfy the changing requirements of the color printing and signmaking markets, and elevate our users' abilities to capitalize on new technologies.

There will be three other buttons as follows: History, Family of Products, How to contact Us. The last button will contain a map of the world. There will be roll-over sections for the address and phone number to pop up for that part of the country. There will also be the phone number for technical support as well as 800 number for Domestic use.

8) Guidance Counselor

Also know as the help button.This will give the user detailed information on how to navigate the CD-Rom. There will be a separate help button for different interface sections.

9) Credits/Quit

The quit button on the Main menu will lead the user to the credits, then ask the user if he wants to quit. The credits will contain the names and titles of all the participants for the project. They will scroll up on the right side as the corporate logo is animated on the left.

Copyright ©1997 Amiable Technologies, Inc.

Fig. 19.11. Design proposal, *PhotoPRINT Training* **CD-ROM. Copyright 1998, Amiable Technologies, Inc. Reprinted by permission.**

Marketing Strategies

There is a crucial need to educate the end users of Amiable products in order to promote usefulness of the software as well as lessen the load on technical support calls. The total length of the CD-Rom is estimated to be two full hours. This includes over one hour of QuickTime movies and some animated slide shows for product descriptions and concepts. Production is estimated to take three months with a total of 1200 man hours utilizing inhouse talent. The outside costs will be approximately $ 10,000. This includes CD-Rom mastering and duplication of 3000 CDs, computer system enhancements and software purchases for production and outside resources (such as training and music).

There is no real cost for advertising as this product will be shipped with every package sold. For those who purchased an OEM product and would like training they can purchase the CD-Rom for $29^{95}. Promotion of this product will be by word of mouth.

Future incarnations of the PhotoPRINT Training CD-Rom will include nine major languages for international support. These include: Spanish, Portuguese, Simplified Chinese, Japanese, German, French, Dutch, Italian, and Arabic.

Below is a sample production schedule

January 12	Initial meeting with production crew / review assignments.
January 30	Production meeting with participants and Director of Marketing.
February 9	Initial review of interface and completed sections. Review of comments and suggestions for revisions.
February 23	Final production review to prepare for Alpha release. Adjust dates if needed.
March 2	Release Alpha version for a 1 week testing and review.
March 9	Receive comprehensive list of revisions and general comments. Meet and distribute assignments.
March 20	Release of Beta version for 3 day testing and review.
March 26	Review comments and revisions. Distribute assignments.
April 2	Release of Gold Master to duplication house.
April 13	3000 CDs ready for distribution.

Copyright ©1997 Amiable Technologies, Inc.

Fig. 19.12. Design proposal, *PhotoPRINT Training* CD-ROM. **Copyright 1998, Amiable Technologies, Inc. Reprinted by permission.**

Staffing Biographies

Brigette Callahan - Producer

She has over 18 years experience in the graphic design industry with 12 of those years producing multimedia. She has worked for Amiable Technologies for 5 years as Art Director then Creative Director. She started the Amiable Art Department with a staff of 1. Currently she manages a staff of 7 artists and 1 administrator. She works closely with the Marketing and Sales departments to maintain Amiable's corporate image. This year The department generated over 125 unique 4-color advertisements, 4 product brochures, countless direct mail pieces, corporate slide shows, and training videos. They are also responsible for a 150 page Web site that is updated weekly and all of the tradeshow graphics. Her primary duties for the PhotoPRINT Training CD would be to manage the project and lend assistance with script writing and QuickTime movie production. She is also one of the voice overs.

Tom Gundlock - Graphic Designer / Programmer

Tom comes to Amiable with 4 years of work experience in graphic design and production. He's been with Amiable for 1.5 years starting as a Graphic Artist and moving up to Graphic Designer. He has taken it upon himself to learn the complexities of Macromedia Director and is now a self proclaimed multimedia artist. He is also responsible for the "look" of the project. He has a degree in Illustration from Long Beach State University.

Eric Presley - Graphic Artist / Web Master

Eric came to Amiable 9 months ago from 2 years of freelance multimedia art production. He worked with Graphic Zone on some of their projects. He has since been given the responsibilities of maintaining Amiable's website, both for content and programming. He also has a degree in Art from Long Beach State University. His primary duties will be to create most of the graphics and videos, as well as generate the 3D logo animations. He will also create all animating buttons and assist in any programming.

An Nguyen - Marketing Support and writer

An has been with Amiable for 1.5 years and comes with experience in research and surveys. She is assisting in the script writing as well as doing all product research and proofing of the project

Joe Oakes - Voice Over

Joe is one of Amiable's talented graphic/production artists. He has been recruited as a voice over talent for his deep, clear voice and his easy coachability. He also has time on his hands.

Copyright ©1997 Amiable Technologies, Inc.

Fig. 19.13. Design proposal, *PhotoPRINT Training* CD-ROM. Copyright 1998, Amiable Technologies, Inc. Reprinted by permission.

PhotoPRINT Training CD sample storyboards of interface   12/10/97

1A   **Main Screen - Table of contents**

After the logo animation this is the first screen that the user will encounter. Listed are the main topics or "chapters" of the project. This example shows the core curriculum section.

1B   **Navigational bar for Movies**

This window illustrates the use of a large QuickTime movie. The size is almost the full screen. The navigational bar only takes up a small portion of the visible area. This allows the user to pause the movie, go back to the main menu, advance to the next movie, go to the previous movie, or quit.

1C   **Electives Screen - detail 1**

This window illustrates the use of a colorful graphic with text rollovers for detailed descriptions.

1D   **Electives Screen - detail 2**

This screen is a simple slide. There are no animations or rollovers.

1E   **Dean's List**

This window shows the PhotoPRINT Family of software and each logo is a rollover for detailed information about the particular product.

Copyright ©1997 Amiable Technologies, Inc.

Fig. 19.14. Design map, *PhotoPRINT Training* CD-ROM. Copyright 1998, Amiable Technologies, Inc. Reprinted by permission.

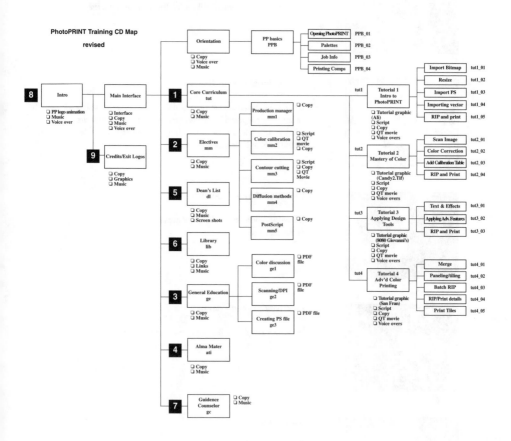

Fig. 19.15. Design map, *PhotoPRINT Training* **CD-ROM. Copyright 1998, Amiable Technologies, Inc. Reprinted by permission.**

INTRO TO PHOTOPRINT SCRIPT

Length 0:28	**Importing a bitmap** After starting PhotoPRINT, choose New from the File menu. A dialog box appears, prompting you to specify a drawing area. Click OK.
Import Ali.Tiff	From the file menu choose Merge Bitmap. Select your image and click Open. *[Pause for the importation time]* A bounding box appears on the drawing area so position your mouse and click to place the image. The bitmap is displayed and is ready to be edited.
Length 0:49	**Resizing an image** PhotoPRINT offers several ways to resize objects. Select the object with the Arrow tool by clicking on the edge of the image. Drag the desired control point. If you drag one of the center control points the image will resize from the center. If you drag from one of the corner points the image will resize proportionately from the opposite corner.
	To see the actual object change rather than a bounding box, choose Show Preview from the Layout menu. You can also resize an
Length = 24"	object by using Resize from the Arrange menu. Notice that you
Height = 22.5"	have a couple of options: Either type in the height or length or specify the scale. For this tutorial, we want to enter a length that's appropriate for the printer we have selected. Click on the drawing area to place the image.

PhotoPRINT Training CD SCRIPT • Tutorial 1: Intro to PhotoPRINT 12/7/97 **1**

Fig. 19.16. Sample screenplay page, *PhotoPRINT Training* CD-ROM. Copyright 1998, Amiable Technologies, Inc. Reprinted by permission.

Length 0:44   **Importing a PS File**

If you have the Adobe Postscript option you can merge a Postscript file as follows: From the file menu select Merge Adobe Postscript. Select your postscript file and click open. A bounding box appears on the drawing area, so click the mouse to place the image. You can move the image behind the bitmap by selecting Move to Back from the Arrange menu. Here we are importing a frame to go around our picture.

Now resize the image to fit around the photo.

Next, select both items and center them by selecting Align from the Arrange menu and choosing both centers.

Length 0:42   **Importing a Vector File**

Let's import one more graphic. From the File menu choose Merge...Select a vector file. This will be a name plate for the frame. Resize the image by clicking on one of the outer points. Hold the shift key while resizing to maintain the preportions. Position the name plate in the general area.

At this point, let's go ahead and Save our file by selecting Save from the File menu. You should save your work periodically to guard against file loss.

Length 0:45   **Adding a printer setup**

Before we can do any color printing we need to set up our printer. This is done using Production Manager,™ which is included with PhotoPRINT.

From the Edit menu choose Setup and Output Device. Click OK when prompted to choose a Production Manager connection. If your printer is attached to another computer over the network, select the Network option.Select the manufacturer and model of your printer and click OK.

PhotoPRINT Training CD SCRIPT • Tutorial 1: Intro to PhotoPRINT 12/7/97   2

Fig. 19.17. Sample screenplay page, *PhotoPRINT Training* CD-ROM. **Copyright 1998, Amiable Technologies, Inc. Reprinted by permission.**

Set the port to which your device is attached and click OK. Your setup now appears in the Configure Setups dialog box. Click Done.

Length 1:17

RIP and Print

Click on a blank space in the drawing area to make sure nothing is selected. Choose RIP and Print from the File menu.

Select your ink and media from the Media/Ink Calibration list. If your materials are not listed, select a combination that best matches the materials you are using.

Center the design on the media by selecting the Vertical Center icon from the Centering menu.

PhotoPRINT offers several outputting options to best suit your needs. For this exercise, select Hold in List from the RIP pull-down menu and PhotoPRINT will rasterize the entire file and then hold the job in Production Manager until you are ready to release it.

Click the RIP button to begin rasterizing the design. The time it takes to rasterize an image varies, depending upon the speed of your computer and other variables.

When the design has been rasterized, click the icon in the upper right of the RIP and Print dialog box to switch to Production Manager. Make sure your media is loaded into your printer and the printer is online. Click the Release button to start printing your job.

Production Manager starts sending the job to your printer and works in the background, so you can return to PhotoPRINT to design and rasterize more images.

Total Time: 4:45

PhotoPRINT Training CD SCRIPT • Tutorial 1: Intro to PhotoPRINT 12/7/97 **3**

Fig. 19.18. Sample screenplay page, *PhotoPRINT Training* CD-ROM. Copyright 1998, Amiable Technologies, Inc. Reprinted by permission.

V.

Frequently Asked Questions

Q : How can a writer "survive" and "grow their career" in this rapidly changing, digitally dynamic industry?

That's an interesting and challenging question that deserves a multiple answer:

1. Differentiate yourself from every other Tom, Dick, and Mary struggling to carve out a career in the wonderful world of multimedia. If you can't, you are only selling an alternative. Be a frontiersman. Don't be afraid of standing out in the crowd. Make a name for yourself by putting your unique stamp on everything you create.

2. Show passion in everything you do (it's instantly recognizable and highly contagious). Learn how to express that passion in your writing, your design, and in your verbal presentations.

3. Hyperlink socially. Whether you know it or not, we all live six degrees away from somebody who can assist our career. Networking (join a new media organization, mingle with the crowd at a trade show event, join an online discussion group) is more than a mere social exercise for meeting new business contacts. It is essential. And don't be afraid to use your friends and acquaintances to help you along the way. You never know when an old buddy will be in a position to lend you a helping hand. Just make sure that when you do call in a favor, you're smart about it. Be prepared. Be gracious. Don't overstay your welcome. Send a thank-you card.

4. Take elocution and singing lessons.

Getting a project off the ground is not always rewarded to the person with the best idea. I am reminded of a phrase from Budd Schulberg's endearing novel *What Makes Sammy Run?* When asked about the secret to achieving a successful career in Hollywood, one of the characters answers, "Take elocution and singing lessons." The implication being that success is measured more by who you know and how you present yourself, rather than the talent you possess. I tend to think that successful writers in the new technology industry owe a little bit to both—the quality of their ideas and the way they express their ideas to others.

5. Give something back to your community (good deeds are always rewarded).

6. Stuff your brain with knowledge. It is ridiculous to assume that you

can do business in interactive media without having taken the time to understand the history, the technology, and the products you will be helping to create and promote. Imagine marketing a feature film without ever having watched a movie! Don't be such an eager beaver. Enroll in a creative writing course. Go to an arcade and play games for an entire day. Explore a Web site you'd normally never visit. Ask your friends to save all their junk mail for a week, then spend an afternoon studying the marketing messages. Visit a museum. Sit in on an investment seminar. Open up an old computer and examine its guts. Seek out knowledge.

7. Don't lie, cheat, or sleep your way up the ladder of success. The world is full of Sammy Glicks—guys and gals who are all-too willing to derail someone else on their way to the land of sweet success. Honesty, integrity, talent, and hard work are a writer's greatest assets. Never underestimate their importance.

8. Rid yourself of financial baggage. It is impossible to think clearly when you are worried about financial concerns (such as paying the rent). Try to stabilize your financial situation before you attempt to become the next Douglas Adams or Chris Roberts. The hype surrounding interactive media may be compelling, but don't let it be your sole motivation. As an emerging new industry, you will probably make less money and do more work writing an interactive media project than should be allowed under the law. When you find ways to free your mind of financial headaches, you may just open yourself to new creative and business possibilities.

9. Don't be enamored by technology! Technological advances have provided businesspeople and artists with exciting new tools to help them tailor their craft. But technology alone is useless without human input and creativity. We are living in a time where the technology tail is wagging the creative dog. Interactive product can dazzle us with its 3-D graphics, animated characters, photo-realistic environments, and intelligent agents, but if the story or underlying message stinks, the product will too. It's that simple.

10. Be fearless in the face of overwhelming odds. This is a tough industry filled with very talented people who are all vying for the same piece of technology pie. To succeed in this business, like in any competitive industry, you must take advantage of all opportunities while adhering to a few basic principles:

- Know yourself
- Practice your craft
- Recognize your limitations
- Be a good listener
- Be open to new opportunities
- Trust your instincts

Q: *What are the top five mistakes novice writers make when approaching the process of writing an interactive game?*
Interactive writer/designer/producer Jeffrey Sullivan answered this question after carefully reflecting on the mistakes he himself made early in his career.

1. Too little interaction. Don't get carried away with your great storytelling skills. The "clicks per minute" in a game must be high; you must give the player something to do.
2. Unrealistic goals. Creating the *greatest game ever made* (or subsets thereof) is a common mistake. If you don't know what is possible, you are very likely to create a game that cannot possibly be made.
3. Missing important detail. If you ever think to yourself, "Ah, they won't care about *x*—it's only a game," then you've failed.
4. Adding unimportant details. Make sure that everything you put into the game is really interesting to people (and not just there to show off how much you know about something). Games, like drama and other forms of entertainment, are not about reality, they're about the dramatic simulation of reality—a game that feels real, but eliminates the boring stuff that fills 90 percent of any job.
5. Lack of game experience. Know games. Play a lot of them. Love them. If you aren't a real fan, you're not going to know all of the things that have gone before. What failed, what succeeded, and why. Without that knowledge, you're going to be learning lessons already learned by others—and that's a costly route back to the unemployment line.

Q: *What's so fun about working as an interactive writer?*
Interactive writer/designer Deborah Todd says:

There are dozens of ways to say something, and as a writer, you get to use most of those dozens of ways in interactivity. It's not linear. It's not one right answer, or one straight story line, or one interpretation. In fact, you have to prepare for people who will play the game, or explore the title, in ways that you don't necessarily intend them to, and write for that.

The very best part for me in the whole process is the initial brainstorming and how collaborative it is. When a team is really coming together, it's unbelievable how much fun that can be. And the ideas feed upon themselves, so they just keep getting bigger and better and these meetings can totally blow your mind. It's great. Then, once you've got the concept outlined, it starts to mutate and morph and grow and it takes on a life of its own and you get to be there and witness it and work with it and see it turn into something truly amazing. If you have really good character work, with bibles that have significant backstory, everybody gets into the characters and you get to watch them develop into "real" people.

I've been lucky enough to be involved in casting and directing as well, and let me tell you, when you're a writer who gets to direct, *that* is heaven! The most fun I've had was doing rewrites on the spot with our director. We had some lines that weren't doing it for us, so we just stopped and rewrote them in a frenzy, had the talent say the new lines right there, did a little more polish, then taped it. It was great fun. Very exciting. Very in the moment. And it made the product better, which was what we were after.

Larry Kay, says:

I like to play games and solve puzzles. One of the things that drew me to this field was the opportunity for a larger quantity of my writing to remain in the final product, unlike in film and television, where so much of what you write just can't fit on the spine of a linear format. It's an eleven-minute cartoon, or it's a 120-page screenplay, or whatever, and that's that. In multimedia, it's still possible to push those barriers out a lot further.

That doesn't mean a writer should engage in hypercreativity. Every project must have a solid narrative spine, a clear beginning, middle, and an end. If you do not know what the end of your game is before you start writing, you will probably get lost trying to get there. I spend a lot of time creating this macrostructure before I actually write the design document and/or screenplay."

Q: What is the best way for a writer to lead a creative life?

I've been asked this question more times than perhaps any other question—especially when speaking at writing seminars. Whenever I hear it, I am reminded of L. P. Wilbur's book *How to Write Books That Sell,* where he quotes the words of David Dortorf, writer, teacher, book enthusiast, and former executive producer of television's long-running hit series *Bonanza:*

Nothing is as lonely as the empty page. But the divine spirit moves us to fill it. Homer filled such a page three thousand years ago. We writers are custodians of a proud heritage. We are the bearers of the divine spirit. We must write and write . . . whether it sells or not. Writers and authors keep the divine spirit alive. To dare to be creative is to keep the world in something of a state of grace.

The beauty of writing is that it fits into whatever lifestyle you are now living. Practically everything you do and everywhere you go can be subjects of a writing project. The trick is to get into the habit of writing rather than simply talking or thinking about writing. Many a coffeehouse is filled with idle dreamers—pencils rap-tap-tapping on Formica tabletops, eyes clouded in a dreamy haze, an empty notepad beckoning for a few drops of life-giving ink.

Living a writer's life can be a joyous and lucrative experience. Armed with a laptop or pen and paper, you can create anytime, anywhere. The freedom of a writer's life is what lures thousands of neophytes into the "writer's way" every year. It's what also dooms so many to failure. Without proper discipline, many writers postpone what should be done today. Consequently, they really aren't living a writer's life; rather, they are mimicking the lifestyle.

Perhaps the best way to jump-start a creative way of living is to set out on a quest to discover your "writing space." This sacred space is made up of the following:

- A specific time of day you will devote to creating. This will be your magic time. You will write during this time at least five days a week. No exceptions!
- A comfortable location in which to write. It could be an office, the kitchen table, a library, a bench in the park—whatever location happens to stimulate your creative juices.
- A sensory aid that helps you tap into your emotional being—an object or trinket that stirs your soul. It could be your favorite teddy bear, your Marvin the Martian coffee mug, a tattered photograph of your great-grandfather, or a favorite book. Make sure that your sensory aid is always within arm's reach. Better yet, surround yourself with several items that inspire you (writers need all the help they can get!).

My last piece of advice, of course, is to *write*. Find your sacred space, write to your ability, and do it as often as possible. Your creative life is now under way. Make the most of it!

Q: How much money can you earn writing interactive media?

Half as much as the last gal and never as much as you need! Actually, it varies, depending on the job, the time schedule, and your level of experience.

For design proposals, a writer may have to create the entire work on spec—in order to demonstrate an ability to conceptualize her approach to a subject. I would advise against working for free at all costs—unless the potential employer is a prestigious corporation or a prominent publisher. For any other firm, a writer must insist on some form of payment. A $3,000–$7,500 fee paid to a writer who creates a detailed design proposal would not be uncommon.

Writer/designer Carolyn Miller claims that top interactive writers working on interactive entertainment titles are making rates comparable to that of Hollywood movie-of-the-week writers—somewhere in the $40,000–$50,000 range. That's for delivery of a complete design document.

Noted interactive attorney Richard Thompson, says that the general range for his clients is around $30,000–$40,000. Writers with experience and credits may get $60,000–$70,000. If you are simply copyfitting (adding dialogue or punching up previously written material), a writer may earn as little as $10,000.

Q: Do interactive writers need agents and attorneys?
Attorney Richard Thompson answers the question this way:

I think that in any case where you need either, you need both. The kind of person who doesn't necessarily need any kind of representation is somebody who has a relationship with one company where they've worked a long time and they just want to keep on doing the same deals over and over again. They are prepared to be paid a fairly modest wage for their work, and don't aspire to gain control of their own destinies.

If you want to be paid better or if you want to develop more industry relationships, or to gain control over your own destiny, then you probably need representation. Very few writers are capable of doing those things on their own. And it's not the best use of their time if they are, because they should be writing. That's what they do best.

Agents are very important in helping to get the word out about writers, to help them develop relationships and to get particular projects submitted to the appropriate buyers. The buyers are going to start looking to agents more and more [in this industry] because they are going to want them to perform the screening function of weeding out the good material from the bad for them.

I suppose there are deals for which an attorney is not required, because the deals are nonnegotiable. But it may still be a good idea to pay an attorney to review the deal to help the client decide whether to accept the non-negotiable terms or walk.

Talent and literary agent Carl Bressler had this to say about the role of an agent:

To me, what an agent does is procure, negotiate, advise, and counsel. Procuring is finding work. Negotiating is getting the best terms for the client without making the buyer hate the client. Advice is of the day and counseling is long-term. In other words, the agent is a mirror. This is where you said you want to go. Are you doing that or do you see yourself falling away from your dream plan?

Q: *During the deal-making process, what are the major deal points writers should insist on in a contract?*
Once again, Attorney Richard Thompson shares his thoughts:

Point number one. Lots of money.

Point number two is to define as closely as possible what work the client is really doing and when the client gets paid for it. There's a real tendency for these projects to spin out of control and go on forever. Writers usually don't earn much money on an interactive deal so it [the project] really shouldn't take up a year and a half of the client's life. You won't be able to eat if you do that. It is also important to try to define what the writer actually has to do to get the money.

Another thing a writer should insist on is a royalty. There are situations when a writer can't get a royalty. For example, the writer is coming in on something that is a preexisting property or something that has a lot of design work already done on it. Many software companies don't want to pay royalties. The reality is, that once a writer who's any good gets involved in a project that is already under way, the whole thing oftentimes must be substantially redesigned. It turns out to be a huge amount of work for the writer and that warrants a royalty.

A writer needs to figure out the scope of the work. If the work is more than just coming in and laying some copy on top of something that's essentially done, then I think it's something that merits getting a royalty. It's an important deal point.

Another important deal point is credit. Since there is no such thing as Writers Guild protection for credit in this business, the only credit that writers are entitled to is what they negotiate for in their contract[s]. And even though software people tend to think that credits aren't important, credits are important. In large measure, they define who people see you as in the business. Your stature and your ability to make future deals is heavily dependent on what you've already done."

Q: *What's the best way to pitch an interactive project?*

Pitching is the art and business of taking your content idea (whether it's a work-for-hire project or an original idea) and convincing someone on the other side of the desk to support it (usually by funding the project). Seems simple enough. In fact, many writers are great at pitching. However, for every writer who can really work a room, there are probably ten others who are lousy at it. And that's unfortunate because poor presentation skills will lose you work in this highly competitive industry.

Larry Kay, an accomplished interactive writer/designer and producer, gives his thoughts on pitching:

Before I pitch an idea, I put together a fairly full proposal. Sample writing, navigation maps, concept illustrations. I pitch somewhat selectively, and try to prequalify that a producer might be interested in this particular category or may consider me for one of their assignments. A successful pitch more often leads to a writing assignment than to actually placing my spec project. Placing a spec project happens very rarely, but pitching one of my own original creations gives a producer an idea of what my own peculiar passions and voice are all about.

Multimedia guru David Greene shared some of his thoughts on the pitching process:

It is very important to understand the individuals you are going to meet with. Are they technical people who are more interested in the technology than the story, or are they marketing types who are more interested in the demographics than the specifics of the project? You will often find yourself modifying your pitch for your audience. Granted, this is a pain, but you need to target your pitch to your audience; otherwise, you stand a good chance of losing their interest rather quickly.

If possible, try to do more in-depth research on the individuals you will be meeting with. A lot of companies actually have bios of their primary officers listed on their Web site. You don't want to pitch your new concept "CyberChrist with an Attitude" to a company run by a born-again Christian. A little research might save you time, effort, and embarrassment."

Jon Samsel's Top Ten Tips for Pitching Your Interactive Ideas:
1. Start off with a teaser (hook the audience, then reel them in)
2. Emphasize elements that will keep audiences coming back for more
3. Pitch with conviction and passion (your idea must be infectious)
4. Humor helps (used sparingly and in the right situations)
5. Pitch from a common frame of reference (use of terminology)
6. Show your ability to create hybrid entertainment that can be franchised to other mediums such as television or books (think of the ancillary rights and merchandizing possibilities)
7. Concentrate on the most exciting aspects of your project, rather than all the minor details
8. Try not to resort to reading notes (if you can't eat, sleep, and breathe your pitch, you're probably not ready to deliver it to a room full of people)
9. Take command of the room (confidence sells)
10. Have fun! (don't take a pitch meeting too seriously; many great ideas are rejected the first time they are offered to others; keep your chin up, smile, and try again another day)

Q: *What are nondisclosure agreements?*

Nondisclosure agreements (NDAs) are typically one-page agreements whereby each signing party agrees to share proprietary or confidential information and each side agrees not to divulge that information to a third party. Why are NDAs used so often in the interactive media business? It is not so much distrust as it is legal maneuvering by attorneys to protect a client's interests at all costs. Many companies have been sued because a writer pitched them a project that was similar to something the company was already developing. Which side had the idea first? A dated NDA helps establish when the exchange of ideas occurred, a date that can be cross-checked with the copyright date on the original source material.

However, the main reason NDAs are used so often in the interactive media industry is to prevent people from talking about the other side's "intellectual property" in advance of that knowledge going public. Intellectual property may include story lines, characters, design structure, source code, authoring tools, interface methodology, graphic design elements, intelligent agents, walkthru environments, and marketing strategies.

Q: Prototypes and demos: are they necessary?

To show proof of concept, many writer/designers painstakingly produce working prototypes or demos of their ideas. Sometimes this is done to secure financing, sometimes to demonstrate concepts or to showcase a new technology. But more often than not, creating a prototype is the final stage in bidding on a job. Especially in the online arena. Online networks, publishers, even major corporate Web sites are now in the business of "shared risk," meaning they want to work with writers and designers who understand their needs. Demos have become the test bed for sorting out the wanna-bes from the true contenders.

What is a prototype? A prototype is an application made up of several key elements loosely thrown together to demonstrate a basic sense of the project's interactivity. The prototype can be as simple as a QuickTime movie with several screen shots, a musical score, and some narration. A prototype may also include sketches, maps, and/or interface designs "borrowed" from other projects for comparison. Total user play-life for the prototype is under five minutes.

What is a demo? A working demo looks and feels much like the final product. A demo might include an opening interface, several subscreens that illustrate basic navigation and interactive methodology, a music score, sound effects, and sample puzzles or other obstacles. Total user play-life is anywhere from five minutes to over an hour.

Beside the obvious benefits (landing a gig), prototypes and demos can also serve a myriad of functions:

- They're an inexpensive way of conducting market research
- The laborious act of creating a demo or prototype serves as a crash course in multimedia production
- They can be used as a marketing tool (giving away free demo copies can be your interactive résumé)
- They can function as shareware (introduce consumers to two or three levels of functionality in the hopes that many will "try before they buy" and purchase the upgrade)
- They help writers and designers "road test" new ideas before the product is put together

Q: *How do interactive writers deal with writer's block?*
Larry Kay says:

I can't really afford writer's block. There is nothing like a good swift deadline to kick in the creativity!

I think writer's block often occurs when you don't trust your ideas. Creativity is like a muscle, the more you use it, the stronger it gets. I don't subscribe to the notion that every writer has a finite amount of stuff to say and uses it up. But, on the other hand, I know that I, like most writers, must be careful not to burn out. I definitely have some days that are surprisingly productive, while other days I have to trudge through on technique. When I get a little rest between projects or drafts, I'll start a little fresher and be more free and spontaneous with my creativity. Ideas generate more rapidly, I feel free to throw out a lot of material on my way to finding the good stuff.

Bibliography

Apple Computer, Inc. *Human Interface Guidelines: The Apple Desktop Interface.* Reading, Mass.: Addison-Wesley, 1987.

Andrew, James Dudley. *The Major Film Theories: An Introduction.* Oxford, England: Oxford University Press, 1976.

Andrew, James Dudley. "Realism and Reality in Cinema: The Film Theory of André Bazin and Its Source in Recent French Thought." Ph.D. diss., University of Iowa, 1972.

Arnheim, Rudolf. *Film.* Trans. L. M. Sieveking and Ian F. D. Morrow. London: Faber and Faber, 1933.

Arnheim, Rudolf. "On the Natures Photography." Trans. L. M. Sieveking and Ian F. D. Morrow. *Critical Inquiry.* September, 1974: pp. 148–61.

Arnheim, Rudolf. *Art and Visual Perception.* Berkeley: University of California Press, 1967.

Barfield, Owen. *Saving the Appearances: A Study in Idolatry.* Middletown, Conn.: Wesleyan University Press, 1988.

Bazin, André. *Qu'est-ce le cinema?* 4 vols. Paris: Les Editions du Cerf, 1962.

Bazin, André. *What Is Cinema?* Vols. 1 and 2, *Qu'est-ce le cinema?* Berkeley: University of California Press, 1967.

Becker, Howard S. "A New Art Form: Hypertext Fiction." In *How to Read a Hypertext,* ed. Mark Bernstein. Cambridge: Eastgate Systems, 1998.

Borges, Jorge Luis. "The Garden of Forking Paths." In *Labyrinths*. Harmondsworth: Penguin, 1970.

Borst, Terry, and Frank DePalma. *Wing Commander III*. Austin, Tex.: Origin, 1995.

Brooks, Kevin M. "Do Story Agents Use Rocking Chairs?" Working paper. Cambridge: MIT Media Lab, 1997.

Brooks, Kevin M. "Programming Narrative." Working paper. Cambridge: MIT Media Lab, 1997.

Bush, Vannevar. "As We May Think." *Atlantic Monthly* (July 1945).

Collins, Russell, eds. *The Spot*. New York: Fireside, 1996.

Davis , Robert Con and Ronald Schleifer, eds. *Contemporary Literary Criticism: Literary and Cultural Studies*. Reading, Mass.: Longman Publishing Group, 1986.

"Digital Hollywood." *Hollywood Reporter, Special Issue*. Hollywood: BPI Communications, 1994.

Dunnigan, James F. *The Complete Wargames Handbook*. New York: Quill, 1992.

Galyean, Tinsley. "Narrative Guidance of Interactivity," Ph.D. diss., Massachusetts Institute of Technology, 1995.

Goodlad, John I. *A Place Called School: Prospects for the Future*. New York: McGraw-Hill, 1984.

Halperin, James L. *The Truth Machine*. New York: Del Rey, 1996.

Hirsch, E. D. *The Schools We Need: And Why We Don't Have Them*. New York: Doubleday, 1996.

Hayles, N. Katherine. "Dinosaur of Postmodern Mutant? Narrative in the Age of Information." Speaking Digital: Media Theory Practice (*www.guggenheim.org/speakingdigital/hayles.html*). New York: Guggenheim Museum, Soho, 1998.

Heim, Michael. *The Metaphysics of Virtual Reality*. New York: Oxford University Press, 1993.

Heinich, Robert, Michael Molenda, James D. Russell, and Sharon E. Smaldino. *Instructional Media and Technologies for Learning*. Englewood Cliffs, N.J.: Prentice Hall, 1996.

Kac, Eduardo. "Holopoetry and Fractal Holopoetry: Digital Holography as an Art Medium." In *Holography as an Art Medium*, ed. Louis Brill Leonardo. vol. 22. Oxford: Pergamon Press, 1989.

Kann, David. *The Literate Writer*. Mountain View, Calif.: Mayfield Publishing, 1995.

Kaplan, Michael, and John Sanborn. *Paul Is Dead.* Los Angeles: MGM, 1997.

Joyce, Michael. *Of Two Minds: Hypertext Pedagogy and Poetics.* Ann Arbor: University of Michigan Press, 1993.

Laurel, Brenda. *Computers As Theatre.* New York: Addison Wesley, 1993

Murray, Janet H. *Hamlet on the Holodeck: The Future of Narrative in Cyberspace.* New York: Free Press, 1997.

Murtaugh, Michael. "The Automatist Storytelling System." Master's thesis, Massachusetts Institute of Technology, 1996.

Negroponte, Nicholas. *Being Digital.* New York: Vintage Books, 1995.

Norris, Christopher. *Deconstruction: Theory and Practice.* New York: Routledge, 1991.

Perrine, Laurence. *Literature: Structure, Sound, and Sense.* New York: Harcourt Brace Jovanovich, Inc., 1988.

Perrine, Laurence. *Story and Structure.* New York: Harcourt Brace, 1983.

Propp, Vladimir Aioakovlevich. *Morphology of the Folktale.* Texas: University of Texas Press, 1969.

Riding, Chris. "Drowning By MicroGallery." In *Resisting the Virtual Life.* San Francisco: City Lights, 1995.

Samsel, Jon. *The Killer Content Workbook.* Cupertino, Calif.: Apple Computer, 1997.

Solnit, Rebecca. "The Garden of Merging Paths." In *Resisting The Virtual Life*, ed. James Brook and Iain A. Boal. San Francisco: City Lights Books, 1995.

Stephenson, Neal. "Daymare." 1997.

Stephenson, Neal. *Snow Crash.* New York: Bantam, 1993.

Truscott, Robert. *The Essentials of College and University Writing.* Piscataway, N.J.: Research and Education Association, 1995.

Warren, Robert Penn, and Cleanth Brooks. *Understanding Fiction*, 3d Ed. Prentice Hall, 1979.

Wimberley, Darryl, and Jon Samsel. *Interactive Writer's Handbook.* Los Angeles: Carronade Group, 1995.

About the Authors

Jon Samsel (*jsamsel@pacbell.net*) is a technology consultant and an interactive writing instructor at the UC Irvine Digital Arts Program. Samsel is the co-author of ten books, including *The Interactive Writer's Handbook, How to Write Books That Sell,* and *How to Write Articles That Sell.* He is also the author and producer of *The Killer Content Workbook,* an interactive multimedia developer guide for Apple Computer.

Darryl Wimberley, Ph.D., is an author and screenwriter who has had two of his screenplays produced into films and more than a dozen others optioned. His first novel will be published by St. Martin's Press in 1999. Formerly a graduate screenwriting teacher at the University of Texas, Wimberley now writes full-time. He lives in Austin, Texas.

Index

Page numbers in italics refer to illustrations.

Books from Allworth Press

How to Write Books That Sell, Second Edition
by L. Perry Wilbur and Jon Samsel (hardcover, 6 × 9, 224 pages, $19.95)

The Interactive Music Handbook: The Definitive Guide to Internet Music Strategies, Enhanced CD Production, and Business Development *by Jodi Summers* (softcover, 6 × 9, 296 pages, $19.95)

Arts and the Internet: A Guide to the Revolution
by V. A. Shiva (softcover, 6 × 9, 208 pages, $18.95)

The Writer's Internet Handbook
by Timothy K. Maloy (softcover, 6 × 9, 192 pages, $18.95)

The Business of Multimedia
by Nina Schulyer (softcover, 6 × 9, 240 pages, $19.95)

Business and Legal Forms for Authors and Self-Publishers
Revised Edition *by Tad Crawford* (softcover, 8½ × 11, 192 pages, $19.95)

The Writer's Guide to Corporate Communications
by Mary Moreno (softcover, 6 × 9, 192 pages, $18.95)

The Writer's and Photographer's Guide to Global Markets
by Michael Sedge (hardcover, 6 × 9, 288 pages, $19.95)

The Writer's Legal Guide, Revised Edition
by Tad Crawford and Tony Lyons (hardcover, 6 × 9, 320 pages, $19.95)

The Internet Publicity Guide: How to Maximize Your Marketing and Promotion in Cyberspace *by V. A. Shiva* (softcover, 6 × 9, 224 pages, $18.95)

The Photographer's Internet Handbook
by Joe Farace (softcover, 6 × 9, 224 pages, $18.95)

The Copyright Guide: A Friendly Guide for Protecting and Profiting from Copyrights *by Lee Wilson* (softcover, 6 × 9, 192 pages, $18.95)

Legal Guide for the Visual Artist, Third Edition
by Tad Crawford (softcover, 8½ × 11, 256 pages, $19.95)

Please write to request our free catalog. To order by credit card, call 1-800-491-2808 or send a check or money order to Allworth Press, 10 East 23rd Street, Suite 210, New York, NY 10010. Include $5 for shipping and handling for the first book ordered and $1 for each additional book. Ten dollars plus $1 for each additional book if ordering from Canada. New York State residents must add sales tax.

If you would like to see our complete catalog on the World Wide Web, you can find us at ***www.allworth.com.***